F**K THE RIDE

F**K THE RIDE

Dave Courtney

This paperback edition first published in Great Britain in 2006 by
Virgin Books Ltd
Thames Wharf Studios
Rainville Road
London
W6 9HA

First published in hardback in Great Britain in 2005 by
Virgin Books Ltd

ISBN 0 7535 1122 3
ISBN 9 780753 511220

Typeset by Phoenix Photosetting, Chatham, Kent
Printed and bound in Great Britain by Mackays of Chatham

CONTENTS

This book is dedicated to:

My Stormylicious, and Malcolm Vango,
who has saved my life more than once

time it hits him square in the face, we're laughing our tits off already. 5-4-3-2-1-Bingo! Right in the mush.

And then he's started screaming.

Because I hadn't actually started my meal, I had no idea that the tomatoes, like every other cunting thing on the plate, had just come straight from the microwave. (That's seriously VIP treatment in Romford.) And the thing with microwaves is that the outside of a piece of grub might be warmish, but the innards will be like hell's kitchen. Guaranteed. Which is what I think he was trying to convey as he got up clutching his burned-up face, and stumbled round the room like Frankenstein's more clued-up brother, knocking over tables, chairs and the occasional pensioner. Say goodbye to Romford, mate.

So I like a bit of fun. But most of all, I like a bit of attention. I've said it before and I'll say it again: I'm a flash cunt. And that really does tend to get you noticed.

Despite my best efforts, the police didn't care about me until I arranged security for Ronnie Kray's funeral. And did they sit up and take notice then. I don't blame them. When I looked out my window and saw 150 of the top boys from all over the country standing in my garden, all waiting for my instructions, I thought, Never mind East London, I want to invade fucking Iraq!

The thing is, I didn't shoot Ronnie Kray; I threw dirt on him. But I showed the British public that I can call up an army if I want, and that was enough to get the police saying, 'Shut this guy down.' Apparently people like you and me aren't allowed to have our own armies. Funny that. So suddenly I was this world gangster figure to the authorities. Public Enemy Number One. And they couldn't have that, now, could they?

Am I better off now than before? Financially, no I'm not, not in the slightest. How can I be? If you expect me to say 'crime don't pay', well you're sort of wrong.

Because crime does pay until the day you get caught. That's why there's so many fucking criminals, of course it fucking works. Then the day you get caught and stuck in this tiny cell in Morocco for twelve years and raped and rogered by some hairy cunt, you find it's not paying so well. All those years of swanning around the West End in your soft-top BMW with a gorgeous bird next to you mean fuck all when you're inside.

But the irony is, as soon as I became famous for being naughty, I had to stop. It's a bit hard robbing banks if your films are on sale at Blockbusters. So I haven't been active for ten years, which suits me down to the ground, because I'm a much better entertainer than a gangster – I love showing off. What do you mean you hadn't noticed! The only criminal thing about me these days is my jokes.

If I'm honest, I don't even know what I'm famous for any more. All I do is talk about myself or what I think about stuff. I philosophise, and my whole input into anything is unique. 'Cos I'm a silly fucking romantic care bear and I know people care about what I say, I think about every word that comes out, and if I can help you out with some pearls of wisdom I will. You can get that in my movies, my records, my TV shows and in my books. And because it's all real, and I'm not an act, it's all the same message. It's all basically me. I'm just selling Dave-ism. And the best thing I do is talk. So instead of getting nicked and going to the copper, 'No comment', I'm like, 'Well, officer, what happened was this ...' Once they give me an opportunity, I can hit them with full-force Dave. Put me in a fucking dock and I'll be there for three days. I want them lot in the jury going home pissing themselves with tummy aches from laughing, going, 'He's a funny cunt.' You know what I mean? I'll answer any fucking question, even what my favourite colour is. As long as the subject is me, I'm away. Even when I was a doorman, I weren't the best fighter, I'd just stand there and have them all laughing. And once you realise that, you know I was made for telly. They fucking love me.

Personally, I think I'm tailor-made for *Big Brother*. But since the authorities won't let me near the place (and I'll tell you all about that later), I'm actually having it done to my house. I'm Big Brothering up my own home. It's gonna cost me five and a half grand, and, if you're lucky, you'll be able to pay to watch it on the internet. Certain rooms will be turned off at certain times of the day, 'cos some of my visitors won't want to be filmed. I'll have untold people in here doing untold things. Naughty ladies, the lot. I don't give a fuck, do I? I'll be sitting here smoking joints, you'll see my house in all its glory, you'll see all my mates who just drop in. And on Saturday night there's a chance I'll bring home a naughty lady and shag in the front room, so on Saturday nights I'll be earning fortunes on that pay-per-view. That's the plan, anyway. You can set your clock by it, every Saturday you'll have Dave Courtney shagging. Between one and five past! Ha, ha. *Stop it!*

That's gonna be absolutely fucking easy for me, I think. I will be swanning about in the Rolls-Royce, I will have all the chaps dropping round, it will have the sex, the drugs and the rest of it. People are gonna love it. Me personally, I don't mind being on screen 24/7. There's nothing I wouldn't mind being filmed. I don't mind sitting there having a shit, or having a wank – I've been in prison, I've had to have a shit in front of loads of people.

All what would make everyone else go, 'I couldn't do that on TV,' it doesn't matter to me. I've lived with the embarrassment of having a shag, doing a shit, being called this, having my wife call me that. Live with me 24/7 if you want to have an opinion of me. That is my dream. To say to the world, 'This is him.' I would love that opportunity, please God. Five grand. *Touch!*

Actually, the only people who haven't clocked that I'm on the straight and narrow are the boys in blue. Don't they read my books? Everything I do, they're looking for the 'real' motive. If I gave a million pounds to charity, they'd say, 'It's drug money.' And that ain't nice. So what I want to do is get it all up and running then tell the police watching my house, 'Oi, mate, you don't have to sit over the road freezing your bollocks off to film me secretly, just pay ten quid every half hour and you can see me in glorious Technicolor.' But watching them chase their tails can be fun. And I've got to tell you about this one.

The scariest thing about the police is their imagination. Listen to this: there's these two traffic wardens working part-time near where I live. They're both working girls – and they do a bit of work for me. One of the perks of the job is they get to use the police canteen down at the local station. And they're good-looking girls too, so if they make eyes at some high-ranking officer, what's he gonna do? Well, you would, wouldn't ya? So I get all this pillow talk and the inside track on what's going on in the world of plod. And let me tell you, it ain't pretty.

What's that got to do with imagination? Well, when I first decided to turn my house into Camelot Castle, with turrets around the roof, tin soldiers out the front and everything, one of these birds reports back to me. She can hardly speak for laughing. 'Dave,' she says. 'The police think you're planning a siege in your gaff.' They'd heard about the renovations, put two and two together and come up with twenty-two. She actually heard them say, 'Dave Courtney's *"fortifying"* his home – if we're not careful we're gonna have another Waco on our hands!' *Touch!*

So that gives you some idea of what I have to put up with. And that's without mentioning the bugs in my car, in my house and on my telephone. Or all the trumped-up charges, the attempt to label me a 'grass' so I'd get taken out, or the fact that the authorities try to shut down everything I do. But what they don't realise – and this is the thing that really cracks me up – is that, if they'd left me alone, you lot probably wouldn't be reading this book. The police have actually made me become multitalented – and even more famous.

If they'd let me get on with writing books rather than use everything in them as evidence against me, I wouldn't have started making records. And if they hadn't interfered with that, I wouldn't have got into movies. You understand what I'm saying? So thanks to them (sort of) I've made porn films in America, I have my own radio shows, I write magazine columns, I work for charities, I do stand-up comedy, I even spoke at the Oxford Union – the only time my mum has been proud of me! What else do they want me to do? Juggle lighted midgets?

I fucking do the lot, mate. And it's all thanks to the Old Bill. Which must piss them off. *Sweet!*

A lot of stuff has gone on since my last book, *The Ride's Back On*. A lot of real juicy, heavy stuff. You might have read about it in the papers – oh, silly me, of course you haven't. How could you when there's a 'D Notice' on Dave Courtney (that's plod language for media ban). The thing is this: the authorities think I'm more dangerous now than I was when I was a villain because I'm popular. Guilty, as charged (and you won't hear me say that very often). And since they've embarrassed themselves in court so many times trying to get me put away, they've decided to stop me getting any platforms to talk from instead.

Newspaper journalists have been told: you don't write fuck all about Dave Courtney unless it's shit. So even when my daughter ran away they stitched me up. They put a picture of *me* in the paper saying: 'Dave Courtney, the friend of the Krays and South London informant, who lives at ... – by the way, his daughter ran away.' They didn't even mention she was black. *Please!*

What the police don't understand is this: these journalists have been writing about me for twenty years and I know some of them really well. They're mates of mine, they come over the house and tell me things. And some of them aren't even journalists any more, they're editors or higher, you understand me? They tell me, 'Dave, we've been blacked – we haven't got time to argue the point to put that story in. The legal team call the shots.'

In other words, my missus could throw a mental on my cars and try to get me arrested and I could even go into court dressed in a Barbie wig with a suitcase full of vibrators and no one would ever hear about it.

How can I be so sure? Because all those things happened to me and the police made sure they was hushed up. Just like that. Just like they make sure they book court appearances for me on the most inconvenient days (you can set your watch by 'em).

The weirdest thing was with my film, *Hell to Pay*. Every single cinema in the country wanted to show it. Who wouldn't want Dave Courtney playing Dave Courtney with real gangsters? And then out of nowhere, without me getting in touch with any of them, they all came back – the Odeon, Warner's, every fucking chain – and said they didn't want to be associated with the film. Funny that, and all within a couple of days of each other. Even two chains that I didn't ask rang me back and said they couldn't put it on.

When I called my first book *Stop the Ride I Want to Get Off*, I was referring to my criminal life. That was over for me then, and I was trying to go straight. But life itself is a rat race and I found myself saying *The Ride's Back On* in my second book. Well, for the last few years I feel like I've been proper back on the ride – and it ain't been fun. Sure there's been moments of adventure, love, success and downright naughtiness, but overall, no. Sometimes I look at the heavens and imagine Him up there going, 'How else can we hurt Courtney? I know, we'll run him over – zap! Then we'll get his missus to leave him.' So, when they asked me to name this book, it was one of those times when I was looking up there. If they'd asked me another day, it might have been called something worse, believe me!

So, all in all, it's not been a good couple of years. I've had a car accident, been smashed up, gone through a divorce, been arrested and took to court by my wife, had my assets drained and my work put back by two years – I've just about been getting up from one kick in the bollocks and I've had another severe one.

In fact, I can honestly say I've got no nice memories of the last two years apart from getting very close to a good friend of mine, Miss Jodie Marsh. (Sorry, did I get your attention then? I'll give you the details later.) Mwah, mwah. Love you, Jodie.

While we're on the subject, I've just re-read this book and I come over like some Casanova on heat. I promise you I ain't like that normally. You don't actually realise how much a break-up from your missus screws you up until you look back at how you reacted to it. So if I seem a bit more laddy or a bit too full of myself where the ladies are concerned, you know the reason why. This being a single playboy lark is fun at the time, but it just ain't me. Just so you know …

But I'm a big boy and I believe I cannot be given this many kicks in the bollocks, which are ultimately learning experiences, without a reason. They must help you further down the line, even if they do fucking hurt at the time, mustn't they? And after all the crap I've been through in the last few years at the hands of the authorities and the police, I now actually believe I have a job to do, to expose the way they run this country. It's like it's my passion, my mission to get everything I know out there. After all, when the police have tried to kill you, it would be fucking criminal not to.

Sorry, didn't I mention I think they tried to kill me?

Looks like I've got some explaining to do . . .

1. ALL SHOOK UP

Car crashes and cover-ups

My mate Tommy Mack said to me the other day, 'I heard about your bit of car trouble, Dave.' He's one for understatement is Tommy. Lovely geezer, but, if you ever need a brain donor, ask for Tommy's – 'cos his one is brand new, still in the box, never been used. But he had a point. I reckon trying to widen one of England's busiest roads single-handedly in a Range Rover counts as a bit of car trouble, don't you?

Don't worry, I'm gonna tell you all about it, but let's get one thing straight first. People talk about me being in a car accident. Well, trust me, there was nothing accidental about that little shunt. And what's more, I believe I know who was responsible. I'll get to that in a minute, but first, all the gory details.

It was my pal Don Crosbie's birthday party and I'd been down to his pub in Maidstone to help him celebrate. I popped in to see my pal Tucker on the way there, so, as usual, I was running fashionably late. By the time I turned up there was just Don and Al Benson knocking back the Jack Daniel's. Al's a funny guy – he's the comedian on my *Dave Tells It How It Is* DVD – but he didn't make me laugh half as much as the sight of Don lying face down in his Chinese meal. He's a fantastic bloke is Don, so we wiped the chicken chow mein off his chops and I drove them back to Don's gaff, all part of the Courtney Cars service, sir, before I headed back home.

It's gone midnight, a lovely clear sky and I'm belting down the road in my mate Brendan's Range Rover. I've got Elvis on the CD player and I'm singing my lungs out. It's just me and the King, knocking out the hits together, right fucking *X-Factor* material and a real treat for the copper on the other end of the bug they have in all my mates' cars. I know Mark Fish, Jamie and Stormy all enjoyed it when I phoned them on my hands-free. Apparently 'who's strangling the cat?' is 'street' for fucking cool.

So I'm flying home in the fast lane when I see in the mirror these main beams in the distance. A few seconds later and this car is right on me, so close I can see it's a white Volvo with these two army-looking geezers in it. This was before they all went Arab-bashing in Baghdad, so I thought nothing odd about that. But 'cos I was doing a hundred mile an hour I thought, Fuck it, I ain't pulling over into the middle lane, 'cos Range Rovers go a bit wobbly at that speed. Then the Volvo's gone out of my mirror, and I'm thinking, Great, they're gonna overtake on the inside. The next thing I know, I feel a nudge up my backside and it's 'Hello, central reservation'.

It's about now the car goes on its fucking Torvill and Dean cartwheel thing, and it rolls over twelve times. Perfect 6.0 each time (except for the Russian judge as usual). But it doesn't go over sideways like normal, it flips top to toe, front bumper to fucking back. The very first smash shattered my pelvis on the steering wheel and then, because I never had a seatbelt on, I was just flipped about inside like a kitten in a spin-dryer. Imagine being the penny rattled in some charity cunt's collecting tin (before you've nicked it) and you're getting warm.

I thought I could kick myself for not wearing a seatbelt – and then in the next few seconds, as the car started playing origami with my limbs, I very nearly did. With one spin I felt my ribs go, and on the next bounce my head got squashed between the pedals, which fractured my skull (as well as making me look like the kid who got his face shut in the lift doors). Then I broke my knee and ankle, tore my spleen, punctured all my ribs on the other side, then I hit my fucking pelvis again and broke that some more for good measure.

Normally when you're in an accident it goes like this: tyre squeal, crash, then the pain. In that order. That's how pain works. Even if you've never crashed a car, we've all kicked a table, right? I sometimes think shins were only invented to find sharp fucking furniture in the dark. Well, when that table does get discovered by your leg, the agony always comes half a second later, don't it?

But 'cos my accident took twenty seconds with all the rolling over, I had too much time to hurt. So I was going, bang, bang, bang, smash – then I'd come up, then came the hurt, but it wasn't the end of the accident. I was being thrown about so much I couldn't protect myself, 'cos I didn't know which way up I was gonna be. The pain just kept coming and coming so I was thinking, Please! Just hit me on the fucking head and put me out of my misery.

Them life-threatening situations are normally only a couple of seconds long, so you can remember them all in really great detail. If someone's asking you about a holiday, that's a lot of hours to remember, you know what

I mean? But twenty seconds where I wasn't unconscious and I was just getting broke up, all my body parts bending the opposite to how they should be, seems like yesterday to me. It's like a video nasty in my head that I can rewind and pause any time I like. Every crunch, every snap of bone, every thought about wishing I'd get knocked out. And fuck knows how I was thinking anything, 'cos I had this skinny head where it had smashed between the pedals and fractured me skull and bent me up a different shape. Another inch and my bonce would have exploded all over the leather interior, like when Travolta accidentally opens up that geezer's head in the back of the car in *Pulp Fiction*.

It was mad, right? But the maddest thing of all was that during the whole accident the CD player didn't jump once. Didn't fucking jump once. I'm getting my head kicked around like a football on Cup Final day and Elvis is still giving it full volume. And guess what was playing? 'All Shook Up.' That's the truth. I fucking love Elvis, but that's taking the piss.

If that weren't bad enough, this is the thing that really fucking freaked me. When a car's rolling over, it goes quick, quick, quick, slow, quick, slow. You know, as it falls and goes up again, but a bit slower every time. The sunroof had gone AWOL on one of the first spins – at one point I actually touched the road through the roof – and the driver's door weren't long after it. So as the car goes up for the last time, I fell on to the steering wheel and out the door. Yes! I thought. A bit of luck at last – but the fucking Range Rover's still got to come down. I'm lying there proper knackered up thinking, Don't tell me – I've gone through all that and the cunting thing's gonna land on me!

Luckily it fell down beside me, next to all the bits of concertinaed crash barrier and half a dozen lampposts. But that weren't the end of it 'cos then all I could hear was all these cars behind me. I thought I'd landed in the middle of Brands Hatch so I was gonna get fucking run over now. So with my one leg that worked, I was trying to push myself up the road away from it all. Actually, I don't know what I was fucking doing, but I was trying to do it all on one breath 'cos I couldn't get any air in, my lungs were proper fucked.

Pain is something that goes so far, then it stops being physical and it becomes mental. You understand what I mean? You can only take so much pain, then that's as far as it goes. I've been shot, stabbed, had me nose bit off, and been hit with anything that weren't nailed down, and a few things that were, so I think I know what I'm talking about. You reach this point where it can't get any worse physically and, once you've been like that for a long time, you're just lying in the road, it's all going on in your head and it feels like you're waiting for the ambulance for about two weeks.

Actually it was about 25 minutes, I've since found out, which is better than a fortnight but pretty shit when you're lying with half your bones in the wrong holes. I'm on one of the major roads in London and it took nearly half an hour to rustle up someone with a first-aid badge? Makes you proud, don't it? But there just happened to be a cop car ninety seconds behind – ain't there always? – and if I was lucky they would've managed to get past page one of the How Not to Let a Bloke Die handbook they hand out at Hendon.

I've never believed in healing hands. And this night fucking proved it. The people who were touching me, whoever they were, I felt shouldn't have been touching me as hard as they were doing. I was in fucking bits, I was proper broke up, but these cunts were pulling me around like I was already dead. I was like, Jesus Christ, are you trying to snap my wishbone and make a fucking wish? Get the fuck off me!

Eventually the ambulance strolls up and they get me inside. A bit later someone finds first gear and we head towards the hospital. From the moment I started my cartwheel display to actually arriving at casualty seemed like a fucking age. I've seen hospitals built and shut down in less time than it took to get me there.

During all this time I was actually conscious. I wish I weren't 'cos it would have been a whole lot more comfortable, but I was. There was no way I was shutting my eyes till I saw a friendly face and for some reason the policeman travelling with me on the way to the hospital weren't exactly trying to do his best Florence Nightingale impression. Who else gets a fucking police escort inside an ambulance?

Things got weirder with this copper at the hospital. By now I have closed my eyes 'cos I think I'm safe, but this policeman refused to leave me. He was actually in my room with me till about four o'clock and the bastard's even written out one of them producer things – you know, 'You have seven days to produce your documents at your local nick or else'. I couldn't produce piss in the next seven days. It's only when Brendan and a few of the boys turned up about four hours later, and said, 'Listen, Dave does not want to see you here, fuck off,' that the geezer got the message. (Thanks to Seymour, John John, Jim, Gary, Mark, Steve, Pierre, Cowboy, Phil and Dave for passing it on.)

Do you remember that scene in *The Godfather* when Al Pacino goes to hospital to visit his dad who's just been shot by a rival gang? He gets there and finds the police guards have all been sent home and he knows the other mob will make another attempt before the night's out. Well, all this is going through my boys' heads. I'm lying there all ripped up, and they didn't know what had happened or what to expect, 'cos I couldn't tell them. So I had two people stand at the end of my bed, the boys, 24 hours a day for the whole time I was out of it, which turned out to be a month. Not one of them had to do it, and I would never have asked any of them had I been conscious. But knowing that they did 'cos they wanted to ... You'll never know what that feels like till you've experienced it (and I sincerely fucking hope you never do).

But all the uncertainty just played into the Old Bill's hands, I realised. The next day, a photograph ended up in a newspaper of me all smashed up in the emergency suite, which is before you get into the intensive care unit, with the headline: UNDERWORLD HIT. I think the only person who could have took that photograph was the policeman who decided to go with me to the hospital.

Now all that got me thinking. All the time I was waiting to go to court for the case of the bent copper Austin Warnes (which you'll all have read about in *The Ride's Back On*), the police were putting it about that I was a grass. They knew full well that I would win the court case but they also know the criminal fraternity breeds and breathes testosterone. It is actually really fickle and jealousy runs high. The police know that by throwing the cat among the pigeons they'll cause chaos, and they knew there'd be some people who'd start believing what was being said (you know who you are) and maybe even one daft cunt who'd try to do something about it. Do I think they'd stand in the way if someone tried to have a pop at me? Put it this way, I've got more chance of getting a wank off the Pope than help from that lot.

Even though Warnes was bent, he was still a copper and if he thought he could help in stitching Dave Courtney up he would. And he did. So by pleading Not Guilty, his police mates could keep saying, 'Courtney's a grass, Courtney's a grass.' On the day of the trial Warnes actually changed his plea to Guilty, which meant my evidence against the Old Bill wasn't heard in public. But by then they'd already been going around saying stuff about me for eight months. The jury was only out six minutes before they found me Not Guilty. I thought, Why the fuck did we go to court for that? And you could see the jury thinking the same thing – 'Courtney had a tape of the copper confessing – what the fuck are we doing here?' But the police look at the bigger picture. Those twelve jurymen might see all the facts, but the majority of the country just hear whispers and snippets and headlines. I've learned that the hard way.

Where's all this leading? Christ, if you haven't worked that out, are you sure you're holding the book the right way up? I don't have one shadow of a fucking doubt that my so-called 'accident' was nothing of the sort. I was on a dead flat bit of fucking motorway, I wasn't pissed and I'm not a bad driver. That white Volvo clipped me off the road on purpose. And the police want everyone to think it's an underworld hit in revenge for Dave Courtney being a grass.

If a villain had decided to get rid of Dave Courtney, there's a hundred different ways he'd think of before he came to 'I'll hit him while he's doing a ton in a Range Rover on a road where it's all camera'd up.' You know what I mean? That's another type of person's way of doing it. You watch one of them TV shows, those *Stop Police Action* things, and you know the police know how to do it. They know exactly how to get a car off the road without hurting themselves. It's 'bing!' and the car's off.

If it was a criminal underworld hit, they would have come back and finished it by now, three years later, and they haven't. It's not like they don't know where to find me. I live in a white fucking castle and every move I make is done in public. Which leaves the real culprits in a dilemma. Now I'm making it public what they're doing and what they tried to do to me, they have got to do something about it. The problem they've got is it's gonna be very obvious when they do. I'm fully expecting the motorcycle and black crash helmet bit, followed by the anonymous phone call about the underworld hit 'cos I'm a grass – and that's what they don't want, 'cos that's what I've predicted will happen.

Now a lot of you reading this won't want to hear this sort of thing. It's one thing the Old Bill taking a few short cuts in a court case, but actually trying to off someone who's a bit of trouble? This ain't the Third fucking Reich. But speaking as someone who can proudly say he bought his first ever TV licence this year, let me tell you this. The police are no different to any other cunt the world over. There's good ones, bad ones and ones who are happy to take a few liberties with procedure if it means less paperwork. We all do it. If you're an insurance assessor and you want to clear your in-tray before you go on a long weekend with some brass from your boozer, I'm sure the odd claim gets passed or failed without too much checking. Or a decorator might skip a layer of emulsion 'cos his meter's running or he's on a promise that night. We all do it, we all take the easy route at work, and being a policeman is just another job. If they have to lose the odd bit of paperwork or forge the occasional signature to speed up the justice process, they won't think of it as doing anything wrong.

So you don't have to be Stephen fucking Hawking to work this one out. (By the way, what is it with him? He gets a bit of fame and suddenly he's speaking in an American accent.) But if you are inclined to go, 'Oh, it's Courtney bleating on again' – and believe me, that's what the police have tried to make people do – let's consider a few facts, m'lud.

Because the police have the advantage of information –

the bugs in the house, the bugs in the car, the bugs in the phone – they know my whereabouts constantly. They are looking at everyone I meet to see what connection they have with Dave's business. Everyone who comes to my house is clocked. It might be the bloke to fix the washing machine or a Jehovah's Witness (smart cunt, that Jehovah, having his own witnesses) but, as far as the Old Bill taking pictures across the road are concerned, they're all part of Courtney's firm. So they knew I was on my way home from Maidstone about twelve o'clock, they knew I was alone and they knew I wasn't drunk.

I know what some of you are thinking – where's my proof? That's where it gets interesting 'cos, apart from the two bugging devices in Brendan's motor which the insurance assessors found when they declared it a write-off, the most convincing evidence of all is the evidence I haven't got. I don't think the Old Bill expected me to survive the crash, not if their boys had done it right and, looking at the bits of Brendan's Range Rover spread up the road (sorry, pal), it looked like they had. That's why I think the copper at the hospital was hanging around like a fart in a phone box, to make sure I wasn't going to pull through. But the worst thing for them was I did, and I'm a stubborn cunt. As soon as the doctors did the old *Six Million Dollar Man* thing and put me back together again, the fact that I didn't die just makes me more determined and gives me more ammunition to go after them. And so I started asking questions of my own.

First of all, I wanted to see the CCTV pictures taken that night. I fucking hate those Big Brother cameras every-where, but I thought they could do me a favour for once. If they can spot me picking my nose from the dark side of the moon, they should have been able to catch which junction the Volvo geezers came on at, where they shot off to and what their number was. Most importantly, they'd have caught me getting a tickle on the rear end. But how's this for coincidence? According to the police, the cameras weren't working on that side of the road for the whole night, which is absolute fucking garbage. That is a main road from the coast to London, right? Are you telling me it's a coincidence that somebody had taken the old films down to Boots and hadn't bothered picking up any new ones for any of those cameras? Like I say, if I'd have died, it would have been, 'Oh, Courtney the silly sod crashed into the barrier,' but suddenly I'm actually asking for the film, and it's caused a fucking big embarrassment.

I also asked to see the witness statements. Unknown to me, 'cos I was flaked out at the time, those coppers on the scene had actually taken thirteen statements from other drivers. Which I'm sure must make blinding reading, except – get this – every single one of those statements has mysteriously been lost. Every fucking one. When my solicitor, Ralph Haeems contacted the police he was told this: 'Mr Courtney may not understand the workings of an office, but things do get lost during filing.' And that was it, that was their excuse.

Now if you ask me, those police fellas were a bit dim admitting they'd interviewed anyone, but it does make me think they never thought anyone would ask to see them. You understand what I mean? But they also fessed to shutting the road behind and in front of the crash rather than chasing the bastards that ran me off the road. Except, of course, despite being virtually up my arse themselves, they didn't see any other car.

There's one thing that they haven't been able to cover up, although nobody has explained it either. Like I said, it was 25 minutes before the ambulance got there – this is all recorded in the hospital records. But when they first rang 999, they actually called an air ambulance, which would have been there in half the time. Then eight minutes after that call, someone conveniently cancelled it. Nobody actually knows why, although it probably wasn't to increase my chances of pulling through, if you follow me. But it's all on me hospital records. It's all there in black and white.

So knowing all this, you have to look back and wonder why that copper was so interested in climbing inside the emergency room with me, don't you? Why was it so important to him to be there when I woke up if all he wanted to do was pin one of those producers to my saline drip? Unless they didn't want me to wake up at all. The authorities even concocted this mysterious phone caller who apparently belled the hospital threatening me. He called himself George the Butcher, and claimed he was a big cheese in the underworld. In his underwear, maybe, but he means fuck all to me. But of course, since he'd phoned the hospital and I was legally their property now, they had to follow the rules and – you guessed it – inform the police, who suggested that for my own safety they put a man in my room. Whatever the reason, the fuckers went out of their way not to let any of my lot know what had happened to me, 'cos I think they knew that, as soon as my missus Jen or the chaps got wind of it, they'd be down the ward and the plod outside would be history. So even though they knew the Range Rover wasn't mine, they didn't officially tell Brendan, the car's owner, about the crash for eleven days. And this is the worst bit. Their way of informing my next of kin was to creep up to my house and pin a fucking note to the front door. I was in more bits than a jumbo jigsaw and they didn't feel it important enough to knock on the door and wake someone up. Luckily, someone on the hospital staff got in touch with one of the boys and I believe it was Brendan, Seymour or Mark Fish who eventually said to the copper, 'I will smack you in the mouth, you cunt, if you don't go.' They've got a way with words, those lads.

I know I've been a bit naughty and, it's true, I do like putting one over on the authorities whenever I can. Closing entire streets for a photo shoot with a hundred blokes and real guns? Yeah, I've done that. Turning up at court in a full jester's outfit? Yeah, guilty of that too (I nearly said 'Not Guilty' then out of habit). Glamorising crime through my own films, books, TV appearances, records and sell-out shows? Yeah, yeah, all of that. So I've proper been a thorn in their backsides for years. But to actually rub me out? Are they really capable of that? Ask Charles Spencer or that corner-shop geezer, old Mo Al Fayed what lengths the upper echelons of British society will go to to protect their own. (I'll tell you about meeting royal love rat James Hewitt later, and what he thinks.) Don't laugh – they even used the same language to me. The last show I did before the crash was at the Harlow Playhouse but it nearly didn't go ahead 'cos the Old Bill rang Al Benson (yeah, him again) and told him not to put the show on 'cos it was 'anti-Establishment'. In other words, the authorities didn't think it'd look good in the history books. Just like the mother of the future king marrying an Arab, and look what happened there. (And what a coincidence the CCTV mysteriously stopped working in that Paris tunnel for one night only as well.)

Al's a top bloke so he told the cop, 'Bollocks to you, mate. Dave's a mate and the show goes on.' Or words to that effect. And on I went and I couldn't help myself, I gave the police both barrels of a sawn-off that night. I didn't pull any punches and I was so in the fucking zone that the two undercover plods planted in the audience, and there's always one or two, actually got up and left. I always say hello to them at my shows, 'cos it makes sense they're there, don't it? If the police spend millions of pounds a year following me around, bugging my home, bugging my phone, bugging my car, on an intelligence-gathering operation, they're definitely going to be sitting in my audiences somewhere if they think I'm gonna be up on stage spilling the beans. I'm not silly enough to not know they're in there; I just never know who they are. So if anyone sees anybody talking into their lapel . . . punch him.

But you can guess what these two plainclothes have reported back (or rather gibbered like some scared cunt), can't you? 'Courtney's got too much power, he's got the ears of thousands of people and he's telling them about how we work.' They also knew full well that my book, *The Ride's Back On*, where I dished the shit on their dirty-tricks campaign to paint me a grass when I actually had 27 bent coppers on my books, was due out in two months. All they needed was an opportunity when there were no witnesses and I wouldn't be around to publicise it. I don't know when they planned it, but that was the first night they could get me 'cos I very rarely drive by myself, normally Brendan or someone comes with me. But that night I was on my Jack. Just me and Elvis.

All this working out, of course, I've done in the months that followed. 'Cos at the time, I had more important things to do, like staying alive. I came round in the emergency room in Dartford about twelve hours after the crash, just long enough to see Jen and Brendan standing next to me and tell them that I wasn't pissed and it wasn't an accident. Then that was that. I didn't say another word for five weeks, which must have been a nice rest for the PC eavesdroppers in the ward. I didn't do fuck all, in fact, 'cos I was in a coma. And if you want to know just how fucking scary that is, mate, turn the page. Just turn the fucking page.

2. ONLY THE GOOD DIY YOUNG

Comas, clowns and coming up for air

You might not expect me to say this, but drugs are bad for you. If you don't believe Uncle Dave, take a look at my house. I like a little bit of whizz now and again, but it don't actually do what it's supposed to with me. Other people have a puff and they want to have a chat for a hundred years. I have a puff and it just makes me want to do DIY. And I can't *do* DIY! So if I come home right buzzing, I'm all Handy Andy, and like, Let's build a fucking conservatory! Then as the gear wears off I think, *What* the fuck's happened here?

But I sometimes – actually, that's a lie – I *constantly* risk the side effects and have whizz because I like being awake. There aren't enough hours in the day for me to do what I want to do, especially now I feel my life's been a little bit shortened by that accident, and long term I know they're going to try again, so I can't be sleeping seven nights a week, not with the fucking mission I feel I'm on now. So I take that, I puff, I have the odd E every now and again. I haven't had a trip in ages, but I fucking trip just staying indoors.

What I'm saying is, I'm not anti-drugs. But I don't do cocaine. I'm not one of those geezers what chops up a line of Charlie to go with the horseradish on his Sunday roast. Most of my friends like it, but personally it's not my cup of tea. I'm on too much of a natural high anyway to need cocaine to enjoy a club or sex. I'm buzzing on life as it is. Every time I breathe in it's like popping an E.

But if there was one nice experience to come out of the whole motorway dodgems episode, it was the fact that the first thing the hospital did was plug me into the morphine dispenser. Woo fucking hoo. Had I been pissed as the police tried to claim, the doctors couldn't have administered it, so the fact they shot me up with this gear straight away had the other benefit of clearing my name of that little accusation for starters. And I proper needed something because within a few hours of arriving I'd slipped into a coma and they needed to operate on me as soon as they could get me in the theatre.

But that morphine is some proper shit and, without it, who knows how I'd have got through five weeks unconscious. It's just like, Wow! Any other painkiller in the world affects the nerve endings and slows you down, makes you tired and dulls everything. But morphine actually affects your brain and makes whatever is going on with you fit in with the dream you're having, so nothing actually hurts. In a dream, you can get shot and it don't hurt, does it? Morphine puts you in a dreamlike state where you think, Oh, my hand's come off – maybe it would look better if I chopped the other one off? And you can and it genuinely wouldn't hurt.

The morphine adds reality to your dream for such a long time you think it's real. You know sometimes, if someone's knocking on your door when you're dreaming, just before you wake up the knocking fits in with your dream? It's like that in a morphine coma, but you don't actually wake up. Everything fits in with the never-ending dream. If someone's tapping your leg, that's what they're doing in your dream, do you understand what I mean? So when they put that air mask on me to help me breathe, in my head it was a flying helmet and I was a fucking fighter pilot chasing Germans. 'OK, Ginger, Jerry at two o'clock.' It was mental.

There were loads of other funny things that happened while I was on that gear, though. However the doctors touched you while you're dreaming, you knew about it, which proves you're not in fact dreaming. One of the things they used to do to me was push this three-foot-long silver thing down a hole in my throat and into my stomach. I had pneumonia as well, and it sucked up all the mucus and phlegm and that, and then they took it out.

So I'm sort of aware of all that, but in my morphine world, a clown, a proper circus clown, came into my room, pulled out this big sword, had a look round then grabbed me by the head and stabbed me right through the neck and into the pillow. I saw it, I felt it, I felt my head being held. I was thinking, Hold your breath, Dave, this could be your last one. So I did, for about two weeks, and I lived. But it was weird, fucking weird, and I was shitting myself because I remembered someone was shot in a hospital three or four years ago by someone dressed as a clown. That was in my head.

Then two months later, this lovely old nurse came in who introduced herself as one of my coma carers. She said it used to be her job to hold my head and put that sucker down my throat. I'd never seen her before but, as she was babbling away about how happy she was I'd pulled through, I couldn't help staring at her make-up. She was sixty if she was a day, but going on twenty-four, with all this colourful slap on her face. She looked like she could have driven down from Gerry Cottle's Circus in her exploding car, but something about her was really familiar. And then I realised what it was. I thought, Fuck me, it's the killer clown. That really cracked me up.

I had weird dreams happen to me as well that you can't explain. You know you hear about these out-of-body experiences, where you see your body from above? In that coma thing, I don't know how I knew this, but I could see all the charts at the end of the beds of everyone in the room. It freaked me 'cos they were all the same. Our temperature, heartbeat, pulse rate, they were all exactly the same. So all morphined up like I was, I thought we was dead. And that pissed me off because I thought, I can't do this for another 28 years, just hanging around looking at corpses – although I've got a few mates who do that for a living. It was only when I was better and I asked someone about these charts and they said that, because, in that unit, everyone's on a life-support machine, all the heartbeats are going to be the same. All of our pulse rates and all our temperatures were all being regulated by the machine. It made perfect sense, but fuck me if I know how I read those charts from where I was.

But even weirder than that, if you can imagine, was this. Who do you think was having it large in there with me? Elvis Aron fucking Presley. And we were proper cracking on. I think it's fucking fantastic they released all his old number ones and they all went to the top again. What a compliment. I don't even need to tell you he was the fuck-ing bollocks. Nearly thirty years after you're dead and you're doing it all over again. But I'm lying there, drugged on this serious bit of kit, and the King says to me: 'Ah haw ha.' The old lip curl and everything. And he says, 'Stop fuck-ing about pretending you're all bust up in an accident, boy.'

That's a fucking touch, I can tell you, getting a visit from Elvis, especially when he should be working in that chip shop. (He was a bit of a porker when he went, though, weren't he? I'm thinking they should rename some of his old songs. Instead of 'In the Ghetto', what about 'In the Gateaux'? Or 'Love Me Tenderloin'. Or 'Lunchbreak Hotel'. Sorry, Elv, just kidding.) So he was with me when I crashed and he followed me to the hospital, and he didn't wait for visiting times, neither. Respect. Anyone who's done a stretch is all right with me, and the old jailhouse rocker more than qualifies. But even though I was away with the fucking fairies, after a while in the coma I could hear everything that was going on around me. And some of the things I heard I didn't like one fucking bit. And the worst thing of all, they were things I'd actually told people to say ... *Prick*.

The thing is, I'm a great believer in the pre-emptive move. Here's an example. I once actually knocked out an ex-heavyweight boxer. Spark out. One punch on the dance floor at Stringfellow's. Which ain't bad for me, considering I'm the only boxer who ever retired with a cauli-flower bum. But what happened was this. I was upstairs with Peter and a load of my mates testing out his new in-house CCTV cameras. So amongst everything else I've got a full close-up view of my missus downstairs throwing some sexy shapes on the dance floor when up behind her comes this boxer. He grabs her arse and says what hot stuff she is. And she goes, 'Listen, don't hit on me if you know my old man is in the building.' And I'm watching her on a screen the size of Saturn and I'm thinking, Oh fuck, don't do this, mate.

Now this boxer wasn't the greatest fighter to hit the canvas, but he was big. Even if you knocked him out, he could hurt you just falling on you. So he goes to Jen, 'Count yourself lucky I'm not hitting on your old man.'

Shit. There's only so much a geezer can take when you're watching it in glorious Technicolor with all your mates, so I said to everybody in the office, 'Watch this.' So I went downstairs and crept up behind him, like you do, and said, 'Mate, a little word.' Now if you actually wanted to punch someone and you said, 'Excuse me, would you mind putting your chin right there so I can reach it?' they'd go, 'Fuck off.' So the way you get away with it is this: pretend you want to whisper to somebody and before you know it they're bending right over and it would be rude not to. Boom. Down they go. Duster back in the pocket and thank you very much.

So that's what I mean by pre-emptive strike. Get in first. Take the initiative. That's how I've always worked. If I was in no doubt whatsoever that there was going to be a punch-up, and I'd identified a guy who was going to be one of the major players, I would be first, without a shadow of a doubt. 'Excuse me, mate, can I have a word.' Works every time. The uncomfortable bit, if you think about it, is you are putting yourself in the role of God to some extent. You think you can walk into a nightclub and hit someone in the mouth, knock him spark out because you think he's going to be trouble later. No one should have that right really, but the time we're in, with the lager-drinking football hooligan, the rules are different. That mob treat kindness as a weakness and you had to be better than them for them to listen to you. And by better I mean harder. If you could beat them up, then they would do what you said. It was primitive but it was real and you knew where you stood with people like that.

Now all this knocking big fellas out might sound impressive, but like I always say, I'm not the best fighter in the world. I employ those people. What I am is a cute cunt and if I can think my way out of trouble, that's what I do. (Fourteen Not Guiltys and counting.) And if I can do that *before* the situation arises, I'm as happy as a dog with two dicks. I'm a great believer in working out all the different things that can happen to you, just in case one of them does, 'cos then you already know what to do, rather than making a decision there and then. What's the worst that can happen? If those situations never occur, you've wasted fucking half a day's thought on it. But if they do happen, you fucking slip into modes that other people can't manage 'cos they're still running around on emotions and you've already got it worked out. I'm a great believer in that. Remember when Roger Cook tried to catch me out with his *Cook Report* at my house? I knew it might happen one day, so I was ready for it. I took the time to speak to him instead of sticking my hand over his camera; I already knew what I was going to say and I came out of it smelling like fucking roses dipped in perfume. As usual.

Now, if you look at the way I live (or used to live, officer), the things that might normally kill you, I fucking did all the time. I drove fast, I played with guns, I took drugs, drank, smoked; maybe even made a few enemies of the wrong people. Anything fucking bad, I did it. So I'd already had the 'what if . . .' chat with my missus in case the worst should happen. And if I weren't killed outright, she knew what to do then and all, and I know full well she would have done what's necessary, too. She would have killed for me, I know it. Without any fucking doubt I know she would have, because she's had to fight for me.

So I'd already told her, if I was in that situation of being hooked up to R2-fucking-D2 just to stay alive, then she had to put me out of my misery. She would take whatever shit she had to take – do the fucking year in prison for 'assisted suicide', or whatever – rather than let medical science keep me alive like a fucking vegetable for the next ten years. And she said, 'Yeah, I'll do that for you, Dave.'

Well, that fucking conversation was proper ringing in my ears big time when I heard them giving me the last rites!

The downside of Dave's theory on the pre-emptive strike is this: I've never once not known what to do. I've sat here working out a million scenarios in my head, so if one of them happened I'd know what to do, I'm ready. And even if with all my Mystic Meg bit it doesn't go exactly to plan, I'm pretty good at the old ad-libs, and I fucking love a challenge, you know what I mean? When I did my first robbery, I didn't know what I was going to say to make them hand over the readies, did I? But I walked right up to the girl at the counter and said, 'I'd like to make a large withdrawal.' The bigger the event, the more I like it. I'm like, Come on, bring it on. Whether it's a massive ego or whatever it is, I thrive for them moments that everyone else winces at; you know, in the spotlight, the Big Day, the night at Caesar's Palace, I fucking grow for those times.

I'm just saying how my head works. And why it is I didn't know what panic was. I thought I did, 'cos I'm a cocky cunt. But I never did, not really. You cannot be natural leader material if panic is a quality you have. Some people get it when they're in difficult situations. You might be the bravest, coolest cunt in the world when you're saying, 'Stick 'em up, give us your money,' and people do as they're told, open the safe and all that. You're great bank robbers then, you've done ten jobs, you're fucking brilliant because everyone's done what you've said. But you only need one guy to say, 'No, shoot me,' and you're in trouble and you panic.

While we're on the subject, here's a tip for anyone starting out in that business. If you're tempted to be a robber, don't try to rob a Pakistani or an Indian. Don't. 'Cos they actually think the money is their own. And they've got this technique for dealing with robbers. Picture the idyllic scene: It's a post office. You burst in wearing your balaclava looking as scary as you like and start screaming, 'Everybody stay calm! And you, open that fucking safe before I put a hole in you!' and then this happens. The geezer behind the till says, 'No.' You think, No? Let me check the manual ... Nope, not in here. So then you're fucked, because if you wanted to be a murderer you'd be murdering people. You don't actually want to hurt any cunt, you only want money. So it's 'Open the fucking safe or I'm gonna shoot your missus.'

'There she is. I don't really like her anyway.'

And by now he can see you crumbling so he feels sorry for you. 'I'm not opening the safe. Now take a Curly-Wurly,' he says, 'and fuck off.' And you probably would.

So anyway, I'm lying in my bed hooked up to all these Space Invader machines in Darent Valley hospital, draining the National Grid single-handedly. I've been sparko for fuck knows how long and I've got some of my hearing back, although it's like a weak radio signal, it keeps fading in and out. You know when you're pretending to be asleep on the settee and working out who's in the room and what time of day it is? It's like that.

So I can hear my mum and I can hear Jen. And there's this geezer there too, a priest my mum got in to fucking baptise me, who actually gives me the last rites for good measure. And that's when I discovered what panic was. And the thing is, once it starts, you can't stop the fucking cunting thing. It's like jealousy, it's an illness. It completely possesses you. Nobody knows I can hear them, I can't do anything to get their attention, and all I'm doing is remembering that chat with my missus telling her, 'Pull the plug out, I don't want to be a fucking vegetable. I don't care if you get caught, if you get banged up. Don't let me rot. Pull the fucking plug.'

So I'm running round inside my own body trying to open a fucking eye or something or move a lip or use ESP to say, 'Move away from the fucking plug, you cunt!' and I'm listening to the priest geezer going, 'He's in no pain, he's going to the other place,' and I'm screaming, 'Shut it, you fat cunt!' and then the whole world went dark. I thought, Is that it? Is it all over? and then I drifted back again, but I didn't know if it was the next second or the next day, I was so fucked up.

And this went on and on. I kept remembering that conversation every time I woke up, then I'd tear around my own body trying to get something, anything, to work to give them a sign. And then it would be dark again. And that was the first – and only – time in my life I experienced panic. And do you know the best thing of all? No fucker saw it! I was running round, saying, 'I'm all right in here! Don't hurt me, don't hurt me!' trying to use mind over matter, going mental, mental. But no one saw all that and that cracks me up. As far as any other fucker knows, I was the king of cool in there, having a kip and enjoying putting my feet up (although since I was in traction, I had no choice where my feet were).

But while it was going on it was a different story and I was having the worst time of my life. When I was awake, I was gripped by this fucking terror. And then I'd slip back into the darkness and the panic would stop but I'd think I was fucking dead. So you wake up and the panic comes back and you can't stop it. So coming round was actually freaking my head out. I was frightened of the awake bits because they weren't nice and I didn't even know if I was still alive.

And then suddenly it stopped. Just like that. For whatever reason, one of the times I was beginning to wake up, and I'm starting to hear the talking in the room again, and the panic was building up, it was as if someone said to me, 'Shut the fuck up, you're gonna be all right. Enjoy the rest. Chill.' Just like that. I didn't hear voices or anything like that – Elvis had fucked off so it weren't him. But the panic didn't come, and I just knew I was gonna be all right.

I don't want this to sound namby-pamby. But it happened. I didn't see lights. But it was as if there was outside influences helping me out a little bit when I was proper in trouble. Try getting your head round that, it's fucking mental. I'm not saying it was God or anything like that (but I'm not saying it weren't, neither). I'm not even saying I heard a voice. But as soon as I could start hearing the real world again, it was as if something went, 'Don't worry, you're gonna be all right.' I'm not saying it was that, I'm saying it was 'as if' that happened – 'cos for no reason at all, right in the middle of one of those attacks, it was OK. I knew I was gonna be all right. And I *was* all right. I had two more of those black bits, and each time I came out of them, I thought, This is it! and each time I went back asleep. Then another one came round and I thought, Don't fucking waste this one! and the same thing happened. Another one wasted. Then all of a sudden, I was halfway through one, really struggling, straining, and it was like I punctured it. *Pffff.* And that was it. Welcome back, Dave.

I'm not saying it was a godly thing, I'm not saying anything like that. I'm just saying how it was. I needed a bit of extra help and I got it from somewhere. I'm not saying it was God but I'm not saying it was me neither, 'cos that would be throwing bouquets at myself – and I'm not really what you'd call a flowers kind of person. But something was going, 'Stop being up yourself, Courtney, you prick,' and if you know what it was, answers on a postcard to Who Gives a Fuck, Camelot Castle . . .

But speaking of religion (even though we weren't really), for some reason when I could hear the vicar telling my mum, 'He's going to the other place,' I envisaged all the walls in my dream being blue. Since that's got fuck all to do with the story you'll have to find out yourself whether I was right or not, but the point is I was relying on my ears alone. I know my mum's voice, I know Jen's and I could imagine their faces as they were talking and listening. But I never saw the priest. Then months later, after loads of different Father Teds had come in to see me when I was recuperating, you know, 'How are you doing, my son?' and all that, this Irish geezer walks in and goes, 'Hello, so you pulled through then?' and I immediately knew who he was. That voice had been in my head for a fucking long time – 'he's in no pain, he's going to the other place' – so I knew instantly it was my priest. I fucking remembered him, all right, I was goose-pimply and all that. I'm in no pain? I'm in loads of fucking pain. And as for going to that other place, I fucking don't even know there is one. You're the geezer who said to my mum you were gonna give me the last rites. Cunt.

If I could have moved more than my eyelashes I might have called him over for a whisper in his ear. But there's plenty of time to bash the bishop later . . .

going. If I was a baker, I'd be the flashiest loaf-flogger ever (you've gotta earn a crust). The words 'flash', 'cocky' and 'cunt' would probably find me whatever I ended up doing.

But the thing that sort of sets me apart in the police's eyes is the way I make jokes about the nastiest shit that happens to me. But that's no act. When you're leader material and people look to you for how to behave, you don't ever want them to see things getting you down, and I make proper sure of it. It don't matter what I find myself up to my neck in, if I can't make a joke about it you'd better check my pulse.

And speaking of which, even hospitals seem to bring out the comedian in me, which isn't always a good thing. When I was in years ago having my dodgy leg seen to, me and Brendan was cracking up so much the doctors had trouble believing how much pain I was in. The fact that my leg was swollen to the size of one of Jordan's tits didn't seem to convince them. But trust my luck, the first doctor to see me, this Indian geezer, comes along and turns out to be a fan. He says he reads my column in *Front* and thinks I'm a top bloke. 'You have no duster on you, please,' he says, whatever the fuck that means. Then he tries to stick a needle in my right hand for the drip to be hooked up to, but for some reason it's not breaking the surface. So he tries the other hand and says, 'I hope it works in this one.' I looked him straight in the face and said, 'So do fucking I, doc, 'cos I'm running out of arms, you cunt!' Which, to be honest, didn't exactly help him find the bull's-eye, he was laughing so much.

That same time was when Brendan used to come and fetch me with a wheelchair and push me out for a sly fag. These old dears watching us used to think he was just taking me for a nice ride, not to light up out the back of A&E. But the best thing about that stay was one Sunday when Brendan, Micky Taylor (who you'll hear a lot more about later) and Outlaw Phil, one of my motorcycle mates, came to visit on their way to Madame Jo Jo's in Soho. I mean, it's just not fair, is it, to pile up to a bloke with a drip sticking out his arm and say you're off to one of London's few Sunday-afternoon drinking gaffs – legal ones, anyway. No way was I missing out on that, so I got dressed, told the nurse I was just stepping outside to light up, then legged it as fast as a bloke plugged into a saline bag can move.

Micky had a Shogun, Brendan had his Range Rover and we took the proper piss out of hurtling down to Brewer Street. Red lights, pavements, one-way streets, we ignored the fucking lot. I've never seen the doormen at Madame Jo Jo's panic so much as when these stupid great 4x4s screeched up outside the club and these nutty-looking geezers started piling out. But they realised it was us and let us in, although one of them took a look at my drip and said, 'People sometimes leave this place with one of them but you're the first cunt to turn up with one.' Anyway, seven hours after I nipped outside for a puff, I slipped back into the ward. Apparently there'd been a bit of a search party for me and, when I suddenly turned up ever so slightly the worse for wear, they weren't none too impressed. I honestly never realised nurses knew so many naughty words. I only said, 'I've heard of losing your patients, but not like that.'

I soon had them laughing again, though, when the doctor doing his rounds stopped at the bloke opposite and asked him, 'Do you do much physical exercise?' His wife was visiting at the time and she piped up, 'Well, he had a Bullworker about thirty years ago.' We pissed ourselves at that, especially hearing it through the curtain they had round this geezer's bed. We couldn't help it, when the nurse finally flung back the curtain, me and my visitors are all sitting there like we're using Bullworkers.

The day I came out of my coma was a great one for me, obviously – and for all my family and pals who'd been with me solid for that time. But then they showed me a mirror. I'm not amused at the sight of me with hair, let's put it that way, and for the first time in years I had a beard and five weeks' worth of hair, which looked fucking crazy. Left to its own devices I've got a naturally pure grey Afro, like Don King on a bad hair day.

It says a lot for my vanity that that was all I cared about, 'cos the condition that my brain was in after the crack in the skull, the water on the brain and the morphine, I was completely off the cake when I come round. Completely round the bend. The medics actually thought that pulling me through was a touch. Now they were worried about whether I was brain-damaged. It didn't look good when I was in that special unit, with all the other people in there in comas just dying. Their hearts are going at the same rate, their pulses are, everything's ticking along at the same rate because of the heart-support machines. I think I looked quite horrific, and not just my hair.

This is a funny one. When I woke up, I didn't know I had these sort of table tennis bats strapped to my hands where all the tubes were going in. As I'm lying there, this is exactly what went through my mind. All you men out there, tell me if I'm right or wrong about this. When the doctors are talking to me they're sticking pins in my thigh and saying, 'Can you feel this?' Nah. I can't talk so I'm just blinking yes or no. I had a tube in my throat. So a doctor moves to my foot and I can see by his face that I should have felt that one. So he's got pins into me everywhere and I've suddenly realised my legs are paralysed. Fuck, I'm paralysed, but I'm alive. I remember thinking that for about half a second and then it was, Do I want to be alive if I'm paralysed? And then all of a sudden, into my head, I thought: my cock.

Now I fucking completely forgot my legs. All I could think was, Is my cock paralysed? So I thought I'd try to touch it and check. I didn't know I had these bats on my hands, so I've moved my arms over and I couldn't do it. These things were banging together over where I thought my cock was and stopping me, but I just thought I was touching it and not feeling it. I can't feel it, I'm proper paralysed. I had this catheter tube going into my cock as well. Then the doctor went and Jen's there and I started crying. I completely forgot my legs were paralysed too.

But this is the thing. As a man, if I said you had to decide between one leg and your cock, what would it be? Of course, you'd say goodbye to your leg. Then the next day, when you thought it couldn't be any worse, you're asked the same thing: last go, the other leg or your cock. And you'd have to go, 'The other leg,' wouldn't you? I know girls would find that really fucked up about men, but if you break it down like that, fellas will all agree, won't you? I don't care if my legs are paralysed, it's my cock I want back.

So I'm welling up in tears in front of Jen and she goes to me, 'You all right?' No, I was actually being emotional in front of her. 'What's the matter with you? You crying about your legs? It'll most probably be temporary because of the broken vertebrae mending.' I managed to make her realise it wasn't my legs I was worried about. And this look came over her and even though I had a catheter on, she went, 'Shut up, you wanker, if you had no legs your cock would still work,' and she's put her hand under the blanket, grabbed hold of my cock, which I actually felt – 'cos I'd missed it with those bats on my hands. And, even with a catheter on, she sucked my cock. It went hard, I felt it, she bit it. Whether I come or not I can't actually remember 'cos I was still drifting, but she left me in no doubt my tackle was in working order.

Whether or not everything else would ever be in showroom condition again was touch and go.

I just had to not go to sleep, which is really hard in there. It's so easy to drop off. All you have to do is close your eyes and you're away.

In my head I discovered what is meant by 'fighting for his life'. When you are all broke up inside, and that's how I felt, you learn how hard it is to actually breathe in; I'd punctured my lungs and broken my ribs so it was really hard to physically inhale. I was in that much pain that if I wanted to die it would have been as easy as breathing out and not bothering to breathe in. You would have gone 'urrrgh' and died. I was in that much pain when I was breathing that I was afraid to go to sleep in case I couldn't breathe then and I wouldn't be able to fight and keep going. Would I be able to keep doing it if I was asleep? It's like the devil up there going, 'Look, you don't want to do this for another eight months, don't bother breathing in. Simple.' And you could have died. To stay alive you had to put the effort in. It's like being in a rugby scrum and going to your mates, 'Come on, come on!' you had to keep doing that to yourself to keep going. One more, one more, do it slowly. It was so easy to throw in the fucking towel, pick the card the devil's holding out, 'Fucking die, die!' To live you had to hurt yourself just to keep going.

Loads of things were never written down, but I must have smashed me jaw on something, because my mouth and my teeth really hurt. My feet were bent back, not quite broke. And how about this for a kick in the bollocks. Literally. All you men out there will wince at this and you ladies will say, 'So?' But as I was driving down the road, the first whack was into my bollocks. Smash. It shattered my pelvis, pushed that into my back and broke my coccyx off. And that hurt.

I had two bits of broken vertebrae but it was too risky

to cut open my back through all the nerve bits to operate. You can paralyse someone if you cut the back open. So what they do – and I think this is fucking wicked – is this operation they do all the time, which is a fucking Caesarean. They cut you open and pretty much give you a termination. They take your bowels out, and your liver and your kidney, all of it still connected, so your insides are empty. Then they put their hand in and operate at the back. You understand what I mean? Then they put it all back. How mental is that! They put this gel in to set hard, then put all the bits back. Where my pelvis was shattered, they've put an iron bar across the front and hope the bone grows round it.

I take my hat off to the medics in there, they proper saved my life. And, like I say, the Bionic Man's got nothing on the way they rebuilt me. But the weird thing is, I definitely feel different. You know you read about when an old white bloke gets a new heart from a young black guy and suddenly he's into rap, dancing and can do a hundred yards in three seconds? (And I'm not even gonna mention the ones that get bits of pig sewn in them.) There's no real scientific reason for it, but the geezer himself feels different. And that's how I feel, too.

Don't get me wrong. They've put all the bits back in the right place, 'cos they know what they're doing and those boys at Darent Valley are the best. But if your settee was on the same bit of carpet for forty years, it would actually leave a hole. So if you move it, you can put it back almost right and no one in the world would ever know, but you might be a little bit out, not quite in the groove. That's what it feels like in my body. They've taken everything out, put it all back in the right places, but there are grooves that things should have been wedged into. They're not in exactly the right place.

I feel loose. It looks all right. You can get a write-off car and it would have 'write-off' stamped in the logbook. But there are some garages who can do this and do that and, with a load of filler and a good spray job and new carpets, it looks all right and someone will buy it. But if you had it from new, you'd know it didn't drive the same. You know, it always used to pull to the left, and now it don't. And you know it wouldn't take another whack. That's how I feel. I feel I've had a good paint job, a few sun beds and stuff like that, but there are a few rattly bits inside that are all loose. You don't know what the noise is, it could do it for ten years, but you know it weren't there before the crash.

Three years later, it's got knock-on effects. It's made me put on a lot of weight – that's my excuse, anyway. I haven't run for three years, I just can't, which if you're in my line of work can be a bit naughty, do you know what I mean? At my fittest I could probably have done 100 metres in about 13 seconds. Although with a blue light behind you, an Alsatian hanging off your wrist and a fucking VHS under your arm, you can usually do it in nine, no problem. These days I'd struggle to do nine minutes. In a car.

I've still got this pain which swells up underneath my foot. There's nothing they can do about it and if I walk on it it's like cracking the bones with every step. If I allow it to swell up it's like standing on a balloon. You have to push yourself right through the balloon until you're standing on the floor, then keep pushing through this fucking liquid and then walk. And every time you lift your leg up you want to put it down again in case it starts swelling in that couple of seconds. Fortunately the best anti-inflammatory in the world is whizz, and I happen to have that pretty much on repeat prescription.

Coming out of that coma, though, just meant I was through the worst of it. But in other ways it was the thin end of the wedge. Altogether I was actually in that hospital for six months, and I'll be forever grateful to Don Crosbie, 'cos he's the geezer what paid for all my private treatment and later took me off to America, to Miami, to convalesce. I'm just happy I met some people in the same fucking industry as myself while we were over there and I was able to finish off a little problem for him during our stay to start to pay him back. A proper gent, Don.

But here's a funny side effect of being on your arse for half a year. When you're lying down in hospital, gravity can't really take its toll. Normally, for your food to turn into shit, gravity has a lot to do with it, 'cos you're walking about, you put something in the top, gravity pulls it through and it pops out your arse. But when you're lying there for six months, gravity has another effect on you. You put something in your mouth and there's nothing at all pushing it out the other end; gravity would make it fall through the back of your throat, more or less. If you're in a coma, you can't even swallow. It just sits there.

Anyway, a few close friends of mine happened to be visiting me when I sat up for the first time. Lucky old Dieter, my German friend, Andy Gardner, Mr Lahif, Clare, Craig, Lynne, Leon, Cain and Storm, that's all I can say, 'cos did they get a fucking show, or what? You have never seen a turd as big as the monster that tipped out of me the second gravity got hold of it. It was the size of a Pepsi can. It was like giving birth. It was so big it had a fucking personality of its own; in fact, it had had kids who'd grown up and pissed off. Do you get the picture? And it shot out of me like one of them log rides at Alton Towers. It's a beautiful memory.

Speaking of memories, coming out of the coma was a touch, and gradually being rebuilt with a new bit here and a one-careful-owner bit there made me feel proper grateful. But that didn't mean I wanted anyone to see me like this, even with my hair cut. There's too many people who draw strength from my fight against the authorities. All those geezers or birds who write to me or call me or get their mate to tell me I've made a difference to their lives in some way 'cos I showed them how to handle stir, or stand up for themselves against the law or whatever. So I was proper pissed off when a picture of me at my weakest was published in one of the tabloids. They didn't write nothing nasty, but how was my kids gonna feel when they saw their old man like that? I was gutted when Brendan told me they'd all seen it, but that just made me want to fix it. 'Right, bring the razors and the fucking coconut butter – we're doing an update!' And we did. They cut my barnet, slapped a bit of colour on my chops, I gave it full-beam smiles and *snap!* We had a new picture to show the world of Dave Courtney on the mend. And before you could say 'vain cunt', there I was, healthy as ever, sticking two fingers up to all those faceless scumbags at the top who'd been trying to hold me under. 'I'm still here,' I was saying, 'and you'd better believe I'm gonna come after you lot when I get out.' And you know they're gonna be frightened by that, 'cos they was the ones that put me in there in the first place.

Me pulling through must have sent the shits through the police, but it had a funny effect on my nearest and dearest too. One of them I'll tell you about later (and that's a fucking juicy story, I kid you not). But Brendan's gotta make you laugh. Just before I went into the coma, and I'm telling him I weren't pissed or nothing, he says to me, 'You must look at this as your crucifixion. You will be back.' And I can hardly even move my eyeballs, but I managed to say to him, 'Sorry about the cross' – it was his car I'd totalled, after all. And he said, 'So am I, you cunt, that was a nice Range Rover.' But to be fair, Brendan didn't give a fuck about that pile of metal while I was out of it. It was only when I came out of the coma and they said I wouldn't have brain damage and he started to think straight again that he went, 'My fucking car!' Ha, ha. Poor fucker.

Before I worked out how to make my gob work, they made up loads of letters out of paper and I was able to communicate with people by spelling out the things I wanted to say. Well, some of them, at least. Talk about wishing you'd paid attention at school. There's me thinking I'm revealing something that's gonna bring down the government, and they fucking answer, 'About four o'clock.' Come back, Elvis.

But, laughing aside for a minute, seeing all those faces around me every day gave me a little leg-up every time I opened my eyes. My kids Beau and Genson, Storm, my invisible army of technological wizards Mal, Donna and Ria, my brother Patrick and his wife, Seymour, Brendan, Dave Quelch, Tony Oakley, Scott Walsh, Ross Bossack, Steve Holdsworth – dozens of familiar faces turned out daily to sit with me and keep my spirits up. And eat my fucking grapes.

There was plenty of laughs going on while I was out of it, though, I learned. Mark Fish took the 'quote of the month' award from Bren. He's got a heart of gold and he's real funny, but he's rung Brendan after he's been with me in a coma all day, and he's asked how I was. 'About the same as he was the last time you asked me, you cunt,' went the answer. And he's gone, 'Well, it's just I've got two thousand revolving Santa Clauses and I wondered if Dave wanted them.' It's the middle of fucking August, I've said fuck all for three weeks and Mark Fish wants me to buy 2K of spinning Father Christmases. Anyway, he turns up at the hospital a few days later and Brendan's there, of course, so he says, 'You and Dave missed out on the

Santas, I've done a wicked deal on them, but you can still have the reindeers at a good price as it's only September.' Stupid cunt me for not going for those Santas when I had the chance.

Another geezer, this Adrian, gets the award for wishful thinking, though. He rang Brendan, who was pretty much my arms and legs at the time, and went, 'Do you think Dave will be about next week?'

'Well, considering he's been in a coma for a fortnight, I very much doubt it.'

'Oh, that's a choker, I've got him booked for a show.'

He weren't the only one I'm afraid I let down. I should have been in Middlesbrough the night after the accident at this place called Cassidy's. My friend Maria organised that one and I'm afraid I probably dropped her right in it by not being conscious enough to attend. If they'd been clever, they could have done a 'Pope' on me and propped me up like a fucking Thunderbird at the window for a bit of a wave.

Still, you can't blame a bloke for trying to earn a crust. It would be like me not wanting to look my best – and have a laugh at the same time. Looking back, the hospital might not have liked my boys stationed at the end of the ward while I was in the coma – apparently it intimidated the old dears visiting the virtual flat-liners in the other beds. But a couple of unsmiling skinheads was a walk in the park compared to what I put them through once I woke up and was getting back to myself a bit.

One of the things I wanted to make me feel better was a sun bed. There was enough switches in my room to power Beagle II, but none of them was going to give me a tan, so I ordered one in. Four geezers to carry it, two to lift me on it, one to plug it in. Don't ask how many of my boys it would take to change one of the bulbs if they'd gone, 'cos we'll be here all day.

It was beautiful to watch as these finely skilled master craftsmen carefully moved about half a million quid's worth of top medical equipment out of the way – just by using their feet, arses and the corners of the sun bed. There was a slight altercation with one of the machines that go 'ping' but, since I never died, it couldn't have been that important. (Although, funnily enough, the bloke in the room opposite went a bit pale soon after.) Then it was a case of 'After four', and Dave, Gino and the others lifted the thing over my bed. Bingo. Welcome to Orange County. I've just been Tangoed.

Unfortunately, the hospital quacks weren't as delighted as us by the little ray of sunshine we'd brought to the place. Especially as they'd lost power in two plastic-surgery theatres and the gent's lav as soon as we plugged in. (If you're one of the couple who was operated on in the dark, I apologise. But I'm told breast implants on men will be all the rage next year.)

So anyway, one of the Dr Kildares says, 'Look, I've got two thousand people in this hospital and you're treating it like a hotel.'

'Well, I'm just feeling a bit off colour,' I said. 'You don't want me to have a relapse, do you?' Apparently they didn't care if I did because, four sweaty men and half a day later, the sun bed was given the old heave-ho.

Another time I had a bit of a party with about thirty of my closest visitors. There was Stuart, Beau, Genson, Donna, Ria, Mal, my brother Patrick and his wife, Mark Fish, Micky Taylor, Jamie from Scunthorpe, Dave Archibald, Micky Goldtooth, Seymour, Storm and a bunch of the Outlaws – all crammed in my room posing with machine guns and that. The pictures look the bollocks. I think some fucker outside posted a bit of a complaint, though, but I conveniently came over all drained and emotional so they sent Brendan up to see the

South East area manager for the NHS. Apparently I wasn't doing his credibility too much good. But if I could just sign this book for him, we'll say no more about it.

Which reminds me ... I was staying in this hotel in Portsmouth while we were down there filming the ending of *Hell to Pay* and having a bit of a party in my room. It was four o'clock in the morning and the bass was turned up, if you know what I mean. Boom, boom, boom, let me hear you say, way-o. Anyway, there's a knock at the door and – well, no fucker can hear it. So the hotel manager uses his key and lets himself in. He takes a look around the room at all these gangster geezers and premier-division hard bastards all dancing around with guns from the film set, and he starts wetting himself. But he's in now, everyone's looking at him, so he says to me, 'Er, Mr Courtney – the man in the room next door has complained about the noise three times now.' I just looked at him. 'Anyway, I've told him if we get another complaint I'm gonna move him.' How do you like *that*!

Another time in the hospital I had this fucking GoPed scooter delivered which really messed with the doctors' heads, 'cos I'm lying there with a broken back, strapped to my bed – and wearing a crash helmet! I didn't do many miles on the thing but it made me smile every time I looked at it.

I made that room look like a corner of Plumstead while I was there. Versace curtains round the bed, big fuck-off poster of yours truly on the door – I'm just sad they wouldn't let me paint a mural on the side of the fucking hospital. I had a wall of guns, just like at home, a drinks cabinet, my paintings and thousands and thousands of cards hung everywhere, a lot of them from people I'd never even met – so thank you to everyone who sent them in. I had such a constant flow of visitors, from 7 a.m. to midnight, that eventually the nurses started having a chucking-out time. 'Haven't you got homes to go to?' and all that. In a hospital!

One of my regular late-night visitors was my son Beau. If he was on his way back from a club at four or five in the morning and his mates needed to top up with booze, he was like, 'I know where we can get some' – and they'd all pile into my room. I had a little fridge next to my bed to keep water in, but I turned it into a proper minibar. Beers, vodka, white wine or a fruit-based drink for the ladies – you name it, I had it, 24/7. At least I did till Beau turned up, the cheeky . . .

One of the other complaints the hospital got was that there was always this smell of grass coming from my room. Then there were the grumbles about Jenny administering me a bit of her special brand of physio. Apparently when she climbed up on the bed and sat on me, it was a bit too visible through the window into the ward. One time, this nurse strolls in and says, 'Mr Courtney, any pelvic thrust in your condition could leave you permanently damaged.' Which I thought of very carefully as I carried on banging away.

When I was nearly ready to come out, I got a visit from a man called Miles Parker, who does actually owe me ten grand, but I'll forego that because, what I've actually gained through the contacts I've met through him, I've had ten grand. A few years ago when I was starting off in the porn industry, he already had his own sex shops and his own studio. He's now a partner with someone called Ian who I have an awful lot of respect for, so I don't want to bring any trouble on his firm. (Because everyone expects Dave Courtney to be all 'grrrrr' if there's a problem, and handle it in a certain way, when I have a normal gripe like normal people – like, for instance, if someone owes me ten grand and I suggest that perhaps it might be repaid – it's very hard for me sometimes.

Especially as I'm now going, 'I'm not like that no more.' Someone else could have a moan, but if I do people go, 'I-I-I t-t-t-told you.' You hear what I'm saying?)

Anyway, when I was actually getting better, Miles turned up with these Russian identical twins who I'd 'worked with' on a porn film called *Lock, Cock and Two Smoking Bimbos*. That was a film set and a half. We shot some of it in Barcelona with Bev Cox and the rest down at Mick Colby's place in Essex. I like to share my luck so I took along Jamie, Martin, Rob Gomez, Jay, Seymour and Jacket so they could remind me later what a good time I had.

Anyway, talk about bedside manners – Miles arrived at the hospital with these beautiful twins and, even though I was still in traction, one of them climbed on the bed and squatted over me and then they just pulled the ropes to lift my pelvis up and down. (Remember, my pelvis was completely shattered and there wasn't any bone in there, so they put an iron rod in with a flat panel at the front, like Y-fronts, and it's got screws a couple of inches long in the back. My cock actually sets off airport alarms now.) I made a little photographic record of them bobbing up and down in there. It wasn't very good for them I imagine, but for my ego it was fucking out of this world. Identical twins dressed in PVC nurse outfits. You don't get that on the National Health.

What with the smell of skunk coming out of my room all the time and two 24-hour-a-day bodyguards, the myth of Dave Courtney just got bigger and bigger. And the quality of visitors that were coming up: Roy Shaw, Tony, Chris and Jim Lambrianou, Bruce Reynolds, Joe Pyle, Joe Pyle Jr, Nigel Benn, Peter Stringfellow, Goldie, Bill Murray, Garry Bushell, Jo Guest. For a hospital, that's pretty good going. I didn't actually appreciate it at the time, but I was proper looked after.

Another thing I didn't appreciate was that a lot of people don't actually get on with each other, but they all get on with me. That's where my power lies. It's not in what I can do, because I can't. It's very Neanderthal and outdated to think that, because you're the biggest and toughest, you're in charge. That's the old-fashioned way; you're the best fighter, so you're the boss. But that's wrong. The guv'nor is someone who picks the right people for the right hole. I need that fighter for that, I need a sniper there, I need a bridge-builder there, I need an engineer there, air support there, a submarine there. Just because you're the best fighter, it doesn't mean you're good at everything. You do the fighting, but you're not in the dance competition. A lot of the time people who don't get on, sworn enemies some of them, came to visit but in my room they're all shoulder to shoulder and fixed grins. Hysterical.

But it wasn't all fun and games. One day this giant parcel turned up and I thought, Hello, I didn't order no catalogue bride. But it turned out to be two thousand hardback books that my publishers Virgin had thought-fully sent over for me to sign. Maybe they thought I'd get bored in there! But I did it, so, if you're wondering, that's the reason my right arm was so much stronger than the other one when I came out of hospital. Nothing to do with all the wanking at all.

Course, while all of this is going on, I'm getting reports from Brendan and the rest about how business is doing. The film, the book, the appearances and all that were all snagged up by me being bed-bound for a few months. And Brendan's running round like a blue-arsed fly making arrangements to keep me in Dartford where everyone can reach me, 'cos there were serious whispers that I might be moved to Norwich or Oxford, which were the only other places capable of fixing me up. He worked his nuts off keeping me at Darents, 'cos we're sure it was the Old Bill trying to mess things up. Look at it this way: if I'd been moved to Oxford, that's half the family who couldn't get there on a regular basis straight off. So Brendan made arrangements for people to have somewhere to stay in both places, just in case, while he manned the fort – sorry, *castle* – back in London.

The police were sticking their noses in all over the shop once I started to come round. A chap could feel seriously underwhelmed by the level of congratulations I got from Plumstead nick and all their mates. So it gave me great pleasure to make my resurrection as public as possible. As soon as I was looking a bit more human, I started giving interviews from my bed, meeting people and just generally putting the word out that Dave Courtney was alive and well and a couple of weeks away from naming names. You could smell the police shit from Dartford, and I don't mean the horses, neither. They'd had their chance and fucked it. I was alive, I was lucid and I was pissing mad.

But in those first weeks I had to be very careful because I was still weak in my head as well as weak in my body. I knew that what was broke up in me, although exterior-wise could be mended, still had the capacity to hurt me long term if I didn't let them fix it right. So, regardless of the messages I put out to the outside world, my main emphasis was on getting better. Who done it and making them pay was secondary. In fact, every fucking thing became secondary after a while, 'cos I realised I had a much bigger problem at home with an unsettled missus.

4. MENAGE A TWAT

Thrills, threats and threesomes

Here's a wicked little success story to warm the cockles. You'll like this one. A friend of mine did fourteen years and, as if that weren't bad enough, while he was in there his missus ran off, so he's come out to absolutely fuck all. In his last year of prison he was allowed to have this outside job working in a stables. He didn't know the front end of a horse from the back end when he started – which was not only embarrassing when it came to feeding them but meant he couldn't even get a job as half a pantomime horse. But by the time he left prison, he knows it all, and he ends up getting a job looking after racehorses, living in a fucking stables. It's hard work but there are a couple of perks and one day he takes the horses to race at the Arc de Triomphe meeting in Paris and while he's out there he bumps into an old mate. Crimes have changed through the years. It used to be all sawn-off shotguns and now it's drugs, and this guy's rolling in it. So he says to him, 'Are you doing anything?'

'Nah, just looking after racehorses.'

'Have a kilo of Charlie.'

'What the hell am I going to do with a kilo of Charlie? How the fuck am I going to get it home?' But since it was worth thirty grand he took it and thought he'd worry about that later. And what he did was this. You know how it's possible to go all James Herriott and stick your whole arm inside a horse's arse? Your whole fucking arm. Well, this guy's not afraid of a bit of elbow grease (and fucking wrist and shoulder grease and all). So the next day he's walking through customs with about twenty horses, and one of them has got a suppository about a kilo big up its arse. Now if it actually gets found, who the fuck are they gonna nick? It could have been anybody and, in any case, nobody's in any rush to check up horses' arseholes. You'd need the fucking long arm of the law to go there.

While we're on the subject of animal rights (or wrongs), dogs are another good tip for smugglers. Stick anything you can fit up Lassie's backside and go walkies through the green channel. I mean, even if a sniffer dog gets wind of it, what are the handlers going to think when they see their mutt sniffing another dog's arse? And that's why he's man's best friend.

There's another way to screw up a police dog and this never, ever fails. If you're expecting a visit from the Old Bill, get hold of some lion-shit from the zoo and sprinkle it on your doorstep. (Be sure to ask the lion's permission first.) Those police dogs hit the ground sniffing, so, when they get up to your front door, they'll take one whiff of your mat and freeze. There is no fucking way that copper will drag the dog past the step, 'cos, as far as his nose is concerned, 'There's a seventeen-stone *cat* in there. You're having a laugh.' So he's fucked up for the day.

But anyway, my horse mate gets out the other side and, once he's gone through nineteen fucking arseholes looking for the right one, he's thirty grand better off. That was about nine months ago. These days he's a fucking millionaire several times over, he owns his own fucking equestrian farm somewhere in England and life is good. It costs about two grand to enter a horse into a race and people say to him, 'Why are you entering this fat old nag in that little sprint over there in France? What a waste of money.' And he's sitting there thinking, It might not be involved in a photo finish with Shergar but it takes fourteen fucking kilos up its arse, you prick. Talk about Grand National, that geezer was on thirty grand minimum, even if his nag was still running the next day.

Speaking of horses, you know when you put blinkers on a racer or a police horse, it actually makes him a better runner or able to switch off from the horrible mob coming at him with baseball bats. At first he doesn't like the cunting things, but they do actually make him more focused and suddenly he doesn't give a fuck about what's going on left and right any more, he's just interested in moving forwards. That's exactly the same as a wife in a relationship.

Forget what you see in the movies, there's only one type of woman a gangster needs by his side, and I had her. All this gangster's moll stuff, that's just a media phrase. In reality, the professional, successful naughty man has to have an anchor. He has to have some form of normality and reality connecting him to the ground or he gets run away with other people's problems, other people's politics, the Charlie, the eighteen-year-old fucking your mates. And you don't need that.

The stereotypical gangster's moll on the TV isn't necessarily the ideal one to have in real life. There are two different roles where women are concerned in the criminal world. Number one: the 'what they don't know won't hurt them' type who knows you go out to work at odd hours and have some colourful mates, but that's about it. If the police wanted to question them, there's nothing they can say that would hurt you. That's if you're a no-company sort of person. The other role is like what I had with Jennifer. That's the type who knows everything about you and is a rock you can rely on one thousand per cent. I cannot put enough importance on the strength of a good woman. If you have got someone to come home to and two kids tucked up in bed, you don't go out Friday night and come home early Monday morning. Not every week anyway. The rules change.

The wife is the unsung hero in the crime world. People say there are no lady crime bosses, but every bloke is run by his old woman. It doesn't matter that I might be in charge of a mob on the streets, if my missus says, 'I ain't having that cunt in the house 'cos I haven't tidied,' there's nothing I can do about it. So Mr fucking top Mafia boss Gambino has to wait in the car and you have to go and say, 'You stay there, I'm just getting my coat,' or whatever you have to say to stop him coming in.

Or she'll go, 'I don't care if John Gotti's come over to see you special, you've been out Monday, Tuesday, Wednesday, Thursday, Friday, Saturday, Sunday, Monday, Tuesday ... I want you to have a night in with the kids like you promised.' And that's you told. You might feel a bit of a prick but it's worth it for those hidden benefits you get. Your wife and your mum are the only two people who will ever give you genuine criticism for no other reason than they love you. Everyone else has an ulterior motive, you know what I mean? So those are the two you listen to – whether you fucking want to or not sometimes.

When it comes to wife material, Jennifer ticked all the boxes and I had the best of both worlds with her. Like I said a few pages back, she would have killed for me, I know it. Without any fucking doubt I know she would have, because she's had to fight for me. Verbals, cunning, fists – she's used the lot. And then there were other times when she's not got in the way like a 'normal' wife when I've had to do what I've had to do. When we had that little run-in with the Tenerife chapter of Gangsters R Us (that I told you about in *The Ride's Back On*), she was absolutely solid. Seymour's being kicked to the floor, some Costa cunt's tapping his head with a pistol and all because he's a mate of mine. I've got my family with me and the last thing I want is to endanger them or let them see me get hurt. My famous catchphrase 'Run away! Run away!' is on the tip of my tongue, but I looked at Jen and said, 'I've got to help him.' And she said, 'I know. Go and do it.' Of course, by the time we had two blacked-out Espaces full of heavies with automatics pointing at us, I wish she'd kept her trap shut for once.

But the main reason I say I had the best of both worlds with her is 'cos not only was Jen my rock, but we had what the Dear Deirdre brigade call an 'open' marriage. Which is to say, if it was open, I'd forget I was married. Let's be honest, not everyone's up for that kind of lifestyle. But Jen was the kind of missus who'd let you become a porn star in your forties. Which is just as well, really, considering what I got up to.

Actually, and this is a confession I never thought I'd make, the first porno I did was about fifteen-odd years ago, when I didn't tell anyone it was me. It was an *Electric Blue*. Remember them? That was round about the time I was at my peak in my other line of work. Fuck knows what sort of reputation I'd have got in the debt-collecting game if that had got out. It's like if you see a policewoman in a bar you just automatically assume she's a strippagram and offer to take down her particulars. Ask her to use your truncheon and all that. What fucker was going to be scared of me when he's seen me up to my nuts in East European action. I should imagine it's still available on Betamax if you're lucky. You'll know me when you see me: I'm the one whose cock is twelve inches. Wide.

Since then I've worked on *Lock, Cock and Two Smoking Bimbos* (you might have heard of the movie it was based on – *E.T.*), I was in the *Bev Cox Experience* (and believe me, that is an experience) and I did another voiceover in my mate Mick Colby's house which brought a smile to the face of the bloke from Scunthorpe who'd come down to meet Dave Courtney for the first time. I said I'd be at Mick's mansion down in Essex if he fancied the ride, so he turned up and there I am making a blue movie. 'What the fuck is all that about?' his face seemed to be saying, although the rest of him seemed to know exactly what was going on.

I've just done one where I'm the doorman of a nightclub, in charge of the VIP lounge. All naughty little goings-on occur up the VIP end, so the film ain't that far from the truth. My friend Dave, who runs the biggest porn internet site in Great Britain, a real slash-dotcom bigwig, he just wanted me in it to add a bit of authenticity as the doorman. I went, No, listen, I'll fucking jump on it and bang it. If it's nice and I can make myself look the bollocks and I can leave my shirt on to hide me fat belly, count me in.

When it comes to the UK porn scene, though, Cathy Barry and her husband Phil are pretty much the king and queen of the business. I've been fortunate to 'work' with them a few times, which is pretty mind-blowing. One film that was up for loads of porn Oscars was called *Cathula* – I'll let you figure out what that one is about, but it involves Cathy sinking her teeth into my neck (and pretty much everything else). Fangs for that, love. Another one was called *The Gangsters and Tarts Party*, which would have been rude to make without asking me – considering how good I look in fishnets. And then there was one I shot in California with another crew called *The Freakshow*, which we actually promoted at Cannes. Can you believe you get paid for being in these things? Most of us would pay just to watch. I'd be the fucking cameraman if they wanted me to, as long as I could operate it with one hand.

The criminal fraternity and the kind of girl that would be involved in pole-dancing, porn films, glamour modelling and escort agencies are all mixed together in the same pot, which is how I got into this particular little line of 'work'. My first job was actually supplying a couple of porn stars to a company called Sin City in America. I went out there for six weeks while they were making films, and they wanted some English girls who weren't Pamela Anderson lookalikes. White, pale skin, a bit pear-shaped figures and not bleached blonde hair. They just wanted something different. There was a complex of villas with a swimming pool in the middle, so the accommodation was where they were actually doing the film as well, to make it cost effective. I just got involved in the whole thing while I was there, watching how they do it, how they edit it and how much money they make from it. The porn industry is about ten times bigger than the normal film industry – they release about 11,000 new DVDs a year, which is fucking unreal. You'd need a right-arm transplant to get through half that lot. And their Oscar awards are visited by mainstream stars as well and are bigger than the 'real' ones. I'll admit I was blown away by that. I was blown quite a lot over those weeks, as it goes.

I got the distinct feeling the sort of gangsters they were used to dealing with were a bit different to me, 'cos they were saying to me, 'Everyone knows the criminal fraternity is behind the pornography industry but it's not often that someone comes out of the shadows.' I went, come out of the shadows? I want to stand in front of the camera! Know what I mean? *Shut up!*

Look at it this way. I'm a fucking realist, right: a bit of a past-your-sell-by-date, short, fat, bald sort of cunt. All of a sudden someone says, 'Would you like to shag this one, this one or this one in a magazine?' It's like Tart Trumps. 'Oh, and we'll take you to America to do it. And I'll give you some little rude tablets to make sure you're the bollocks. And I'll give you five grand.' Give me half a second to think about that one, will ya?

Another time I met Hugh Hefner at the Cannes Film Festival and he was quite smitten with Dave so I went on to his yacht for a party, where I was met by these identical twins dressed up like Pocahontas, whose first words to me were, 'Is there anything I can do to please you, sir?' I think the words 'come on your boat' might have featured in my reply. I finally got off there two days later – now that's what I call a jolly roger – by which time my wife and my mum had gone home.

A lot of blokes would get back and find their clothes parked on the doorstep for that – *unironed* – but that's what I'm telling you. My missus was up for that as long as it weren't serious. So many relationships get ripped apart by lust but, as long as it don't interfere with your genuine love for your other half, where's the harm? And if you can share the workload, all the better – remember I told you last time about Cathy Barry turning up in Vegas to give us the sort of present you can't order from the John Lewis wedding list?

But we also had our own things. You know what it's like, sometimes your missus ain't around when the mood takes you. That might not be a problem for some people – I've got a few mates who couldn't pull a bird in a brothel. But where I've always had a bit of a gift, I suppose, is in chatting up women. I guess it's in my genes. And in her jeans a few minutes later if I'm lucky.

I'm not saying this to make anyone jealous or to paint a picture of Dave Courtney leading this Hollywood life. People have natural gifts and everyone gets up to what seems normal to them, whether it's being a prostitute, knowing how to take an engine out of a car, putting your hand up a cow's arse all day as a vet – or being able to talk two women into bed at the same time. I'm forty-odd years old and I've been able to do that all my life. But because it comes so natural to me, I'd still find it more impressive to take a car engine out in a fucking day and put a new one in on the next day than meet two birds and have them know about each other when you're shagging them. You know what I mean? To me some of the other things that other people get up to as part of their normal life I find mental. I can't get over how some people get up at six in the morning to spend two hours on a train to go into London, and spend two hours on a train to get home by half-ten at night and spend nine hours at work asking 'Can I go to the toilet?' and all that to take home three hundred quid, I find that fucking unbelievable.

I'm a bit flattered that people think I live a better life than them, but the truly mental thing is that half the people saying that to me could get hold of Dave Courtney and fucking screw me up and beat the crap out of me. It's all about confidence. You might be four hundred times better looking than me and have a cock with an extra six inches to mine, but if you haven't got the bottle you'll be going home alone. I don't want to offend my ladies, but it wouldn't matter to them if I was Quasimodo (although it might give them the hump). The press have now portrayed me as a naughty man and an awful lot of women find that attractive. It wouldn't matter what I look like, they find the power thing sexually attractive, and I'm not exactly slow in using that.

My mate Brendan seems to have been blessed by a fair amount of luck with the ladies too, and he's the first to admit that hanging around with my little outfit has certainly helped there. I went round to his once because it was the birthday of this bird who was doing a bit of cleaning for him. A bit over the top for a lady who does, you might think, but this one certainly did and he said she was worth celebrating. Anyway, she asked Brendan to pick up a McNugget meal on his way home and, it being her birthday after all, he splashed out on the twelve-piece bucket with the barbecue dips and all the works. No expense spared. Brendan got in as she's wandering around with just a towel wrapped round her, and she said, 'Have you brought Dave as a birthday present for me?' For a minute I thought it was *my* birthday. The next thing is she started to give me a blow job and, halfway through, Brendan said, 'Do you want a dip?' and gave her this little paper cup of barbecue sauce. And with that she's slapped it on the end of my knob and started sucking again. A second later and my flaming Jap's eye's on fucking fire, I'm hollering the place down and she just thinks I'm enjoying it. What the McFuck was that about?

Like I say, you and your missus have to really love each other for this sort of relationship to work. The biggest danger you face is one of you finding there's more outside the relationship than you planned. And this is what happened to me and Jen.

I'd love to tell you I was the one who moved on, but I wasn't. As far as I was concerned, I had the perfect set-up. What happened was this: Jen was growing away from me, although, to be fair, I didn't exactly do too much to help the situation. I might have seen it had I not been so focused on my own thing. To be honest, when I was being battered by the whole 'Courtney's a grass' thing, an awful lot fell by the wayside and I neglected an awful lot of people and things because I was on a fucking mission to clear my name. I was most probably guilty of neglect at home, and that's what probably helped it along. Little did I know what a fucking messy divorce that would lead to. Now obviously a big part of what has happened to me since my last book has been my divorce, but I don't want to waste any more time on it here than I need to when I could be writing about me.

Jen had been growing away from our marriage and it's escalated so it appeared that Jen's discontent has started to override her love for me, and, although she might not even have realised it at first, Jen's opinion of me had changed. Suddenly she'd gone from 'even your shit smells nice' to 'anything you do is wrong' and I'd done nothing for once, good or bad, to warrant it. It's like the police. If I give a million pounds to charity, they go, 'Drug money.' There's nothing I could do to stop them thinking that because that's how they think of me.

So, once that way of thinking had set in in her head, it didn't matter if I was Prince Charming, I was never going to get her back – although I did try on a few occasions, sometimes chemically propelled, and sometimes put up a good performance. But normally I fell asleep halfway through.

I soon discovered that this had been going on in her head since before we got married in Vegas, but in the end, what actually happened is, like in most cases, one party is not actually aware that the other party is preparing to leave, whether it be the man or woman. One person is normally planning the 'I'm fucking off out of here' speech long before you know they're going, so Jen's made prepa-rations. She's not gonna just announce it during an argument and leave cold, 'Oh fuck it, I'm off.' You don't do that, do you? You put in the planning first.

I allowed our relationship to carry on, even though it was becoming fucking volatile. Whatever I did just got on her tits (and not literally, neither). Even if I tried something nice, it would come over horrible. We'd gone from 'your shit smells like roses' to 'wash your own shitty pants'. That's when you know you're in proper trouble, when just being normal drops you in it. But the writing was on the wall (fucking graffiti kids) 'cos she wanted to be somewhere else but she didn't have the nerve to come out and say it.

Instead, all the same tricks that blokes use, she'd done with me. Starting an argument so she could storm out. All the usual stories. I think I was actually prepared in my head that we were gonna split up, and I was happy that it was gonna be amicable because I've seen some messy ones. Seeing I'm such a public person, that's all I wanted. I didn't want her to make me take her on. I'd rather be nice. That's how I wanted it to end.

So I was aware of that and thinking about my own life in the future and then, just as we get something sorted, the police try to take a pop at me and fuck up all our lives more than they could imagine.

Looking back after all that's gone on, I'm afraid the only good thing to come out of that car crash is the fact that it fucked up Jennifer's plans to leave me. It didn't stop her but it made it hard for her, which, considering some of the things she did subsequently (you'll have to read on for those), is almost wank material for me now.

At the time of the crash, Jen had actually been living with a friend for about two weeks. We'd done our goodbyes, had a kiss and a cuddle and she had moved out of Camelot Castle. No hard feelings, good luck to her. Let's stay friends for the kids, and all that. But then I've ended up at death's door and that's proper put a spanner in the works for everyone.

Did the crash bring us together? Actually it tore me apart, as it happens – *shut up!* But when I woke up at the hospital, Jennifer was there. And because everything was so fucked up in my head, I'd forgotten she'd actually left me. She got there about six, seven hours after the accident and I was able to talk to her and all my mates. And then it all went black for a few weeks. But the first night, I knew she was there.

It was then, while I'm fucking about with killer clowns and larging it with Elvis, she realised the predicament she was in. It was very hard for her to have everyone going, 'How's Dave?' and saying, 'I don't know, I'm not with him any more,' so she's actually made the decision to come back to me, although I'm virtually flat-lining and don't know this. Whether she did it through love or 'cos Drew and Genson were still at my house or what, I don't know. I think she was genuinely upset at the thought I was gonna die, and it was seriously touch and go at the time, and she thought by moving back in she could help.

Look, I completely understood why she'd gone in the first place. I'm a selfish cunt, I'm a lazy cunt and I'm a pervert. But for a lot of years we got on like the best couple in the world and even when she'd moved out we were still on good terms. So in all the emotion of everything, she didn't think twice about coming back.

But then as the weeks passed and it started to look like I was gonna come back like a vegetable, cos I'd fractured my head, I was talking all stupid, I was on morphine – then she started to realise. 'I had done the hard thing and left, now it's impossible – how can I leave him now?' It was hard enough telling people she'd left me before, but if she leaves me when I'm in that state she's gonna get slaughtered by our mates.

The good news for both of us was that I started to make a full recovery. Because of all of the time she was sitting on the bed when I came round, you actually talk more than you do at home. When you sit in hospital there's no distractions. So I explained to her that I knew what she was feeling. I'd been in there three months and I knew she wanted to leave so I said, 'Why don't we split up now? I can't do anything about it.' If we split up when I got out, I might be running around after her making myself look like a cunt. Right now, I thought, I've got another half a year in here. 'So, if you need to, now would be the ideal time to do it,' I said. 'I'll be all right, I'll live, I'm hurting anyway.' Then she went, 'Thank you, I love you, I'm glad I met you' – then fucking left me. *Cunt!*

Did that one proper backfire! If you wanna leave, off you go – and she does. Ah, plan B . . .

So off she went. She was gone for a couple of weeks but again she came back out of necessity. She couldn't live with all the 'How's Dave?' from everyone and so, for completely the wrong reasons, she said, 'I'm coming back.' In hindsight, I should have been man enough to go, 'Don't come back now, babe. It'll be hard for you to leave later.' If I'd been of sound mind and body, I would have. I don't know if I was hoping it would all get better or whether I knew I needed her to help me get better. All I know is, we both knew it was the wrong decision pretty soon afterwards.

Jen's problem was she's already been and gone twice and now, as I got better, she's got no reason to leave Dave Courtney again. So she doesn't really want to stay, she wants to set up home elsewhere, and she's come back for all the wrong reasons. The longer it went on, the more she realised she'd screwed up and the more she realised she needed a fucking good excuse to leave me now. And if she couldn't think of one, she'd have to invent it.

So she did.

5. JAMAICAN RUM 1

Excuses, exits and end of an era

Did you hear about the lag sent to prison who wasn't worried about serving his full term. When the judge asked him why he didn't seem bothered, he said, 'Because my wife never lets me finish a sentence.' It was a bit like that with me and Jen, 'cos both of us like the sound of our own voices and both of us are fucking pig-headed when it comes to getting our own way, even if we went about it in different ways. She was the talker and I was the listener. Actually, she was the fucking screamer and I normally just sat there and did fuck all till the storm had passed, then I'd find a few carefully chosen words to get my point over. Silent but violent, and all that.

I realised as soon as I was released from hospital after the coma that things were kicking off at home. We both knew she wanted out of it but, if I'm honest, I thought I needed her around to make me get better. She was my carrot, although as it turned out she made a blinding stick. And because of the pressure of not being seen to leave Dave while he's sick, she was just trapped there, always looking for reasons to fuck off. She'd start fights just so she could flounce out, and when that didn't work she was putting fucking sleeping tablets in my drink so she could fuck off for a bit and I wouldn't know – all the fucking stuff that I'd do, she done! You know, 'I put an extra sugar in your coffee, babe. I know you like it sweet.' *Cunt.*

The thing for me is loyalty. I do love a bit of hand on heart. I was blind to the fact that it wasn't actually like that for real any more. She was actually turning people against me. Because I'm older, I could see how it could turn out and, even though I didn't want her to go, I was trying my hardest to help her get out of it, but she had other plans. She was egging me, I now realise, to publicly give her a clump or hurt her, anything so she had an excuse to march. That's how I genuinely feel. I can't see any other reason for her behaviour than that. And one day she got lucky. She got this row going so she's standing in front of the mirror saying, 'That's why I don't want you, you fat, crippled cunt!' Proper full on, nasty.

To be honest, I'd had more clumps off her, in front of people, than she'd ever got off me. Full-on, mad, nutty Jamaican smacks. If you've never had an argument with a Jamaican lady, you've never had an argument. Until you've had a nose-to-nose confrontation with her face against yours, pushing you backwards, you haven't experienced anger. So I'm afraid there have been times when it's been, 'Shut the fuck up'. You know, let's twist again – *clump.*

At the time I was wearing crutches to get around. The type with the arm grips, so, if you let go, they're still on you. It hit me that minute that there was too much venom going into that particular argument. As an argument it would normally be on a 3. But this was a full 10 every time. And with bass! *Bzzzzzz.* I thought, She's got to be doing this on purpose. So I said, 'If you think I'm gonna fucking hit you –' and she went for me. It's a little girly attack, hands all over my face and body, just annoying really. It's like when I took on that Chinese restaurant in *Stop the Ride* ... These Bruce Lee geezers with the chicken noises might slap you a million times a second but it's only like being hit by a flapping budgie, it don't really hurt. So I grabbed Jen in this bear hug to stop her arms flailing, but then, when she pulls away, I can't walk, can I? So she's stepped back and, 'cos I'm on crutches, I can't go forwards. And 'cos I'm holding her I start to tip like a fucking domino. And I fell on her. Crash, right through the door on to the bedroom floor, and I'm stuck there lying on her 'cos my hands are right round and our joint weight's on them. But the thing is, when I've landed on her, I've broke her rib. I didn't know that but she's obviously felt it go. *Snap.* And she thinks, There's my way out. He's a woman-beater, he's broken my rib. I'm a celebrity wife, get me out of here.

Suddenly she's screaming in my face, 'Let go, let go of me!' I'm trying to, but we're both lying on my hands. As she's eventually got up she's going, 'Thank you, thank you, you fucking wanker!' I thought, That's a touch. I didn't know all she needed was a little rugby tackle every now and again to keep her happy. But, like I said, I didn't know she was injured and, as arguments go, it weren't really that out of the ordinary for us at the time. You know, we were like one of those cartoon families always on it, that's just how it is. Anyway, she ran off and I got myself downstairs 'cos Don Crosbie was due round to take me to the hospital for some private treatment on my leg.

So Don turned up and he's seen me covered in all these scratches. 'What happened to you?' he asked.

I said, 'There was six of them.'

He said, 'What? Steps?' Funny geezer, Don, but he knew where I'd got the cuts and that I'd actually been a victim. They didn't hurt, they were just superficial, but they were visual ones, and, importantly for me, he saw them, which came in really handy later.

After we'd gone, Jen's said to Johnny Jacket, who was staying with us at the time, 'Ring me an ambulance.' So he does, but she goes, 'Tell them I'm unconscious, they'll come quicker. It has to be an ambulance 'cos I want this reported.' The wicked thing is, all this is recorded by the emergency operator the other end and you can probably guess what happened when we heard it later. Proper wanking material that was!

So that was the excuse Jen needed to leave. By the time I got home that afternoon she'd moved in with a friend and she had the perfect story. 'Dave's a wife-beater, I can't live with him any more,' and all that, which is exactly what she'd been trying for.

Bad as it sounds, though, that weren't even the worst of it. 'Cos I don't like making a scene, the public humiliation, the arguing in public thing – I like my missus to pretend we're getting on, even if we ain't. I don't know whether that's right or wrong. Under normal circumstances, I wouldn't give a fuck. But now I'm in a position where everybody's looking at me, I'm afraid it does matter. I'd like it not to but it genuinely does. If you're trying to spread stability among others, you've got to look stable yourself. I can't be out of my head on Charlie every night, then tell someone off for being out of their head on Charlie when they're out with me. I don't do that. I would most probably make somebody hide something when things were wrong. And Jenny was good at that. She lived among the media world with me, under the magnifying glass for years and years and years. By the time she left, she was fucking good at it. And that's when I realised I'd created the perfect person to hurt me if she ever wanted to. 'Cos when you're that close and that in love, both of you actually give your other half all the weapons to crucify the other before one of you leaves. And the best you can do is hope they never fucking choose to use them.

But Jen did. And it weren't pretty.

6. ANTISOCIAL SERVICES

Kids in the crossfire 1

Here's a question for you: what was the worst day ever for crime in this country? You don't know? Then you are the weakest link, goodbye, you cunt. The answer is the Berlin Wall coming down, and it's got nothing to do with drug prices falling with it or all them East European hardnuts coming over here and stealing our work – and I fucking hate stealing, me.

The reason it was so catastrophic for British crime is 'cos the police suddenly had fifty million quid's worth of spying equipment on their hands and no one to use it on. The Cold War's over, we're all friends now so what can we look at? The loony Arab in the hills in Afghanistan hadn't been invented yet, so I know, let's look at Dave. Whereas the normal police force never had the budgets for that sort of hi-tech equipment (the only reason the blue lights flash is 'cos they can't afford ones permanently switched on), suddenly they had it in abundance and they may as well use it or else it was going rusty in the garage. And what they can't do with all this technology, it's scary. Unless they're going to use the evidence they take in court, they don't even need to have a fucking warrant. They just listen to you, bug your house and hear you go, 'I'll meet you with five kilos.' It's inadmissible in court so they won't say they heard you on tape, but they'll say they had an 'anonymous phone call' and you're bang to rights.

All the authorities want is to stop people liking me. So they do the grass, wife-beating, child-molesting, murdering shit, rumour-mill thing. I don't say nothing now in private that I wouldn't mind being made public, because I know for a fact that my house, my phones, my cars and even my mates' motors are all bugged and monitored round the clock. I don't blame them 'cos I wish I could listen to Dave 24/7 and be paid for it. Because I treat it so lightly, people don't believe me. But I've taken bugs I've found down the police station and gone, 'Are these yours?'

'Er, don't know what you're talking about, mate.'

'They've got "If lost please return to Plumstead nick" written on the bottom.'

'Oh, is that the time . . .'

I could wear a brown tweed suit, drive a Mini Metro and live down an alley in Sidcup and it wouldn't make a difference – the authorities would still look at me in the same way. With their eyes. *Shut up!* Seeing as there's nothing I can do to stop them looking, I decided I'll give them something to look at. I'll do the fucking big picture on the side of the house, another one on the wall up the drive, eight-foot toy soldiers, a sword in the stone and a Union Jack in the garden and all that. Get a picture of that on your satcom.

How about this, though. When I got arrested, they showed me eighteen months of photographs of the top of my house where this helicopter's been up there every day taking pictures. I could not believe that. How fucking different can a load of bald geezers in black leather coats look from up there? And since those choppers do even less to the gallon than my fucking Roller, that's proper wedge invested in that little scheme. So because I thought it deserved some recognition, I got the painter who did the picture on the side of my house to paint a picture of my head on the roof. Just one of my eyes is six foot across, and it's got this great big bubble coming out of my mouth saying, 'What are you fucking looking at?' It's mental. I even put a halogen lamp on it to make sure it was visible, so it's actually costing me money. But I get off on the fact that one bloke that I'm never going to meet is gonna go back laughing to his gaffer at the nick and say, 'You know what that Courtney's done now ...' And now every fucking helicopter that goes anywhere near here makes a point of flying over just to see it.

The other day this geezer from across the road came and told me some coppers had been on the roof of the flats he's the caretaker of, and when they got up there one of them said, 'I've lost my bearings, mate.' Now from up there you can see Crystal Palace, the Millennium Dome, the London Eye, Canary Wharf, every fucking landmark in London, so how anyone can lose their bearings is a bit of a joke. Even Stevie Wonder would know where he was. But the copper goes on, 'So which way is Chestnut Rise?' – which, if you didn't know, just happens to be my address. Then they've just set a camera up pointing directly at my house and cleared off.

As soon as the caretaker told me about it, I thought we could have some fun here. The trouble was, although this geezer could get us on the roof, there was some nasty concierge bastard in the flats who wouldn't let us in the building. So me and Brendan got the old potato printing press out, knocked up this wicked-looking official police document, marched over to the guy on the door and said, 'We've come about the camera on the roof.' He asked for some proof, so we showed him the letter – it's got the full plod letterhead and everything. A proper genuine fake if ever there was one. And I said, 'If you want to check up on it, just tell the station DC Ourtney's here.' How I got that line out without cracking up I don't know – I'm a better fucking actor than I thought! But he's a lazy bastard really and can't be bothered with the hassle, so he waves us through, and we can't get out of his sight quick enough so we can have a proper laugh.

Up on the roof we just danced around the camera like a couple of naughty schoolboys, singing 'You Need Hands to Love Someone'. It was one of those set-ups that doesn't have film in, it was just beaming live pictures back to the station. So we took the battery out and left the fake letter underneath it and scarpered back past the bastard concierge. If someone had pulled a stunt like that on me, I'd have gone, '*Touch*, Courtney, you got us there.' But no, it weren't long before I got the letter warning me about impersonating a police officer. You've heard of the Serious Crimes squad – this lot must have been the Not So Serious unit. *Wankers*.

As that little episode reveals, they scrutinise everyone I'm with, and they see me having a laugh with them. That's why it's so hard for the police to accept I've retired, because I still keep such colourful company. If you look at the Frankie Frasers, Freddie Foremans, Tony Richardsons – when they said they'd retired you believed them because they were seventy-odd. But people look at me and go, 'Naah.' Course, I do know the odd character who is genuinely active and they have to be proper careful around me. They know I'm red hot and it seriously impacts on who and how I can meet.

Even before they tried to kill me in my 'accident', I've known the authorities have a bit of a problem with me and they've even taken it out on my missus and any of the chaps who come into contact with me. After Ronnie Kray's funeral I couldn't really do anything naughty any more, but even the legit avenues were shut to me. They're just legit cul-de-sacs now as far as I'm concerned, so cheers for that, Ron. My doormen were all told, 'If you're one of Dave Courtney's boys you won't even get a licence for a fucking telly, you cunt, let alone for security.' So they all had to stop working for me or lose their livelihoods. They wouldn't let me have a publican's licence for The Albion, in case I actually made some money at it – all they need's a chain of Courtney alehouses up and down the country, can you imagine? But what's even worse is that clubs or theatres that I'm booked to appear at get the visit or the phone call from some suit, like Al Benson did at the Harlow Playhouse, and suddenly they're worried about losing their licences if they put me on. So I get the 'Dear Dave' phone call telling me I'm dumped. And I feel for them, all these fuckers who do the dirty on me, 'cos they all try to spare my feelings and come up with all this different crap about there being a fire in the front row or their accountant's run off with the keys or the usherettes are having a fucking Ann Summers party that night and they've double-booked. They all have a different excuse of why they're cancelling, not realising how many times I've heard it and I feel for them, I do. 'Cos I wouldn't want to fuck Dave Courtney off.

The worst aspect, though, is that people who I consider my friends, or sometimes people who want to be my friends, get picked on too, just because they know me. Brendan's had a load of it, of course, but then he's what the Old Bill call a 'known associate' of the 'criminal mastermind' Dave Courtney. When actually he's just a mate who helps me out a lot. Brendan's had the bugs in his car (which I thoughtfully tried to destroy by writing off his Range Rover), the full fucking going over from the VAT and tax people and even this stunt. Talk about below the belt – this one's lower than a snake's arsehole. Brendan's company did some work on the Channel Tunnel rail link that involved some impressive fucking sums of money. But things weren't going smoothly for him in the accounts department despite all the government cash swilling around and then this bird in the main offices there told him why. Apparently some senior police officer strolled in and said they suspected Brendan of money-laundering and told them not to pay him – their theory was that it would force him into using undeclared cash and flush out the laundered loot. So whereas every other contracted fucker is paid on 30-day terms, Brendan's got 90, 100, 120 days passing before any cunt even starts saying the cheque's in the post.

Nasty fucking cunts whoever thought that up, but I take my hat off to them really, 'cos I'd do exactly the same. If I didn't like you, I wouldn't want anyone else liking you, it goes without saying. So, if I can engineer my friends to fuck you over in some way, I might do that. I think it's the same with the police. If they don't like you, they get the VAT man to fuck you, or the Inland Revenue to fuck you, or your bank manager or traffic wardens. They'll load you up with speeding penalties, parking tickets, fines for overdue books at the fucking library and crap like that till you're on your knees with it all, and then they'll really start to put the steel toecaps in.

It's not only Brendan who gets it in the neck just for being Dave Courtney's mate. I picked another mate up at work, he was a security guard at Asda, and took him out in his lunch hour to buy a dinner suit for when he was working the door. When I dropped him back, his locker had been emptied and he was sacked. 'You can't be security round here if you've got friends like that,' was the reason he got.

Then I spoke to this posh bird, Ashley, who was on the Stock Exchange and who was helping me to get film investment. The same day she put my name in the computer, the suits came down and got rid of her. Downsizing they called it, but fucking funny it was just her.

Even strangers who write to me from the nick don't always know what they're letting themselves in for. I always try to be nice and write back, I'm a regular Postman Pat, but, as soon as the screws see who his new pen pal is, suddenly the geezer's getting a bit more 'special' attention. They might not even give him parole, because they don't want one of Dave Courtney's boys out, imagine that. I could actually get someone an extra year in prison, so I make them fully aware of that before I start a friendship.

On the good side, a lot of people ring with stories like, 'Dave, I got pulled by the Old Bill but your book was in the car so I got let off.' That feels pretty blinding, I can tell you. The fact that actual coppers have read my book and liked it, that's proper wank material, that is. The fact that any of them can actually read is wicked in itself. So maybe there's more good than not out of being around me, but I feel for the ones it goes wrong for. You pay dearly to be my mate so I love you more when you are. I love all the old-fashioned nonexistent rules of loyalty and all that shit. If I was going to be a criminal in today's society, I would have to retire quickly because I would come very second having things like loyalty and respect. I'd just get shot in the back.

All right, so that's mates, strangers and yours truly all dealt with. And I can see that we would be fair game to the coppers, so obviously they're gonna use whatever toys they can to trip me up. But this is where I think they step over the fucking line: when they mess with my family to get to me. And I don't mean my dear old mum or my wife, I mean my fucking kids. Can you believe they would stoop so low as to use my children to score a point against me?

What happened is this. Jen's daughter Drew, who I've raised as my own kid and who calls me 'Dad', went missing. When I've gone down to the police station to report her missing, they've done their little thing and got social services involved. The next thing is the Greenwich Murder Squad has turned up saying they're looking for things in the house, telltale signs, maybe an address Drew put down of where she's going. So it sounded feasible enough. Except five men come in with three suitcases, like they're checking in for a dirty weekend at the Savoy. I said, 'Hold on. If you're coming in to look for something, what are these suitcases full of? Bugs maybe? You should be going out with three suitcases, not bringing stuff in. You should be bringing fuck all in.'

Three times they came round looking for things. Once I found this copper in my bedroom looking inside a vibrator. I said, 'Do you really think Drew is going to leave a note of where she's staying inside a vibrator? Now shut the fuck up and get out of my house.'

So everyone's involved, but the social services get the message from the police, 'Don't worry, we know where she is.' Because they bug my phones and constantly monitor my house, the police knew exactly where she was, of course they did. But they weren't exactly in a rush to tell me. In fact, they took the opportunity to ask her, 'Has your daddy got guns on the wall? Is there white powder in the house?' And she's scared and saying anything they want her to. *Touch*.

After I threw the murder squad out, they started saying

I'm hindering the investigation. Then Drew came home. Now she's told us everything: how they knew where she was, how they were listening on the phones. And that just freaked me out. Because I am fully aware of some of the naughty things they do, I've got a little bee in my bonnet about it anyway. But because the police are aware I'm publicising what they do, I think they have to fuck me over somehow. They have to bring this one down. They use every fucking possible opportunity to hurt me, I know that. But they allowed me and her mum to run around thinking she'd run away from home when they knew where she was, just because they thought they might get something on me. They got the social services to keep quiet. It was just a bit too fucking much as far as I was concerned.

If that's not painful enough, the bastards had a go at twisting the knife with this little publicity stunt. When Drew ran away from home, the *Sun* was informed by the legal authorities, which is the police, and this is what they were told: 'This is the picture you can use, and this is the wording if you want to write about the story.' As I said, these journalists know me very well. They've been writing about me for twenty fucking years. And one of them said, 'This is what we were told to put in.' It's a photograph of me – not Drew – and the story basically gave my name and my address, and called me an informant, murderer, friend of the Krays and everything else, then right at the end they said, 'Oh, by the way, his daughter's run away.' They didn't say she was black or nothing, but they managed to get another kick into me.

Anyway, it weren't pretty. But don't ever make the mistake of thinking the social services aren't part of the same mob as the Old Bill, 'cos they are. And if they can stitch you up, they will.

7. TASMANIAN DEVIL

Ramadan, Roman and revenge

I'm a Muslim, as it goes, and I'll tell you why. I was in a special unit at Belmarsh and inside there was this proper Yardie. Now every black geezer who gets nicked says he's a Yardie, every Irishman says he's IRA, every Chinese bloke says he's a Triad. But a real Yardie is a scary cunt. And this geezer in front of me was a *fucking* scary cunt. It's the last meal of the day, there's only eight of us in this unit, and he's got this pile of sandwiches, a pint of milk, an apple and everything. So I said to the guard serving, 'I'll have that, please.'

And he said, 'No you won't.'

I said, 'Don't fuck me about, just give me the apple then, like him.'

'You can't, that's Ramadan.'

'Well, I'll have some Ramadan then,' I said. I thought it was a Greek dinner, I didn't know what it was.

The guard says, 'No, no, he's got that meal 'cos he's a Muslim.'

I said, 'Well, I'm a Muslim as well.'

He said, 'No, you ain't, you're Church of England. It says so on your door.'

I said, 'Well, no fucker asked me. I remember you lot hitting me on the head with truncheons, saying, "What's your name and where do you live?" but to my recollection no one said, "By the way, what's your religion?"' I'd have remembered, believe me. So they think I'm a Muslim and they serve me up all this Ramadan gear. It was good stuff and it tasted even better knowing I'd annoyed them. Any problem you can cause them inside is a good problem. You know what I mean? Anything to trip them up.

Later that night, about two o'clock and I'm fast asleep after my tenth wank, they've come round, banged on the door, turned the light on and said, 'It's two o'clock.' Thanks very much. And back I go to sleep. Then they're back round again going, 'Oi, Courtney, it's five o'clock.'

I said, 'So fucking what? Has someone bought you a watch?' And they pushed something under my door, like this little Barbie doll quilt, like a blanket for your toe. It's a fucking prayer mat, ain't it, but I have no idea.

So seven o'clock rolls round and I'm in the queue for breakfast. 'A bacon sandwich, please,' I say.

'No,' the guard says.

'Well, why not?'

'It's Ramadan.'

I thought, Ramadan, I've fucking heard of that ... 'Oh yeah, Ramadan – I had that yesterday. Dead tasty.'

'Well that's got to last you twenty-eight days.'

'I've got to eat the same thing for twenty-eight days?'

'No, you don't eat at all in sunlight hours.'

How the fuck do you ever get a fat Muslim? You don't eat in daylight and when it's dark you're asleep, so you're gonna starve to death, ain't you? So they come round at two o'clock in the morning with this mat, and 'cos I don't want to back down and lose face I go along with the Ramadan thing.

What slaughtered me is that in the Koran it actually says you must not wank. Or words to that effect. I understand the 'thou shalt not shag around' and all that but not wank? What's that about? It's the only thing you can do in prison that's free and nice. You can tell how much time someone's done 'cos they come home with one right fucking muscly arm.

Where am I going with this? Oh yeah, religion. That Jesus is a vain cunt, ain't he? I saw him down at my health club the other day – he was getting his nails done.

I used to be an atheist, thank God. But these days I'm definitely not anti-religion. We might have different names for it – Allah, Buddha, God – but all of us are pretty much aware there is something up there, I think. It's not like ghosts – I don't know whether there is such a thing or there ain't; I'd have to see one to believe it. But if anyone needed a sign of anything to make them go over the edge and believe, I think I got it in that coma. I genuinely felt I'd done all I could with the 'Go on, Dave, you can make it' stuff coming from myself. I'd run out of that, but something else made me go on. I feel something helped me.

I'll probably end up a Reborn Christian one day, although it wouldn't change my life. I'd still be a lying, thieving, murdering cunt. Or a Catholic, maybe. Now that's the religion to get into, ain't it? 'Cos it's got the Get Out Of Jail Free card, that religion, repent and you'll be forgiven – *touch!* And there's nothing namby-pamby about it, neither. The Mafia are the most fucking deadly firm of the lot, but before they shoot someone they're in church all the fucking time doing the old 'brains, bollocks, wallet, heart' cross thing with their hands. Then they go and kill someone, a couple of Hail Marys and crack on, repented and forgiven in one go.

Some people might say that, because I'm a naughty cunt, I'm not allowed to believe in God. I'm a murderer, a bank robber and a drunk, so I can't. And that stops people going the whole hog and admitting they do too, because if you're religious you're not allowed to go shagging and catch fucking herpes and be a car thief and all that. But it's a different thing. I don't want to make a mockery of the whole thing by saying, 'Yes I am a Christian,' 'cos to be honest I do and have done a lot of un-Christian things.

But with all that's happened to me, I've realised where my strengths lie and what it is that people get from me, and I have a very strong feeling that I will eventually be helping people somehow. I don't know what you want to call it, but I know I've been responsible for a lot of good out there. I make it very fucking acceptable for dirty big white skinhead gangsters to go out with black birds, for example. I think I definitely helped out there. And I do all the charity stuff, the talks in Borstal. I really get off on helping geezers out, so that's got to count for something, don't you think? And I reckon that's a bit of a gift from old Holy Hands upstairs, don't you?

Have a look at the chaps next time you come round. I ain't some fucking warlord, believe me. Half my boys could beat the fuck out of me. But what I can do is spread a little bit of wisdom, a little bit of knowledge, a little bolster here, a little battery charge there. I'm a fucking Duracell bunny where morale is concerned, 'cos I believe you can achieve anything if your morale's high. You can fucking hold out in the Alamo against the whole of Mexico if you fancy it. Do you understand what I mean? If that's what my job is, giving that, I think it's a help.

Where's all this going? Well, when I've come out of the hospital after six months, my wife's sodded off and I'm feeling and, to be honest, looking like shit, I had this little miracle of my own. I ain't saying it was a godly thing at all, although what it did do was make me think about the subject, which is what you've just read. But when I got to that point in my life where the only reason I'm keeping going is 'cos I know there's thousands of people out there who need me to pull through, where I've struck out when it comes to motivating myself, I needed that little bit of help from somewhere and it only fucking turned up on my doorstep.

When you're a man, and you're ill, proper ill, you need goals to get better for. I'm a real carrot and stick person. For me to go training, I couldn't, I'd be bored. But if I was booked to have a fight for November, I'd go training in June because, if I didn't, I'd get beat up. At the time I was at my worst low, worse than in prison. I was broke up, I was in bits, Jen had left and I didn't have anything to get better for. I'm not doing a 'woe is me', 'cos medically I was getting better, I was fighting, but my soul was not in it and I was being proper trouble.

My mate Seymour was living with me at the time. I've known him since I had a fringe. He had to carry me about, I was weeing out the back door 'cos I couldn't get up the stairs, it was fucking awful, I was in pain. Then there was this knock on the door and this beautiful girl called Taz was standing there. I've hobbled to the door, I'm barely able to stand up to open it and she said, 'Look, I've just moved into the area, mate, and I know you're single at the moment; I fancy a bit of you, what are you doing today?'

Fucking hell. *Touch!* What am I doing? I'm doing you, babe. Come on in! I was looking up and going, Thank you! Jesus might not be able to hold a fucking marble ('cos he's got holes in his hands), but He hasn't lost the old healing bit. Just seeing this bird on my doorstep made me stand up taller than I had for months, and it actually made me leave my stick in the hallway, and walk her into the lounge and sit down. It was total vanity, but that little cutie made me get better in my head. I had all these people saying, 'You'll be all right, Dave' and 'You were lucky to survive' but what fucking good is that? It's no fucking compensation. That don't cut it with me. I needed something to get better for and it turned up in the shape of that woman. Taz made me get better.

The attractive bit about Taz is she's a naughty girl; I'm judged by my past and so has she been. She's a fucking wicked shag who just happens to be stunning to look at (just look at the picture section if you don't believe me). She's got some lovely kids and she gave me the extra bit of vanity I needed to get better. Undoubtedly her best qualities are what nature has given her. She had a lot of catching up to do going out with a forty-year-old and obviously there were our little disagreements, shall we say, because of the age gap, but she more than made up for it in the bedroom. And I am a dirty old bastard! The sex is so good even the neighbours have a cigarette at the end. How dreamy was it for me? My missus had left, I was in a lot of pain, and she knocks on my door. And she never left!

Actually, that's not true, she did pop out at least once 'cos within about five minutes of meeting me she paid a little visit to the excellent Docklands tattoo parlour and got this wicked picture of me and my knuckledusters printed on the bottom of her back. She designed the thing herself and just gave it to the geezer and said, 'Get drawing.'

I imagine there's a fair bit of pressure on a tattooist at that point not to spell 'Courtney' wrong. Or put OBF, OB1Kenobi, or any other fucking thing instead of OBE. That woman who had 'Kelly Homes' written on her back instead of 'Kelly Holmes' will feel a proper tit till the day she dies. And I don't think Kelly was none too impressed, neither. And all those birds who've had 'Westlife' written on them have spelled it wrong too – anyone knows it should have been 'Pondlife'.

Because of where she wanted it, Taz's tattoo was six hours of an awful lot of pain. Which is about the same amount of time she'd known me before she got it done. Believe it or not, it was no suggestion of mine. I actually tried to convince her not to, but you can't tell her anything. You know what it's like, it's all new, you're in love, aren't you, she thinks your shit smells of perfume, and you do daft things. I've done stupid things over women a thousand times. 'Can I have a new fur coat?' Have two! It's true, though, innit?

And so she just went down and had it done. It was her thing and I certainly didn't lead her into it 'cos she already had one tattoo on the right side of her chest, a bloke's name: 'Stuart'. She's had that tattooed over with an angel's wing and she's gonna get another one on the other side so she's got a pair of angel wings on her tits. But she just liked the actual picture of me, it's the one I use on my flyers, my mug with the duster.

At the time she had it done I was having someone follow me around (even though I weren't getting that far from my sofa at the time) making a documentary about me for Bravo, someone called Ian, so he caught it all on film. He took six hours of film of the front of Taz's face with her going, 'Aaargh', 'cos she was topless and he could look at her tits. He didn't bother filming the back of her where the geezer was doing the fucking tattoo. He just filmed the front with her tits out. It was mental.

The tattoo does look proper wicked, but there is one thing about it. I hate to be rude, but when we're doing it from behind it looks like I'm sucking my own cock! How mental is that? That's a dream for me, although I feel right sorry for any other geezer who gets the same view. 'Er, do you mind if I go on top, love?'

But in case you haven't noticed, I do like a picture of myself, yes. I actually belt past speed cameras just so they take a snap of me. I was chucked out of the Jockey Club because I kept stopping at the end for photo finishes. In fact, Burnley Paul was in my gaff the other day and he picked up this old black-and-white picture of me done up like Rocky Marciano in my boxing prime and he said, 'Who's this, Dave?'

I said, 'It's me, you prick. You think I have pictures of any other cunt in my house?' Considering his dad was the one that painted the forty-foot-high picture of me on the side of the house, you'd think he'd know better.

But it seems to be the thing at the moment, people getting pictures of Dave on them. It's just a little sign of the firm, a little gang thing. Ria, one of my publicists who helps me out, she's had one of a knuckleduster on her backside. Wolves Paul and Lee Griffin have got them, so's Mark Fish, and Mickey Goldtooth has a picture of my face on his leg. And then there's Watford James. What a star he is. He was going to have a big tattoo of me in the court jester's outfit but his girlfriend Ellie, who is normally a lovely bird, went fucking mad. I can't understand it. So he's had 'Dave Courtney' written across his leg with knuckledusters each side. (But if you're reading this, Ellie, look away now 'cos he's just come round again and shown me this knuckleduster and my initials that he's had tattooed on the underneath of his big toe 'cos it's the only place he reckons you won't find it. It's absolutely the bollocks, so we took a picture on his camera phone of me kissing it. Obviously he'll have to die if that picture gets out. Dave Courtney, kissing some bloke's feet. Mad.)

Before I forget, there's a geezer called Roman living with me at the moment who's getting one done on his back. It's gonna be me in the pose of Christ during the crucifixion, arms out, head down, crown of thorns, the bollocks, like the bloke on the *World in Action* credits but without the extra legs. I can't wait to see that, it's gonna be fucking wicked. Proper iconic, too, whatever that means.

Roman is my Get Out Of Jail Free card. He's an illegal immigrant and a really nice guy. If he got arrested for anything he'd only do about three or four weeks before he got shipped back to whatever fucking Eastern European country he's from. 'Cos he's got that accent, over here we think he's fucking KGB. I clothe him, I feed him, he lives here rent-free. Wherever I go he goes, if I get laid, he gets laid, if I have a drink, he has a drink. But if anything ever happened to me, like if they walked in my gaff and found whatever, and they wanted to nick me, I'd go, 'It weren't me, it was him.' And he'd go along with that. 'Ees mine, meester.' So they take him down the police station and go, 'Fuck me, you ain't even supposed to be here,' and they send him home. Then he's back here again on the very next train before I've even changed his sheets. Anything in my car, anything in my house, I can't get nicked for nothing. For the purpose of the bugs in the house, how clever's that one, Sarge! 'Who was driving your car when you got all those driving tickets?' Dunno. 'Well, it's your car.' Yeah, but it's always open, I never lock it, any fucker could have jumped in.

It's flattering, though, isn't it, all these tattoos of yours truly? Of course it is. I'm fucking over the moon about it. I'm like, Wow, and because I can see how happy they are getting it done it's like double mental for me.

But speaking of mental, the one downside to the whole Taz thing was that Jen didn't like it. Never mind she was the one what had left me, she did not appreciate me having this young 21-year-old take her place. I guess she felt airbrushed out of the Dave Courtney history, which isn't surprising 'cos that's exactly what I fucking did. Literally. I got Welsh Paula and her friends round to paint Jen out of the mural on the side of the house and put Taz in instead. It's a fucking Michael Jackson trick, one minute the bird on horseback behind me is black, then she's white. But it's a proper excellent job as usual. Hats off to them all.

Only Jen didn't see it that way. So when we've woken up one morning and found all this paint sloshed over the picture, we haven't really taxed the brain cells too much to work out who we think dunnit. Little did I know, that was just the fucking beginning.

8. MY STORMYLICIOUS

Soul mates, support and starting over

It was annoying that Jen was going around saying all this 'Dave's a wife-beater' crap, but if I'm honest I knew she was happier not being with me so it was for the best she went – and until I met Taz I couldn't give a fuck what she said 'cos all our friends knew the truth. I just thought, Cool, I'm happy with that. Johnny Jacket was staying with me, Seymour was around, Genson was living here as well, so I wasn't gonna be a lonely old raspberry. And best of all I had the wonderful Stormylicious staying here as well, who actually just became the most fantastic nurse a bloke could need.

Let me tell you about Storm. Storm is my powerhouse. I get all the pats on the back for being Dave Courtney but this beautiful woman irons my clothes, she worries about my health, my diet, my fitness. When everyone is worshipping the star-spangly bits, she washes my shitty pants. Makes my bed, makes tea for the lovers I've brought home. Gets them cabs in the morning, vets them! She has been a good friend of mine for some six years and I have no doubt that she will be in my life for the rest of my life, please God.

Stormy was there to visit me in the hospital 'cos she was around when Jen was still here. Her and Jen weren't the best of friends. Although Jen was already planning to leave and it shouldn't have mattered to her, she could see there was a spark between us, even if we hadn't noticed it ourselves.

When Jen left, we started going out with each other and it was the easiest and nicest thing in the world. It just happened. And because Storm had been such a good friend anyway, it just worked. I suppose you'd call her a soul mate. She's the closest thing to Jennifer I've ever come across. I think me and Jennifer had something really special and I still think that. What we had was enviable to the world, that's the truth, and when it popped it popped a bubble for a million different people who just wanted that one to work. But on a par was my relationship with Storm, who would love you in what I can only describe as 'the right way'. I need to be loved by a mum as well as a shag. I need to be looked after as much as I need the girlfriend thing, you know what I mean? I'm a useless cunt, right, and I can't fucking remember fuck all. I can't remember where anything is, paperwork gets on top of me, I can't iron, I'm a fucking wanker. And Storm helped me sort all that out.

When I met Taz, Storm was actually living here at the time. But Storm took the view that anything that made me happy made her happy. How better a partnership than that can you have? You can't ask for more than that, can you? But Storm's outlasted everyone else and she normally knows the end result with the others before I do or the other lady does. 'Oh well, anything to keep him fucking happy.'

When I moved Taz in, Storm and I stopped shagging. Then, at the end of my relationship with Taz, Storm and I picked up where we'd left off, which Taz was cool about 'cos she had her own little things going on. Storm swallowed it that I was seeing Taz, and Taz swallowed it that I was seeing her. Taz was totally aware of my involvement with Storm before she came here, so it weren't a bolt out of the blue. She knew that Storm was an intimate friend of mine.

While Taz and I were at the beginning of our relationship, me and Storm were on hold, 'cos she thought I had a chance of happiness there. But later on it sort of evolved that we got back at it. But it wasn't a hidden thing that I was with them both. If I'm honest, it would not be beyond the realms of reality that me and Storm end up together partnership-wise, marriage and all that, 'cos she gives me a licence to play, which is what Jennifer did. It's a hard one to find someone that can genuinely go along with that and not let it eat her up. Like I said earlier, some geezers can strip an engine in a day, some can draw pictures so real they're like photographs, and I can talk two birds into having a relationship with me and not minding that I've got another one on the go. That's life. And it's not a fucking bad one!

I don't want to fill my book up with shitty religious bits, but I do want it to come out that Storm is a Christian, which I found very attractive about her, so I think it's important to mention it. She's also actually a star in her own right. She's been signed up by Universal, she's been in girl groups, she's produced records, she's a writer. She's writing for Emma out of *Big Brother* at the moment. And she *knows* me. Which is very hard for anyone to do. It's not that I'm complex, it's just that *I* don't know me so I couldn't actually help you. But she knows a lot of me. She's very funny, which is very important. We've been abroad a lot together and she's a very important part of the structure of the whole Dave Courtney empire, so to speak, which is being single-handedly sailed, steered and fucking captained by myself – and loads of other people who don't jump up for the glory. They're just there to help Dave and I'm just lucky to have people like that around me. For whatever reason it is, I want to thank them all. I love ya!

There's loads of unsung heroes I should mention, so here's a few more, starting with H. She's a lovely girl I met a couple of years ago through a mutual friend, Mark, who died in a motorbike accident. She's become another of the sort of backroom boys under the Dave Courtney umbrella of people who help me, you understand? We'll have a laugh together but she'll come round here and put ornaments up, do the washing when the washing machine has packed in, tidy up, and all that without jumping up and saying she wants the glory of going to the Brits. Instead, it's 'Give me another Stanley blade so I can clean the floor up, please.' I don't know what I've done to deserve it but I'm fucking grateful.

Another unsung hero is the lovely Ria. You can tell she's one of us 'cos she has the knuckleduster tattoo on her backside. What a hallmark of quality that is. If you want to check out a bird's credentials, ask to see her arse and look for the sign of Dave. Ria's as close to a manager as I've ever got and she deserves a medal for that, 'cos can you imagine managing me? It's like trying to shag the Invisible Man. 'Fuck me, where's he gone now?' Along with her kids Lee, Jamie, Ricky and Eleisha, and her mum – hello, Ria's mum – she's really put in the hours over the years to get me where I am today. Plumstead. *Shut up!* She's sorted out gigs for me and just been a star with general backup. And she does a lot for charity but she's one of those who don't like to talk about it – so I fucking will.

Ria actually runs this kids charity down in Rochester called Misunderstood, which helps look after and generally give a leg up to kids with ADHD – that's attention deficit disorder. To you and me ADHD is fucking naughty kids playing up until their mums, who have no control, hit the little darlings. But now they've realised it's a medical complaint so they've given it a name and everything. And I'm the patron of its charity.

'Cos I've been in and out of stir, I realise that ADHD has always been around – how else do you explain the recurring population of all prisons? Up to a certain age, what you get up to is called bad behaviour 'cos you're a kid. After your eighteenth birthday that same behaviour becomes prisonable, so these kids seriously need a bit of help between the age of learning and the age of being banged up – and that's where I come in.

Ria thought I might genuinely be able to help these kids by telling them about stuff that's happened to me and pointing out how things could turn out for them. And I should know, 'cos I might even have had the thing myself. I was one genuinely naughty kid. It didn't matter how many clumps round the head I got, I just had to do it. I didn't care if I got caught, 'cos weren't it funny! So that's what I do, I give talks and advice. I don't like giving money to lots of these charities 'cos you don't know where it's going. Look at Oxfam. Buy half a fucking rhinoceros – what is that about? Or Red Nose Day. Is that meant to be funny? Instead of dressing up like a cunt on live telly to improve your career, just put your hand in your pocket if you're so worried about all that. *Pricks*. I personally believe a lot of charity-givers do it for the pat on the back, so that's why I'm involved with something I believe in and I think I can contribute to. And the fact that some of Ria's kids have the thing as well means I'd never say no anyway.

Through Misunderstood I was invited by the Prince's

Trust to give little speeches and hand out prizes to kids who'd turned up to school for thirteen weeks without having a day off. What chance have they got in life, poor little sods? But I actually get off on it 'cos the kids I'm doing it for are all people I would try to help if I saw them in the street anyway.

Ria also arranged Party in the Park in Rochester Castle. Hiring out that place is a job and a half, but, like I said, if she can book Dave Courtney to appear somewhere and then make sure he turns up roughly on time, hiring a stately home is a piece of piss. That was a great day out. We had the Crimestoppers there, we had motorbike exhibitions, we had the Lord Mayor come down to do his bit and the whole thing was hosted by Dave Courtney. Obviously as it was a castle, I had to dress up as a king, didn't I, just like I do every day at home. I stood at the top and all the kids down below had to sing, 'You're the king of the castle.' Wicked. Anyone who said 'dirty rascal' was chucked in the moat. And 'cos I had it with the Lord Mayor, then he started inviting me to all these fund-raising events he had going on down there, including a few memorable karaokes. I've got to give it to the geezer, his mayoral chain is serious bling, but that didn't stop him getting up to belt out a few Iron Maiden numbers. He's been a good friend ever since.

Someone else who's gonna get a big shout whether she wants it or not is my Donna Cox. She's another one who's given more free time to helping me than I deserved and she's been the nice voice at the end of the phone selling Dave Courtney for more years than she'd care to remember. She also happens to be the adopted daughter of Reggie Kray, so she's a bit of a star in her own right and I love her to bits. She's now a very busy lady with her new career as a property developer down in Somerset, but that didn't stop her spending loads of time with me when I was in hospital. I look forward to a long and happy relationship with her.

Speaking of long relationships, a geezer called Jerry, who I've known since I was at school, has this website called www.knuckleduster.org, which has my full blessing and co-operation. He just does it for the crack, so Jerry's not into anyone complaining to him about me or getting involved with the unpleasant stuff in my life, but all the nice things about Dave Courtney and his little firm, like pictures, interviews, the books, the DVDs and the records and all that are right up his street. Jerry also runs a very active social calendar through the site which I involve myself in loads. Next time you're down at Skinny's in Brighton, look out for me and regulars like the Wolf, Len and Les. Talk about all things Brighton beautiful ...

Talking of websites, I met Malcolm Vango, a very good web designer, a few years ago through Ria; they're distantly related, and not only was he a Dave Courtney fan but he was also a diamond of a man. So *touch*. He's another classic example of one of my friends who ain't your average gangster's mate. He was just this little country boy from Bude in Cornwall and then he found himself coming up to stay at the house with all the famous naughty boys. He came to Cannes with me, he comes to my film premieres and he's living the life of Riley now and deservedly so. Unfortunately, he recently had a couple of heart attacks, which he says were stress-related, and I just hope that weren't nothing to do with me and my mates!

While we're on the subject of the information super-highway, what is it about these web forums? It's so easy to be anonymous on them that anyone who's bored can ping a few unpleasant words over and no one will know who it was. If you ask me, these fucking websites have taken away real manhood from people. If someone wanted to have a row with you in the old days, they used to knock on your door and go, 'Oi!' Now they type 'you're a wanker, and I'm not telling you who I am and where I live' and they press 'send' and you've got an email volleying you off from someone you don't know. What the fuck is that about? Not being computer literate today is a real minus in your fucking arsenal though. To people like me, forward-slash double-click just means a geezer being stabbed and shot twice. (Have you heard about OJ Simpson's website? It's called www.slash.slash.backslash.escape.)

On the other hand online casinos are another matter. I'm thinking of getting into that in a big way in the next year. It'll be yet another avenue for me to go and say, 'Come and get a load of Dave Courtney.'

And playing online could save your life. The last time I played poker we used tarot cards. I got a full house and eight people died.

you were an old bloke with a bird like Taz hanging off your arm (amongst other things) you'd want to fucking shout about it.

Look at it from my point of view: I don't mind Jen running around telling people I smacked her 'cos anyone that knows us would know that was a lie. And, anyway, I was telling people about the time I took Jen to the premiere of *Godzilla* – and she spent three hours in the foyer signing autographs.

But the thing is, Taz didn't know me that well and the last thing I wanted was my new lady and her family hearing all this 'Dave's a wife-beater' crap, so that's when I decided to tell the true story of Jen leaving me and how I never really clumped her, it was an accident. All I'm concerned about is clearing my name of all the 'wife-beater' shit Jen's been going around saying, and showing off my new bird. So I put out, 'This is exactly what it's about: Jen left when I was ill, I'm quite happy, I'm looking after the kids, I don't want to fall out with anyone. Everything's OK, but that's what it's about. Yes, she did get the occasional clump, but then so did I, yes I did fall on her, yes I did break her rib. But if I was gonna hurt my missus, I ain't gonna jump on her and do a Jonny Wilkinson manoeuvre to break her up.'

I'll admit I probably wouldn't have said anything if Taz hadn't come along – 'Hello, world, I've been dumped and I'm a bit lonely.' Yeah, I really wanna boast about that. *Stop it!* But as I had got a new lady and as she happens to be proper tasty, and as it's fucking embarrassing when the old one's running round saying you're a bird-basher, I'm just going, 'Stop going on about me being a beater and horrible bloke – you're the one who left me.' But it's actually had disastrous effects on Jen.

And then, fuck me, if Armageddon didn't break out. In her anger, Jen's turned into this monster from the blue lagoon and turned her attention to me. So, four months after our little dances with crutches episode, and seconds after I'd met Taz, she's gone to the police to say she wanted me nicked for ABH. Four fucking months after it happened? *Please*.

Now this is proper playing into the authorities' hands, ain't it? I had to go and pick Genson up from the police station shortly after for some other business, and they've gone to him, 'Say thank you to your mum.' And he's gone, 'Why?' And they've said because she's giving them Dave Courtney on a fucking plate. All these years of him slipping through their fingers and now his fucking missus has gone and handed him in on a silver platter. That huge 'yes' you heard then was the sound of a tsunami of spunk as half the Metropolitan Police cracked one off to celebrate.

Once she's got the backing of the boys in blue, Jen can pull a few strokes that normally she'd have been carted away for. And that's what hurt me most, 'cos I know they're sitting there rubbing themselves going, 'We don't even get the blame for it. We just help her and she fires the bullets.' At least I think it was her; see what you think.

Someone sent people here to the house to beat Taz up. People came up here to wreck the cars, to tip paint over the mural and to threaten my witnesses not to go to court to defend my assault charge. I had people ready to go to court to say, 'Jenny's come on to me' or 'I'm too scared to baby-sit for her', and they were told in no uncertain terms not to. This doctor actually was ready to say I looked like I was beat up, I was the worse-off party after the fight, and someone somehow found out about him and paid him a visit. We had the door broken down when someone came to try to get some dirty photos back, then this bird came in and while she's talking to someone on the phone – and I wonder who that could be – she's attacked Taz, nicked a machine gun off the wall, and clumped the fucking baby-sitter round the head with it so she had to go to hospital. All the while giving an update on the phone: 'I'm in now ... she's in the bedroom ... I've got the gun ...'

Why don't you make your own minds up? For example, Taz rang 999 seven times in one day saying there's a woman outside the house with a fucking screwdriver trying to stab her. It just so happened to be the night we was on Men and Motors with me asking her to marry me – you don't think anyone got jealous of that, do you? Anyway, Taz is going 'She stabbed my baby-sitter last week, come and fucking help me!' Seven times? It took six-and-a-half hours for the first policeman to come here after a 999 call. Now it's all on tape, they're all timed, these are official facts. A policeman was actually driving past my house when the intruder ran out with the stolen gun, screaming, jumped in a car and drove off. We went down there and reported it, but they lost all these records, all the records of the damage to the cars. Then I got a court injunction to stop the person I suspected was breaking in here. She's got the hump with that, so she's come round, kicked the door down with her mate when I'm not here, gone upstairs while Taz is in bed, and started rooting round. I'm down the police station saying, 'This can't be allowed.' They're laughing at me. They're wetting themselves, taking the piss that my missus was actually serving up Dave Courtney with a side order of fries. There was a lot of goading, expecting me to respond.

At one point, Drew and Genson were sent up here to nick things. Of course, they're gonna do it, she's their mother. I've found them trying to nick the computer, so I've taken it down to the police station and gone, 'Here's a letter telling you she can have anything she wants. Here's the computer she sent the kids up to nick. Just tell her to keep them out of it.' I've played it one hundred per cent by the book.

So I've co-operated all I can and all I've asked is that someone stop the attacks on my missus and my house. And, surprise surprise, the police wouldn't do nothing. They kept saying to me, 'Did you *see* Jennifer in the garden scratching your cars?' I went, 'No.' 'Did you *see* her come in and throw a pot of paint up at the new picture on the wall?' No, but I believe that only Jen would want to do that. It was only when this girl who attacked Taz got drunk and pitched up the next day with another weapon that the police turned up and the girl ended up in prison for trying to get her.

But as for catching Jen at it, I had a bit of a brainwave. I realised the CIB3 would have seen her, because they're filming my house from across the road. Now CIB3 are not the normal everyday police. They're the internal investigations bureau, in other words, policemen who are just out to catch bent policemen. Which I bet is a fucking full-time job. Because I'd been to court and it had come out that I had a five-year investigation into me with bent policeman, it's all come out in the Old Bailey that I've had bent policemen for fifteen years and I'm still getting that information. Consequently this unit is still stationed outside my gaff. So they're still filming and bugging me and not telling the local police because that's exactly who they're trying to catch. That breakdown in communication was what did for me. I've no fucking idea how to get hold of CIB3, so I wandered into Plumstead nick and asked to be put through.

Guess what they said? Actually, they said fuck all 'cos Plumstead nick denied CIB3 existed. Which means either they're lying or they have no idea they're being monitored, which I suppose is quite satisfying in its own way.

But what the police or Jen didn't take into account was

this: my firm's resident cocksman Brendan was actually having a relationship with Jennifer's sister, Sam, during this time. And we all know what happens with pillow talk. The tongue is a more dangerous weapon in the underworld than the gun. The grapevine is a much more dangerous tool than anything else in the world. Little things spurted out in anger make more of a difference than in any other job. If you're a bricklayer and you go, 'He's a wanker,' it might not mean anything. But in the gangster fraternity the tongue, the grapevine, the spitefulness, they're all dangerous. And I'm afraid women getting involved in men's business is never a good thing.

Let's be honest, a woman can turn your head – and anything else she wants. When your heart or your cock starts ruling your brain you're in trouble. And women have had an awful lot to do with the course of history where gangsters are concerned. So many men's stupid actions can be attributed to what the wife wanted done. And we've all been there.

But, as for the pillow talk, I've had the benefit of it more times than I can remember, in fact I still hear things that have come from the sack. It's a tactic the police have been employing for years, so to be able to do it back to them actually gives me a hard-on.

Now Jen's deal, according to her sister and Brendan, was fifty grand, and the offer to move her to another country if she wants because I'm a self-confessed murderer. 'If you want to help put him in prison,' they said, 'we'll give you that money, criminal compensation; half for the ribs, half for mental cruelty. We'll have it that you're in fear of your life so you can't come into court; you have to do it via video link, that all helps. He'll get guilty. The worse you can make it, the better.'

She's got off to a good start, getting me nicked for Actual Bodily Harm, having loaded firearms and Class A drugs in the house, mingling my kids with known murderers. Not a bad opening move.

Brendan and Sam's relationship was on-off, on-off, but was definitely kept on while this problem was going on. He did actually like the bird as well, but he made an extra effort to keep it going on to find out inside information; you know, bought her some flowers every now and then, remembered her name and all that. Actually, Sam's a lovely girl. Anyway, apart from the cash, Jen was promised a Jag, but most importantly the police actually promised her they would keep everything out of the papers. In other words, she can get me put away, get me done for ABH, and then get on with her life when I'm out of her hair.

The police might have guaranteed Jen they would keep it out of the press, but they were finding it hard. I was on the blower to all the journalists I've ever met, arranging publicity stunts – you name it, I was doing it. But somehow the authorities were getting it all quashed. Journalists are writing the stories, and it's a dream for them, but out of nowhere they're all getting spiked. They've only got to press 'save' on the old word processor and they get a call from upstairs saying the story can't run. I got loads of calls from writers telling me about this. Freedom of the press, my fucking hairy arse.

On top of that, they didn't even report I was going to court. They weren't even putting it in the paper that I was arrested for wife-battering, 'cos they would have had to show both sides. Considering I had almost day-by-day punches in the press when I was being stitched up as a grass, fucking column-inches of insults, now I'm being totally ignored – and I'm going to court on Monday! Surely someone is going to see how much influence the police have over the papers!

But the way it works is this. There are hundreds of

stories breaking every day and a paper can only run so many. If a piece gets chucked on the fire, a journalist hasn't got time to stop and argue each one. It's no skin off the paper's nose, anything for a quiet life.

When I learned what lengths they'd go to to deny me any publicity, I full on went for it big time. And every time a journalist rang me and said, 'Dave, I can't get it in,' (the story, you dirty cunt) I just tried that bit harder. In the end I was turning up at court in a blond Barbie-doll wig and a case full of vibrators. I know how the system works. When they've got these signs up telling you what you can't take in, I look at it a different way: that means everything else is allowed. So I had eight vibrators in a bag, copies of my books, dirty magazines and a tape recorder. I ran it through the security machine and they said, 'Can I have a look?' This geezer opened it up, looked at all these dildos and porn and said, 'Er, can I take the tape recorder?' I said, 'Yes, thank you very much,' shut my bag and walked into the court with all these dildos while this guy's scratching his head. Now I get off on things like that. I'd find that really funny if it happened to me. And I know he's gonna remember that for the rest of his life. He's gonna be telling his mates, 'Courtney came in here in a long blond wig with a bag of vibrators.'

When I get in the court, the judge says to me, 'Please take the wig off, Mr Courtney.'

I said, 'Pardon, sir.'

He says a bit firmer, 'Would you please take that wig *off*.'

I said, 'I will, but I want someone here to write down that I had to take my wig off because you didn't like it. And I want to know when anyone else has been in court and had to take off their wig because the judge didn't like it. I wanna know if I'm being singled out or what.' I'm making a right fucker of myself, standing there in this long blond wig, but the judge is in a dilemma. Let's go through the history books, shall we? A judge don't like your wig so you've got to take it off? *Please!*

So I said, 'All right, I'll take it off,' and he says, 'No, no. Leave it on.' What a wanker! As if judges don't wear wigs to court – I was saving that one up for the next argument.

So I was doing all sorts of things like that and guess what – no fucker would write about it. Now that's fucking scary.

Right, so there's the ultimate weapon, Jennifer, primed and pointed at me. They've got a media blackout as far as Dave is concerned – unless the headline is 'Courtney's A Cunt' – and I'm up on a serious charge of beating up my wife. What else could go wrong?

Actually, quite a lot, 'cos the cunning bastards decided that an ABH charge wasn't enough, so they schemed of a way to get me twice. And Jen, to her credit, played a blinder in this one, although I was wise to it. Nice try, Mrs C, but no cigar.

What happened was this: she met Brendan and said, 'Tell Dave to give me twenty grand and I'll drop the charges.' Bosh, just like that. She didn't want to meet me, just to get me to write it down.

So I wrote the letter, and, yes, I gave her the twenty grand, and then I put on the letter: 'You do know I was giving you sixty grand when *Hell to Pay* comes out and that's without the divorce settlement. Why you're settling for twenty grand now, I don't know, but I'll fucking give it to you. You're cutting your nose off to spite your face. Just because I've got someone else doesn't mean I don't love you to bits.' And I've written it all out in a letter and Brendan took the twenty grand to give her but she weren't there.

A few days later, when he did find her, she had a little

chat with him. 'Look,' she's said, 'I'm getting £50,000 compensation for taking Dave to court.' Not for the first time the police reckoned they had a watertight case against me, and not for the first time they expected me to go Not Guilty even with all this evidence against me, so she was laughing. She's said, 'I'm saying he broke my ribs, he's saying no, and I've got picked up by an ambulance and he's already written a letter admitting he's lied.' He can't get Not Guilty, she thinks.

Now when she's seen Brendan, she's made a miscalculation, because Brendan has been known to be a little bit money-orientated and has the loyalty of a fish finger. But to her absolute disadvantage, she told him the truth, which included this little bombshell which, hand on heart, I did not fucking expect. She said, 'I am now working with Austin Warnes.' Which, in case you've been locked up for the past five years, is the bent policeman who took me to court for being a grass but ended up going down as bent Old Bill. She said she was seeing Austin – not as a boyfriend, but that they were in contact with each other. I now don't know if that was going on in the first place or not, 'cos you know how relationships start. We've all been there, haven't we? 'I weren't going out with her then, but I just started going out with her when we split up.' You know what I mean?

As if that weren't world-stopping news on its own, she's then gone further and asked Brendan to come onboard with her and become a police informant. This is before he's actually handed over the money. But he's like, 'Wow, I've got to tell Dave you said that.' So he left there, with the twenty grand, and came to me and told me she's working with the Old Bill, and that Old Bill in particular.

So now Jen's panicked, right? She's made a serious miscalculation with Brendan and she knows I'm gonna hear all about it very soon. So what can she do? Well, she's gone straight back to the police, told them about the letter and asking me for money and said, 'You'd better lock him up now 'cos he ain't gonna be happy.' So did they throw the book at her for interfering in a police investigation? Did they investigate her plan of trying to extort a bit of money from a suspect in exchange for silence? Did they fuck. They went, 'Dave's tried to pay you to drop the charges, so let's arrest him again for perverting the course of justice.' And that's what they did, even though it was Jennifer's fucking idea. Round one, then, to the Old Bill and their star witness.

10. OOH NEARLY

Videos, violence and verdicts

You've got to be able to think on your feet these days and I'll give you an example. Copper pulls this car over for speeding, opens the door and this fella is fucking battering his dog on the passenger seat. (I know that sounds rude, but it ain't.) The copper goes, 'Hang on a minute, I'm having you for speeding and, more seriously, cruelty to animals.'

The driver goes, 'Officer, you don't know what he's done.'

'Well, what was it?'

'He's just ate me tax disc!'

Thinking on your feet has never been a problem with me. I heard a noise downstairs the other night, so I went down and there's a geezer with a flashlight turning the place upside down. I said, 'What the fuck are you doing?'

He said, 'Looking for jewellery and money.'

I went, 'I'll put the light on and we'll both fucking look!'

I actually believe the phrase 'thinking on your feet' came about because of cheeky cunts like me. Think about it – when they're grilling you in court the bastards actually make you stand up so of course you do your thinking on your feet. If they let you sit down, it would be a different phrase completely.

Once they'd arrested me, the police had to decide whether to charge me. If you don't know how these things work, and I imagine a fair few of you out there are very familiar with it all, they don't necessarily charge you at the time of arrest. So I was given a day to attend Plumstead nick where my future would be decided.

The problem I had was this. Well, one of the problems I had, anyway. You cannot be on bail for two things. It's a clever little law they've got so, if you're on bail for one crime, getting charged with another one not only loses you your bail money from the first one, but it normally ends up with you going for an extended mini-break at Her Majesty's pleasure. So if they wanted to play a bit dirty, for example, the police could actually work that little bit extra hard to get a second charge against you just to fuck you up. Work it out: if you're in prison, you're not exactly in the best position to work on your defence for the other charge, are you?

I'll be honest, there were a few tense days at home before that one, 'cos no one really knew what the outcome would be. On paper I was arrested for trying to use cash to get my charge dropped; in reality that's exactly what I fucking did. I imagine the police thought, This one's a no-brainer, we'll have him by the balls on the next one. It was gonna take a full dose of the Courtney charm to get out of this one.

At home I was very aware that Taz was trying to put on a brave face for me when actually she was scared shitless. Even though she was young, she knew it was kind of her job to keep a lid on it all the time, really, 'cos there were so many other people depending on me. There's millions of people out there having the same thing done to them by the law, but they haven't got the chance to stand up and do anything about it. She knew I didn't have a choice in all this, and I love her for that.

So the morning came and I got all togged up, best bib and tucker and that, and I was driven to Plumstead nick by a good friend of mine in a convertible BMW. The wind ruined my hair. *Shut up!* I'd said goodbye to Taz already. Neither of us knew if I'd be home in the afternoon or in three months; things were that touch and go. But I was ready, duster in my pocket, 'clunk click on every trip' and all that. Bring it on.

Twenty minutes later, I was back outside the nick with the biggest fucking grin since Jaws found himself in a kids' swimming pool on a Saturday afternoon. Events, in case you haven't worked it out, had gone in my favour. The police, Lord love 'em, had decided not to press charges, which meant I was free to walk out of the nick. Two things in particular had swung it for me and, me being the bloke I am, I'm claiming credit for both.

First off, I'd saved myself by adding a last bit to the letter I'd given Jen. I didn't have to explain myself, but I'm glad I did. I made sure I mentioned that she asked me for the money and she arranged for it to be delivered. It was crystal clear that everything I done was her idea. Yes, technically it is perverting the course of justice, tampering with witnesses, paying someone to drop charges. But look at the mitigating evidence – she fucking asked me to!

And then there was this. The day before I went into the police station to get charged, Jen's own sister went down there and said, 'Look, my sister's lying. I was there. She made it up. She asked for the letter.' So when I went in to hear my fate the next day, they weren't too far from dropping the charges already. Of course, they didn't tell me that till they had to. They wanted to see me sweat a little bit first. But then they had to come clean, which is almost my favourite way to come.

How smug was I that they'd now dropped all the charges? Not Guilty, your honour, dotcom and all that. They were so happy to let me off, they're gonna have a charity night for me, a Dave Courtney Benefit. Are they fuck. But they do have the honour of winning the year's first 'Ooh Nearly' award. It's a bit like an Oscar, but the winner gets a statue of me instead of the little gold bloke in his pants. You know in football, when the geezer's going down the wing, he takes a shot and the whole crowd goes, 'AAAAAOoooo' – ooh nearly. It's exactly the same with the various police stations who have tried to get me over the years. You know, it's Courtney on the left wing, he's into the magistrate's court and – AAAAaaaa! And Courtney's under arrest, he's surely going down this time and – Oooo! Not Guilty. So I present an Ooh Nearly award each year to the police station that came closest to getting me. And so far, Plumstead – up your arse!

I have to be honest, I truly was not expecting to leave the nick that day. Yes, I was expecting to get Not Guilty at the end of the long haul, but not then, not for that one. And the reason they failed is: not enough significant evidence. They actually arrested me *then* went looking for the evidence. In fact, I think the journey home was when I experienced my first premature ejaculation in a convertible BMW.

As you can imagine, Taz was moist when I phoned her with the news. She was very happy, Storm was, everyone was. I say everyone – maybe not the Old Bill, I imagine. It's not easy for them to drop the charges, is it? It's like waving the white flag, throwing in the towel when they've actually had me against the ropes for so long. And best of all, they knew and I knew – and they *knew* that I knew – that this very seriously damaged their chances in the next case. Once Jen's been proved to be lying here, it's more believable she's lying in the other one. You follow me? So obviously I made a pain of myself before I left, and I made all the coppers shake my hand on the way out. They all tried hard not to. It's like, urggh, fixed grins and all that.

But that was only the end of round one. The case that I was allegedly tampering with witnesses for was due to kick off on 7 June 2004 in a London Crown Court, would you believe. They'd actually booked a seven-day trial at the Crown Court over a domestic argument between me and my missus. Charlie Manson chopping up Sharon Tate wouldn't have got that. And all the time I was nicked and waiting to go to trial I couldn't do any television, the police took my passport and basically made sure the months leading up to it weren't very nice. And they obviously made Jen feel confident 'cos of all the things she did to me and Taz in the run-up.

The big day came and I turned up at the Crown Court. No court jesters outfits, no entourage, just little old me and my briefcase on a beautiful summer's day. Quite low key? *Shut up!* Take a look at the Harley in the car park.

I actually told everyone not to come because Jennifer had told people I was gonna kill her in court. Fuck knows how I was gonna achieve that little miracle, 'cos her brief and her advisers – who happened to be the Old Bill – had managed to secure this behind-the-screens deal so I didn't even know where she was testifying from. Even proper rapists don't get that. I didn't like it much 'cos it's very easy to tell lies when you can't be seen. And of course she's gonna be good at that 'cos she's had a documentary crew living with her for a year, she's been in loads of programmes with me and even acted in my movie *Hell to Pay*.

And it's fucking hard to be cross-examined if you're not in the same room. You can have a proper row with someone when you can see the whites of their eyes, but if you do it by phone or letter or fucking carrier pigeon everyone has a chance to think rather than coming out with the truth. So I actually asked for us both to be put on lie detectors, 'cos I had nothing to hide, but that idea was thrown out. In the end, I went on my own, 'cos I figured the jury doesn't want to see all these threatening-looking blokes in the gallery, or they'll just start believing the Dave Courtney thing and not see I'm just an ordinary bloke.

When I got there I was feeling pretty confident, like I feel most mornings, 'cos I'm a bit of a flash monkey. I thought, What a lovely day for war, bring it on. As you get older you realise that hell hath no fury like a woman scorned. And that is very true. Men are only the stronger sex on the biceps. Mentally the man is nowhere near as vicious, cunning, vindictive, venomous or spiteful as the woman can be. Not every woman is, but give them the hump and they turn into a creature that you would not want to row with. Believe me. So I'm hoping that it wasn't Jen's decision and that an awful lot of her vindictiveness arose through the cases being manipulated by the police. I'm hoping she was just a pawn, a weapon to get me with. I think it was them loading the gun and making her fire it. But whatever the reason, it's gone past it being sad because I now genuinely hate her.

The only downside was that I knew that, whatever the outcome, Jennifer was not going to go, 'OK, I've lost the case, let's just carry on with our lives.' I never thought that for one minute. But I've still got a little soft spot for her – *just behind the shed*.

I might have been in court on my own, but I wasn't letting the side down when it came to having a laugh. Just 'cos I'm facing a few years for ABH, it don't mean I can't cheer up someone else who's down on their luck. I had recently done a show on TV where I'd given an interview in a swimming pool with just my shorts on. This woman from the case next door came up to me in the waiting room before I was due to go in and said, 'I saw you on telly – I didn't recognise you with your clothes on.' So I dropped my trousers and said, 'Recognise me now?' That actually got brought to the judge's attention and I got told off and threatened with losing my bail.

The actual case itself took five days. And what a fucking laugh that was. One by one me and my brief just tore into Jennifer's stories. The only reason it all took so long is 'cos I was enjoying myself so much. So I'm saying things like, 'If you're in fear of your life, how come you only live up the fucking road?' And she had no answer for that.

She was saying that I had guns in the house, I had drugs in the house, I had villains in the house – and my barrister's gone, 'It took you *fourteen years* to realise that wasn't your cup of tea?' They got out copies of her videos and books called *Gangsters' Molls* – and she didn't exactly look too unhappy about the lifestyle on them. So another point to me.

Then my guy asked her if she was violent. She could see where he was going with this: Dave's up on ABH but could it have been an accident or even self-defence 'cos you've thrown one? Anyway, through the power of television she's gone, 'No.' I had to laugh. It's like a footballer saying he don't like a nice roast or a bear in the woods going, 'I'm not shitting in there.' I'm not knocking her for it and I actually loved her for it, but I believe that violent is something Jennifer is. Violent people all dance fucking brilliant, they fight brilliant and they fuck brilliant. It's in everything they do. So, if you could put up with a headstrong bird and the occasional scratch, you actually got a better shag out of it. And I do like a better shag.

But even though she's in another part of the building and she's listening to all this on speakers and answering into a camera – she can't see us, but we can see her – Jen's still actually lost her temper with my barrister. It was round about the time they showed her photographs of people she'd allegedly beat up with knuckledusters. 'Are you *still* saying you're not violent, Mrs Courtney?' She actually flipped at that.

And that's how it went on. We asked her something, she denied it, we got out the proof, she got a bit more fucked off.

If I'd got any more turned on with proving her lies I'd have had to have a cigarette and a kip. But that weren't the end of it. Jennifer actually thought she was being clever by listing all the times she'd told a little fib for me in the past. She said she'd lied in court to help me, she'd lied to the police, she'd lied to the newspapers and to my solicitor Ralph Haeems. She even said she was in cahoots with Ralph and that, every time I was up in court and she had to speak, he scripted the whole thing. And I should fucking hope so – that's what I paid him for.

So my brief's gone, 'You admit you've lied in court?'

'Yes.'

'So how can we believe you now?'

'Er . . .'

So Jen's not doing too well, is she? It's actually getting a bit embarrassing 'cos her case has got more holes in it than Al Pacino at the end of *Scarface*, but she still won't let it drop that I smacked her on purpose. But then things got really mental when they played the 999 call that Johnny Jacket had made from my house on Jen's instructions. My lawyer goes to her, 'Were you unconscious?'

She goes, 'Yes.'

'Who rang the ambulance?'

'He did – I've already told you, I was unconscious.'

'Right, could you listen to this tape.'

Jen can't remember what she's said and so she thinks this is her winning ace. Try again, love. 'Cos the next minute the whole room hears her going, 'Tell him I'm unconscious!' *Thank you, God!* You don't know how much wanking material that one was!

Watching all this from my seat, I really felt for Jen even though she was trying to hang me out to dry, 'cos she was getting torn to pieces in there. I thought it was degrading to her. She seems to think she got some glory out of it by embarrassing me, but it actually humiliated her. She'd have realised that if she hadn't been beamed from down the hall. Jen lost it in court and was shouting through the TV monitors and to be honest it was a bit unpleasant. Talk about a video nasty. X-rated doesn't start to cover her performance. Luckily Jen wasn't able to see the jury 'cos she weren't there, but I could see them going off her with every word that came out of her mouth. She was only in there on the two days she gave evidence, which was actually a good thing for her, 'cos she would have lost the will to live watching the rest of it. Considering that every point seemed to go yours truly's way, my only question was how the whole pantomime lasted so long.

I don't have to tell you that, after five days (they couldn't even string it out to seven) of being accused by my own wife, I was acquitted of all charges. Even Jen's sister Sam couldn't have held out too much hope. She is not happy with me because she can't really be with Brendan while me and her sister are locking horns, but I think even she saw the writing on the wall.

I know I did. For the last hurrah I was on the blower to Courtney Central getting them all down to the court. I'd only gone down there on my own 'cos I didn't want to give any mileage to Jen's story that she was gonna be killed in the courtroom by her self-confessed murdering husband. I know everyone was going crazy, ringing me every day to find out what was going on. So, as soon as the jury went out to play make-your-mind-up time, there was no harm in a few dozen familiar faces dropping in for moral support and for the moment of truth.

So, when the jury shuffled back in after about three minutes' discussion – I reckon they was gutted they didn't get to stay in a hotel for the night – they had a gallery full of Courtney-ites to stare at. There was Lynne, Brendan, Tel Boy, Ruth, Seymour, Ritchie Hawsley, Martin, Pitbull, Rob Ferguson, Mark Fish, Wolves Paul, Ria, Dave Quelch, Guy, Tracy, my brother Patrick and Sarah, Taz, Storm and loads of others. You should have heard the noise when the foreman got up and gave it the 'we find the defendant . . . Not Guilty' speech.

While all my mates were whooping and hollering, I just nodded a thank you to the jury and the court officials and waited to be let out of my box. A lot of people wanted to know why I didn't do a little dance when the Not Guilty verdict had come through. But the thing about these trials is this: you can't really stand up and go *Yes!* when you get Not Guilty if you haven't done it. The only reason you go *Yes!* when you get Not Guilty is if you really done it. And I should know. So I sort of wasn't surprised, or overjoyed. Just glad it's all over – although I doubt it is for her. Jen'll always be a pain in my side, I don't have any doubts whatsoever. She was in a proper lose–lose situation. I mean, she's stood up now twice and tried to grass me up and now she's known as a grass, it's naughty, she's a silly girl. I know her. She's not that stupid. I know there had to be outside influences to make her do all this. But she still went along with it. And worse for her is, if a court's decided I was telling the truth, then Jen wasn't.

These are all things I thought about afterwards. At the time I was more interested in sticking on one of my trademark jester's hats and having my picture taken. Like I said with the end of the Austin Warnes case when I wore the same thing, 'Why don't people take me seriously?' Pull the other one, it's got bells on.

I seem to recall we did sink a few sherbets the night before, but the real party had actually happened the night before. Even though I knew I was gonna win, all my mates weren't so sure so I thought a little eve-of-war celebration at my house might lift everyone. And you never know, as long as it don't clash with *University Challenge* I might even put in an appearance myself. *Stop it!*

My friend Ruth is actually an entertainer by trade so she brought a full stage and PA system over, which she set up out the back. Karaoke is too cheap a word for it. We were proper singing. Elvis. El-fucking-vis. Beau was there, and all the mob from the courtroom. It was mental. And if I felt a little bit the worse for wear in court the next day, so fucking what. Either I was going down, in which case, who cares? Or I was going home. Ditto.

But I know what you're thinking. Jen's been given that much rope she could hang my mate No Neck Nick (it's like lassoing a double-decker) and she's been financially supported throughout. She's had all her fees paid, all her technical legal aid. Did I qualify for legal aid?

Did I fuck. If I got Guilty, then Jen actually got compensation, which is why she was so fucking keen to help out. Her plan was to move to Barbados as soon as the blood money started to come in. But I guess I kind of fucked that little plan up by not getting sent down. Not only did I not get legal aid, they actually nicked me for asking. They put the taxman on me and everything, but all that proved is I am totally broke. The only way I'm gonna come into money is if I wank in a till. It's not that I'm hiding it, I just don't need money. I don't pay to go anywhere, I don't pay to go in, I don't pay for my drinks, I get stopped in the street by strangers offering to buy me dinner, I don't pay for clothes, I don't pay for a haircut. If I want work done in the house people just come and do it for free. Just being around my place, things happen for you. I've got big by making everyone else get big. A car salesman might give me a Rolls-Royce but I've fucking sold him 25 in the last ten years. My little set-up is very similar to the Freemasons – and I really do mean Free. It's like I say, one man, one job. If you're a carpet-fitter, I only want you to be a carpet-fitter for me, I don't want you to be a gangster. But the amount of people I get you to do carpets for, you get rich. So when it came to Jen saying I had this and I had that, I've actually got fuck all apart from a film that's gonna make me a millionaire. In pounds, shillings and pence I've got fuck all. I don't have a bank account. Every time I go in to open one up, everyone puts their hands up. I'm like, 'But I want to put money in!'

Here's an interesting postscript to the story. Just when I thought it couldn't get any better than all the papers reporting the court case at last, and getting the facts out there for the masses to read, this little gem came out in the press.

When the policeman who arrested me for ABH had been at my house, he'd come up to me and gone, 'This Dave Courtney gangster bollocks don't impress me. I am not tolerating men who hit women. Got it?' Those were his last words to me. Three weeks later he got arrested for domestic violence himself so I thought that was absolutely the fucking bollocks and I was buzzing reading that. Taz got the full fucking five-and-a-half minutes that night, I can tell you.

11. BEAU SELECTA!

Kids in the crossfire 2

I went to a sex shop and got some of that powdered rhino-horn aphrodisiac. Forty-six quid it was! A full giro. So I bought some, got home and I'm stood there in the bathroom in my undies, posing in my pants like Chris Eubank. Remember him? 'I'm one of the greatest boxers that ever lived. People say to me, Chris, why did you become a boxer? Because my father was a boxer, my mother was a boxer, my grandfather was a boxer, and my auntie was a cocker spaniel.' Yeah, right.

When I looked at this rhino horn in the shop, the only instruction on the bottle was 'take with water' so I nicked a couple of Evians on the way out as well. But it said fuck all about doses, so I decided to take the lot. A full bottle of rhino aphrodisiac washed down with some Martell-flavoured water. Tasty.

Anyway, my missus came into the bedroom, stripped naked and lay on the bed. 'I've got the horn for you,' she said, 'show me what you can do.' So I ran outside and headbutted next door's jeep!

So that was the rhino horn. Another time a mate of mine got hold of a couple of those Viagra tablets. Big fuckers, they are, and unfortunately the first one I took got stuck at the back of my throat. I had a stiff neck all day.

So my mate got me some smaller ones and because they were so tiny I thought I'd better take a few more just to make sure I got my money's worth. So my missus is in bed waiting for me and I'm in the bathroom chucking down a dozen of these Smartie things. I recommend the blue ones. And fuck me, they've started to work. We are talking serious 41-gun salute. Hang your hat on it? Mate, you could raise the *Titanic* with it. Are we in for a night of it! So I've leaped out of the bathroom, gone running towards the bed, tripped on the rug – and pole-vaulted out the window.

Even that didn't dampen my 'ard-on. When my missus looked out the window, all she can see is me trying to get up, crawling on all *fives*.

Look, I know I've made myself sound a bit of a play-boy throughout this book but, in all honesty, that's the effect of a serious marriage break-up for you. It screws you up a little bit, you feel like someone's doing a Rubik's Cube with your insides, and you find yourself sort of rebelling against the things you've done for the last fourteen years. I know it sounds stupid, me being a grown man and that, but I'm an analyser and I've seen it happen to myself. When you've been put through the emotional tumble dryer, it takes a while for things to set-tle back as they were. Shake up some oil and water together and eventually they'll sort themselves out so it's oil on top and water underneath. But before that hap-pens, you have all sorts of interesting patterns going on where they're working things out. And that's where I ended up.

The truth about Dave Courtney is I'm actually a family man, I'm a kids man. And here's a tip – always be nice to your kids – 'cos they're the ones who'll choose your nursing home. But I love the domestic bit, I love the kids bit, I love the cuddles bit, I love the little faces laughing bit. The most natural form of entertainment in the world is a child. I love their honesty and everything. Look at my house. It ain't a castle for a man, it's palatial for kids.

Which is why it fucking hurts me more than words can say – although I'm gonna give it a go here – to report that my kids did not come out of the Jen vs Dave split unscathed.

When I left my old home nearly twenty years ago it was with ten bin liners of clothes and a one-way ticket to this block of flats with a bird with two small babies. It never entered my head that they weren't mine and it's still like that today. Genson and Drew both call me Dad and, apart from not being blood, they're my kids. No different to Beau, Levi, Chelsea and Courtney in my eyes.

When Jen and I started to fall apart, that was tricky for all of us and I'm afraid she used how much I love these kids to get at me. Like I've said, they were sent to the house with a shopping list of things to take back to her to help her in court. I don't blame them for that – they've been brought up to do what their mother says.

What was really shitty for them, though, is that she didn't want them to live with me, did she? How can she go around saying, 'I left Dave Courtney 'cos he's a wife-beater' if her two kids are still living with me? But Jen was living in a tiny bedsit, so where did that leave them? 'You can't live with him and you can't live with me.' Charming.

I was saying Genson could live with me, his mum was saying he couldn't live with her, but she didn't want him living here 'cos it was making her look bad, so he actually ended up living a bit rough for a while, staying at mates' houses and God knows what else.

He had a really bad three months of his life where he was living really like a genuine street kid. He's running around doing a few naughty little things, nicking stuff, running off with motorbikes, breaking and entering – just being someone that I know Genson ain't really like. There's two sets of thieves. There's ones who are just addicted to it. It's like taking drugs, they just go out on the rob to pay for their drugs or 'cos it's an everyday habit. It's just work to them, just normal. 'I'm a thief. That's what I do.' And then there's the other set who are living on someone's settee and they're starving, so some of the things they would do in that position they themselves would consider inexcusable if things were different. But when it's the only way to stop you starving to death, it becomes a bit more acceptable.

Circumstances actually put Genson in a bad light and pushed him into things he wouldn't normally have done. But the police, using any opportunity they could to hurt me, they jumped on that one and tried to get to me by hurting him. It was so obvious they were just messing around to get at me and didn't give a fuck about him. When they hit him with this charge of robbery, they said they had five witnesses and a sample of his blood swiped from the outside of the downstairs window. When it actually got to court, this copper goes, 'I haven't actually got any statements, but five people all told me they saw him. Honest.' So nothing was written down, there was no names, no one signed anything. How is that five fucking witnesses? And the blood they'd found – yes, it was Genson's, but it was from a completely different window. So they had to drop all those charges but, for the three months leading up to the case, they put one nervous fifteen-year-old through the shit.

If you think that's bad, how they actually arrested him I think was quite disgusting. They actually rung me and said, 'Dave, look we're chasing Genson on a nicked motorbike.' I said, 'Well, get off it and use a police car.' *Stop it!* But they went, 'He's being really cocky and, in trying to shake us off, he nearly killed himself. So we're gonna back off but, for his own safety, please bring him down the station tomorrow.' At the time, I think they thought he was still living here. So I got hold of Genson and told him the message and he said, 'Yes, OK,' and he came round to the house. I rang the police and said we're coming down to speak to Mr So and So, but they said he was off-duty – call back in the morning. Because Genson hadn't been in the house for three months, we had a bit of catching up to do, and that was nice. But the next thing we know, there's a knock on the door and the police have piled in mob-handed to raid the house. It was absolutely fucking disgusting. They showed me a warrant for his arrest and just took him away. It was a stitch-up from start to finish.

It ended up they had him on twelve charges, which was enough to keep him in on remand at Feltham for three months, which is no life for a kid, especially one going through what he was going through with me and Jen. She might not have wanted him living with her, but Jenny didn't mind taking all the visiting rights and visiting him once a month, which meant I couldn't go in there. One day in court, she actually had a screaming go at Taz 'cos she'd brought Genson there, and I don't like the scene thing and neither did the magistrates. So they've gone to Genson, 'You can't have both your parents there, which one do you want with you?' and he's chosen his dad. I was chuffed to bits he wanted me there, but obviously it's made a rift between him and his mum, which was the last thing I wanted.

By the time it actually got to court, the police admitted that some of the charges they couldn't make stick with Sellotape, so they dropped it down to robbery and theft. When it came to sentencing, they said he'd already done enough time in remand so he got off with community rehabilitation classes six days a week for three months, and a tag for the same time. But the best bit was he was bailed at my address so he's been back living with me ever since, like he always has done.

Because he's decided to live with me, Genson's made himself an enemy of his mum's family. Obviously Jenny tried to grab as many people on her side as she could for something that was very hard to defend – which was leaving your kids, getting a one-bedroom flat and saying, 'I've got no room, go and live where you want, but you can't live with your dad.' Trying to justify that was hard and she let her mouth run away before her head kicked in. Her gob wrote a cheque her brain couldn't cash. Given a second go round, I'm sure she'd have gone, 'Yeah, you can see him,' 'cos I make a much better mate than a continual target. But she didn't.

By the time you read this, Genson will be a free man again. At the moment, 'cos he's my only child living with me and 'cos I know he ain't going to be here forever, he's actually getting both barrels of love from me. Lucky, lucky boy. I imagine in a year or two he'll have flown the nest, 'cos after being cooped up here with his tag for so long I'm sure all he can think about is being his own man and having his own space. That's his plan, anyway, although the cheeky cunt also informed me he'd be keeping his room at my place. Cheers for that, Genson.

With the Filofax I have, I continually help everyone. That's where my nickname The Yellow Pages of Crime came from, because I have contacts in every walk of life and my great skill is in putting people together. (I used to take them apart, but that's another story.) 'Cos my house is so busy, all you have to do is wait in my lounge and one day someone will come in who can help you make your million quid. If I put my mind to helping someone I can make a success of any person because of my contacts. And I have plans to help Genson. I asked him what he wanted to do work-wise and he said, 'Make some dough, innit.' Let's assume he didn't mean become a fucking baker. I should imagine he wants to get involved with something that's got two wheels on it. Four wheels will do, but two wheels would be dreamy. And I know just the people for him to talk to as soon as the tag comes off.

The worry I have is I won't have any say in what he decides to do because he's like a caged fucking animal at the moment and he can't wait to get out there and do this and do that and make up for lost time. He'll want to go to every fucking party, shag every fucking bird, clump every fucking prick. A chip off the old block.

It's very much concerning me that I will not actually be able to hold the reins when he's allowed out. He really feels like he's missing out and I'm trying to compensate by allowing him more friends round the house than I should do. But he's natural leader material. So full of good morals and honour and code and all that that youths around him actually warm to him. In fact, the only real genuine fatherly worry I have for him is, because he is leader material, he will be a man's man. Not that he will go with the wrong type, but he will probably attract the wrong type to hang around him. There will be people who will just like the feeling of being in Genson's firm. Being popular and leader material is very addictive and he probably won't want to hear any warnings from me. It's very hard to say to a young kid of sixteen who's been to prison, lived in a castle with Dave Courtney as his dad and who is genuine leader quality to not mess around with other people, to stick to a few mates and don't get involved with strangers who want to be your friends. Genson is already, I'm afraid, as the authorities say, set in his tracks. Whatever he does, they'll have their twist on it. It's like when Drew ran away and they kept asking her if Daddy kept any funny white powder in the bathroom. Er, talc?

The other thing with Genson is he's a hench. He's a big, good-looking fucker and he's only ever had one clump off me in his life. I can't remember what it was for, but this is my theory on smacks with children. It might be looked at as a bit barbaric by some, but I guarantee it works and if you ask my kids they'll tell you it made them better people. The continual *slap, slap, slap* is a complete waste of time. It doesn't hurt and, as soon as the kid realises that, he's not frightened of it any more. So what a smack is is a deterrent. Once, Genson got a lot more than a smack. He most probably hasn't had a hiding like that from anyone. I'm not saying I punched him in the mouth, but I proper let him know I weren't happy. But from there on in, the next time I say, 'Don't do that,' he's got something to fall back on and make him not do it – or he's got that decision to make knowing the consequences. If kids are naughty, the odd smack ain't gonna stop them. They'll just start hiding it from you that they're naughty, 'cos they can't stop it. The last thing I want my children to do is start hiding anything from me, 'cos I've got to be their best mate as well as their dad.

That's what prison is, it's a deterrent. They make it nasty so you don't want to do it again. And that's what a smack should be. And in Genson's case, it's made a really good kid. I never had to do it again. And funnily enough, I think prison actually worked for Genson an' all.

I know a lot of people take a look at me – which I'm chuffed about, obviously – and go, 'How else is the boy meant to turn out living with a gangster?' But I promise you he hasn't got a bad influence in the house with me. Just 'cos your old man's a chippy, it don't mean he leaves saws and off-cuts all round the kitchen trying to get you into the trade. Work is work and home is home and Genson's never really seen me do anything naughty at all. In fact, all of the big lessons you might get *not* to copy a gangster, he's actually lived them. I can see the kid across the road going, 'I want to be like Dave: big house, Rolls-Royce, nice clothes.' But Genson's actually lived with the nasty bits as well. He's been held hostage with machine guns in Tenerife, he's been on the wrong end of some police mind games because of his dad, so he knows what's what. All he ever hears me tell anyone who dreams of doing the gangster thing is 'Don't do it'.

I won't say Genson fell in with the wrong crowd when he was living rough 'cos, having me as a dad, he's what most other mums would call the wrong crowd to start with. 'I don't want you playing with that Courtney boy, all right?' I know I've already made a label for that poor little fucker. I learned that with my first son, Beau, so I knew it was gonna happen with the second. There are times when being Dave Courtney's son is no fucking bonus.

I remember when Beau was about thirteen or fourteen and he was just running around playing with BB guns with a few mates. They ended up outside this vet's and someone in there called the police and said, 'There's a bunch of kids shooting guns outside, you'd better send a car round.' So they turned up and just arrested him. Back of the car, down to the station, thirteen years old or not.

The kids had all had a can of Foster's each, and Beau weren't a big lad so it's had an effect and he was probably a bit lairy but that's it. Thousands of grown men are worse every Friday night. But it must have been a slow day 'cos they got him for being drunk and disorderly and firing these guns. Talk about sledgehammer to crack a fucking nut.

I got a call from his mum Tracey who said I should get down there sharpish, but that has actually just made things worse. The coppers have taken one look at me and Beau's gone from getting a slap on the wrist and a lecture to being charged with 'being in possession of an imitation firearm and threatening lives'. Suddenly he's looking at three-and-a-half years in fucking prison for having a game of cops and robbers – well, robbers and robbers.

That poor fucking kid. There was a proper court case and everything. No expense spared in the authority's courageous pursuit of this dangerous felon – *shut the fuck up!* Before I turned up, Beau was facing a ticking off for being drunk and disorderly and playing with toy guns, and then as soon as they saw me it's straight into their *Book of Made-up Charges* and suddenly he's being done for possession of an imitation firearm, intent to harm, threatening lives, murdering JFK and nicking Bernie Ecclestone's wheels.

It was really close in the end and he was advised to go Guilty on three cases on the understanding he wouldn't go to prison. In the end, he got six months' community service, aged fourteen. But he's still got a criminal record and I find that hard to take, 'cos I know they wanted to get at me and Beau just got in the way. He did actually say to me, 'Why couldn't Mum have come down to pick me up instead?' but he knows on a normal day I could normally have helped. He doesn't know I know this, but he told a mate of mine, 'I would always want my dad with me 'cos no one can pull any tricks on him. He knows everything.' Fuck me, I think I've got something in my eye. I love ya, Beau.

The weird thing is, when Beau was at school, having

Dave Courtney as his dad was a proper touch. They'd have had a parents' evening every other week just so I'd go down and visit more often. If they could possibly help Beau out, they would and they'd always go, 'Say hello to your dad from me.'

Beau moved out about two years ago 'cos he and his girlfriend Kerry had a little baby, Taylor. I'll never forgive him for that – I'm meant to be the Godfather, not the fucking Grandfather. But Taylor's great and they've got a lovely home in Colchester. As soon as they moved up there, I popped up for a visit and me and Beau did the rounds of all the clubs. There ain't a doorman in Essex who don't know – and, in some cases, owe – Dave Courtney, so they was proper chuffed to have his son in town. So, whenever Beau goes out, they call him and his mates over to the front of the queues and in he goes free. 'Is your dad coming down tonight? Say hello to him for me, won't you?' And Beau loves all that, don't he?

This is the kid who used to bring thirty kids home every night for dinner. You can see them all creeping in with their mouths hanging open, safety in numbers and all that, thinking it's gonna be Bugsy Malone and his boys in the back room. And I'm in there with a load of my mates having a laugh. They used to say to Beau, 'I thought your dad would be all quiet and moody but he's like a comedian. It's like living in a sit-com.'

And it didn't hurt with the girls. Beau was never, shall we say, too proud to bring a young lady home and go, 'This is my new girlfriend, Dad. She's a big fan of yours.' As he says, 'A girl wants to go out with me 'cos she's heard of my dad? And that's a bad thing *because* ...? Bring it on! You want to meet my dad? Come on down.'

The thing is, 'cos I never bring my work home, my kids have only grown up with the funny side of Dave Courtney and that's how I want to keep it. My only real regret is that, because I have a lot of people who look up to me and come to me for help and advice, sometimes I don't have as much time for my kids as I'd like. But they're cool with that. They know I'm always there for them in the evenings. But daytimes it's like a fucking deli counter in my house. Take a number on the way in and take a seat. Number 48 – how can I help you?

Beau's future is in the record business. For the last five years he's been doing music in a little studio in his house, and now he's doing courses in sound engineering. He's already made a few records for other people and one for me called 'The Ten Commandments', and we're just waiting for the right time to release it. I just go into his studio and sit and chat in front of the microphone, sharing Dave's pearls of wisdom, then Beau cuts them together and puts the music on the background. It's fucking wicked. This album will be proper number-one material, bootlegged, downloaded, MP3'd, the lot.

We reckon he's got another fifteen albums' worth of me to get through so we might have to do an Elvis and release one a week for a few months. I'll have the whole Top Ten sewn up by Christmas.

Beau also did all the music for my film *Hell to Pay*. You've got The Business and Rancid and that doing their songs, then Beau's written all the background and incidental stuff. Oscar-nomination stuff it is, an' all. He's now also making a set of videos for me and he put together a wicked piss-take of a geezer called Gaffer that I'll tell you about later.

Actually, I've just bought Beau his first motor. That's a funny feeling, buying your kid's first car. Seeing them go from the size of your hand and playing with Tonka toys to being bigger than you and now he wants a proper car, that gives you real mixed feelings. Knowing you're buying him something that a lot of kids kill themselves in is a real headfuck. I've spent a lot of time thinking about this and this is what I've come up with. If you buy a little tiny car, like a Clio or Fiesta, obviously it's cheap on fuel, the insurance is low and it's a nice first car, but it don't do more than sixty on the flat and his girlfriend needs to get out and push up hills. But if they can afford to buy petrol, they're just gonna be fucking around driving for the sake of driving. And if you do that, you're just putting the odds up of having an accident. Whereas if you get him a juicy car, yes it's faster, but it takes a lot more fucking petrol so you can't go cruising about in it just for the sake of it. It gets your kids to school, it gets you down the pub, gets you from A to B and that's about it. So, although it can go a bit faster, your kid's not in it so much and, if he does have an accident, 'cos it's a bigger car he's not gonna come off second to most things. So I've bought Beau a Granada 2.1 injection. There's no way in the world he can afford to go cruising all round the place in that monster, and he can't sell it 'cos his old man bought it for him.

I got a new car for the wife once – that was a fucking good swap.

So Beau's going great guns and, to the outside world, Jen's son is now living with me again and I'm bringing him up. But what's got to be remembered is I have not seen Courtney, my daughter by blood who's now six, for nearly three years. If she can't hurt me any other way, Jen thinks she can make me suffer by withholding my little baby from me. And she's fucking right.

But enough's enough and, now I've seen how cold my ex-lady can be with using the children as a weapon to hurt me, I've decided to say, 'OK, I'm not going to see the children until they are old enough to come and see me themselves.' It sounds hard, but I cannot allow myself to give someone who is so against me such a perfect weapon to use on me. Any day she wanted to, Jen could have brought Courtney round here. I've had some real messing around. She calls and says I can see her, she's on her way, but then they don't turn up and I've got all built up and it destroys me. So, rather than let her do that, I've said, 'For my own preservation, I won't allow her to mess with me like that so I won't let them see me until they are old enough to pop round on their own.' But, Courtney, if you read this, Daddy loves ya.

Drew has just had a little daughter and it actually made me cry that I wasn't allowed to go and visit her or baby Renelle. Genson speaks to Drew and visits and he passes on my love, but it's very hard for him to keep a normal relationship with his mum.

I'm fully aware that to some people the situations a couple of my kids have been in will reflect badly on myself. But I truly believe I'm the one who tried to hold it all together. Which is why I've made such an effort to be honest on the subject – all the bits that make me look great and the bits that don't – so that you won't misconstrue what's happened and you can make up your own mind.

The internet is actually a great weapon: it lets you keep up to date with the latest adventures of Dave and it has been responsible for at least one change in the law – so someone in authority is keeping a close eye on it! While Genson's case was going on, I made sure the world was kept fully informed about what toerags the police were being. And then they pulled the plug. I got a legal letter saying all the Genson stuff had to be removed because it was now illegal. 'Since when?' I asked. 'Since you made us change the law, Mr Courtney,' they said. Parliament actually changed the law about what you can put on the internet to do with cases that are in progress. The real reason was I was revealing and predicting all the naughty things they was doing, which meant they couldn't do them, if you see what I mean. So they actually passed a new law that you cannot publicise a court case on the web. How's that – Dave Courtney, lawbreaker to lawmaker. That's gotta be worth an OBE in anyone's money.

So where are we now? Genson lives with me, Beau's as happy as Larry in Colchester (and Larry was fucking delirious last time I saw him), Courtney and Drew are off limits, Jen's living with a friend and Brendan and Sam are still on and off. It was very hard for him to carry on and have a relationship with her when her sister was trying to put me in prison. Obviously Jen and Sam are still mates. But an awful lot of her family have now fell in with what's happened, so things get a bit more strained with them every day.

Can I see a day when Jen and I have a cup of tea and laugh about all this? I would have imagined if anything was going to happen, it would have done by now. But I believe that there's still too much hatred on her part. I'd love for there to be a day where we're all right, but I think Charlie Bronson has got more chance of being asked to present *Pet Rescue* than I have of seeing my Jen on happy terms again. She's actually in the process of writing a book about Dave Courtney and she's been offered money to say this and that so it should be interesting reading. For my lawyers, anyway. And I do hate a court case, don't I?

weren't the brightest thing he ever done, so they've thrown him in stir and automatically chucked him out of the Masons. So now they've got one fucking livid lord on their cases.

What actually happened was this. He had the biggest collection of Ferraris in the world. But he got skint, so he went in the garage at night, turned the alarms off, cut up three of his motors, buried them under the floorboards, reported them stolen and sat back. Unfortunately, the police have turned up and noticed the alarm was switched off at one time but they weren't called for hours later. Then they found all the bits. 'Oops, sorry, I'm a criminal.'

The only trouble now is he's a loose cannon, so they've really stuck it to him. 'Cos he was quite high up in the Masons, as soon as he was nicked, they realised that made him a threat. He knows too much. The only way they can dampen that threat is to make sure everything he does or says is pooh-poohed. That way there's a chance you might not listen to the truth 'cos you've already been programmed not to believe the other stuff. And they've done it to Brockett big time. He's proper got a fucking axe to grind. I'm like it myself so I can see it in other people. So the reason he's fucking about in the jungle with Jordan (and I'd give her bush tucker a trial, wouldn't you?) is to get the police seriously looking over their shoulders. He's a good bloke, and a popular one now, so it's harder for the authorities to slide him out of the picture.

There's nothing the police like less than popularity, which is just as well 'cos they'd always be last in any poll.

Even though they know I'm never gonna pull off the bank job of the century or order Her Majesty to be bumped off, the police are more scared of me now than they ever were when I was active. And the reason is people listen to me. They read my books, they come and see my shows, buy my DVDs, they write to me and they call me.

And I'm saying things about how this country is run that they don't like, and they will do everything in their power to stop that. Anyone can say something controversial, and normally you'll be called a nutter. Look at David Icke. I don't know if he's the new Messiah or just a very naughty boy but, since no fucker takes his turquoise-tracksuit brigade that seriously, the authorities don't give a monkey's what he says. But when you can raise an army of hardnuts with one phone call, and people actually pay in their thousands to hear your opinions, and you're actually talking about how corrupt the ruling classes are in this country, then you're a threat. And believe me, the police do not like to be threatened.

The biggest weapon the police have is the power of the media. They can say anything they want and, just as scary, stop anything they want being said. So the only bad boys that are allowed to go on television and speak are normally the ones that are going to crucify themselves the minute they open their gob. We've all seen that sort of Neanderthal skinhead getting tied up by his own tongue in interviews and wondered what the fuck's he doing on telly. And now you know: the authorities actually encourage that sort of 'kick 'im, stab 'im, hurt 'im' caveman, 'cos who's gonna find that attractive? The last thing they want is to promote someone like myself who actually doesn't do that badly in front of a microphone. Do too badly – who am I kidding? I'm that good I wish I could listen to me sometimes.

So one of their tactics is to paint me out to look worse than I am. When they dragged the Austin Warnes trial on for eight months, they was just trying to get me killed by making me out as a grass. They had no intention of finding me Guilty, they just wanted to spread some shit and hope some of it stuck. No smoke without fire, and all that.

At one point, my barrister went, 'Dave, what they've actually done here is, in their eagerness to get you killed, they've actually made legal history. They would rather collapse a case than produce the informant.' Never before have the police put the name, address and photograph of someone who is an informant on the front page of a newspaper eight months before it got to court. Never, ever.

Everything that I predicted, the whole fucking thing, happened. The copper was bang to rights because I had him on video. But they still said to him, 'You carry on going "Not Guilty" and Dave's a grass for eight months. Then on the day of trial change your plea to Guilty, so you don't have to stand trial, and Dave's gonna get Not Guilty, but it might not get that far 'cos he might get shot.' It was such a joke. I went in and said, 'This is the tape I've got, this is the video I've got.' Game, set and match Courtney.

After the court case, the whole jury came out to the pub across the road and one of them went, 'You're in trouble, mate, aren't ya? We know what you are and what you ain't, we've had to sit there for seven weeks listening to it. And today this is in the paper, so you're in trouble.'

At the time, I knew full well this was the case, but I had no proof. Then this happened, which gave me a very precise read-out on exactly how high up the 'Get Courtney' campaign goes. When I was running for Mayor of London, there was this headline in my local paper that said, COULD YOUR WORST NIGHTMARE BE YOUR NEW MAYOR? and that started some fucking fireworks. Catherine wheels, roman candles, rockets – the lot. The commissioner of the Metropolitan Police actually called an emergency meeting of the editors of all the national newspapers and media outlets in England, at two o'clock in the morning. Two o'clock in the fucking morning! That's the only time all of them had five minutes in their diaries, and they all turned up, they all chucked their mistresses out of bed for a few hours, sobered up a bit and went along to talk about Dave. And the head of the police held up that local rag and went, 'Will someone please tell me this ain't happening.' Now that is genuinely seeing me as a major threat.

What he don't realise is I've got a bloke on the inside, one of my editor mates, and he's rung me up on the way in. 'Listen, Dave, I don't know what this is about but I've heard your name whispered.' So what he's done is left his phone on. It's a bit muffled 'cos he's had to hide it under some papers, but I've heard enough to know this mob are pissing themselves that all them masses, all them minority groups who don't normally vote, but would for me, might actually do it. They might actually turn up in enough numbers and I might actually win the cunting thing. Democratically elected Dave, and there'd be nothing they could do about it. These editors were proper worried.

You remember when Arthur Scargill was being a right boil on Maggie Thatcher's bum? He was considered a proper threat, so they did all this to him. There were top-level meetings to bring him down. They infiltrated his union – his right-hand man was actually CID – bugged his office and tried to jeopardise everything he touched. And they look at me exactly the same. In their minds, every single bit of airtime that Dave is getting, he is picking up followers. All the people the police don't like, they all seem to like this bloke. The ravers, the poofs, the thieves, the blacks, the prostitutes, the junkies, they all like Dave. So the commissioner's probably gone, 'I don't want any mention of this cunt in any national newspaper. I don't want to see his face on telly. I don't want to hear him on the radio.' He's gone, 'We made a documentary on him and called him a grass, but he came out of that a fucking hero. We took him to court and the fucking policeman ended up going to prison.' He weren't, it has to be said, a happy bunny.

One of the ways they try to keep you down is through scare tactics. They will do all they can to make other people not like you. As far as villains in the media are concerned, they're all no good. But that's not right, we all know that. There's good baddies and bad goodies. Poachers make the best gamekeepers, and all that. So, if you robbed a bank twenty years ago, you're an 'orrible bastard today. But the truth is this: just because you do something naughty for a job doesn't necessarily make you a worse person the rest of the time than that brickie next door. It's just a job. A bank robber has his tools just like a sparkie or a plumber. But he don't use them to eat his dinner with when he gets home. You get up, you go to work, you come home and you be yourself. A gangster is just like anyone else when he's not working. I don't sit there with a gun going, 'Make me a sandwich.'

They do not want me to glamorise crime. And not just me – anyone. Did you know that, back in the 1930s, a law was passed in America that said films could not show gangsters in a positive light. The original *Scarface* movie got really fucked over by that, trust me. And that's why the majority of crime films these days are all right for the first ninety per cent of the movie, but then in the last ten per cent they remember, Oh fuck, we're not allowed to show bad guys winning, so they always have it going wrong in the last few minutes.

Like I say, one of the clearest signs I've had that the authorities really are a little bit afraid of my power came when I decided to run for Mayor of London. I think the thing that worried them was when I declared my first decision in power would be to give the Metropolitan Police the year off. And, as Mayor, I could have. Talk about fucking panic stations. They went into overdrive. No wonder they called that meeting. As far as I was concerned, it was a million-to-one chance of me winning, but the police obviously thought I could do it 'cos they pulled out all the cheating stops for that one. It proper pissed me off at the time, but I'd have done the same thing, so fair play to them really.

The way I looked at it was this: there's only fourteen candidates in the race and I know I've got an audience 'cos thousands of people were travelling miles to go to my raves. If I can just get most of them to come down long enough to put an X in a box, I'm in with a fucking shout. And if you look at who my fans are, I've got the hard men, the drug dealers, the drug takers, the prisoners, the prostitutes, the naughty boys, the blacks, the gays, the Triads, the Yardies – you name it, I bring all that lot together. They might not like each other, but they all like Dave. On their own they're not gonna make Tony Blair lose a minute's sleep, but you put them all together and you've got yourself a political fucking movement, mate. That's the masses talking, that is.

And that's what scared seven shades of shit out of the police. They knew that only about three per cent of people vote for mayors, so, if all my mob really did come out, it would be close. So here's what they did. About 24 hours before polling day, I was told I was banned from standing. Why? Because apparently I lied on my application form, when I knew I hadn't. But they've gone, 'The rules state you can't have been in prison in the last five years, and you say you haven't, and yet in your book it says you were in Belmarsh.'

'I was on remand and anyway I got Not Guilty, so it don't count.'

'You've got us there – but we'll have to check with the board, and they don't sit until the day after tomorrow.'

Well, fuck me. The words 'stitched up' and 'like a kipper' spring to mind here, along with a bunch of other phrases. Polling day was the next day and they'd let me know if I could run the day after that. Fucking genius. You've got to admire their balls. To make matters worse, they still nicked my ten grand entry deposit. I'd be called a thief if I did anything like that. They stitched up Jeffrey Archer the same way. Let him pay his deposit then hoicked him out. We've got a lot in common, me and Jeff. We're both bestselling authors, we've both been cheated out of running for Mayor and we've both been up before the judge in the Old Bailey. But that's where the similarities end, 'cos he got Guilty – and I never!

Looking back, maybe we did put their noses out of joint a little bit over that one. There's an unwritten rule that you're not allowed to pose for pictures outside New Scotland Yard. Not many people know that until they turn up with their Instamatic. But I knew, and the fact that I did made me think that would be the perfect place for me to have my 'Vote Dave' campaign pictures done.

So one day me and Brendan, a geezer called Bulldog, David, Mickey Goldtooth, Eamon, and a few of the lads, all met at the end of the street. The rest of them all look normal enough, you know, long gangster coats and that, but I'm dressed as a fucking king, aren't I? Ermine robes, big fuck-off Freddie Mercury crown – the sort of thing P Diddy and his posse wear most days, the *pricks*. So we've started walking down towards Scotland Yard and all these policemen are obviously taking notice but there's no law against making a tit of yourself, even on Broadway in Westminster. But what they don't see is coming towards us from the other way is a photographer. And as soon as we're outside the front door with the blue light, he gives the nod and I yelled, 'Hats!'

And with that, all my mates have suddenly produced

these police hats from inside their coats. Not only that, but I'm now somehow holding a gun and posing like I'm about to take over Scotland Yard in my king's outfit while the photographer clicks away, having a right field day.

That's when it gets all Keystone Cops, 'cos obviously the police milling past have soon twigged what's going on and come haring after us. 'Oi, you lot, stop that!' and words to that effect. So immediately we've all grabbed our hats and legged it up the street and for once I actually wanted the police to chase me – 'cos the photographer had gone the other way. It don't matter if we get caught for wearing bad fancy-dress costumes in a public place (or whatever the charge is) as long as we get the snap.

As it goes, we made it round the corner of the street with this mob in pursuit, and I've gone, 'Woah, there,' and we've all stopped, put our police hats on again and waited for the coppers to turn the corner and meet us. When they did, their faces were a picture and I wish we'd captured that one as well, just to proper piss them off. 'Cos they come bombing round the bend and there's us lot dressed as them going, 'Evening all. What's going on here, then?' You know, giving it all the plod speak from *Dixon of Dock Green* and all them shows. Luckily they saw the funny side. Not! But hopefully it distracted them long enough for us to get the picture we needed.

And did we fucking get it! Six geezers dressed as coppers, one prick who thinks he's Emperor Napoleon, posing with guns outside the home of the British police force. *Touch!* The Old Bill did their nut when that photo started doing the rounds.

To be honest, they weren't that happy even later the same day. On the way home, after a few brandy and cokes to celebrate our little paparazzi coup, we were pulled over by a traffic cop. I don't know how he found us. Maybe the back window being filled with police hats gave him a clue.

Or possibly the 'Vote Dave Courtney for Mayor' signs stuck all over the motor? I don't know, but maybe they're cleverer than we think! It was one of those baby-fresh coppers who wandered over to speak to me, you know, straight from the factory, hasn't had his first prisoner 'fall down the stairs' while in custody yet, you know what I mean? So obviously he's never seen anything like a fucking king getting out of a car. And before junior's had a chance to open his mouth, I've gone, 'Be careful how you speak to me, officer, because I may soon be your new mayor.'

That was hysterical. The mob in the back of the car were pissing themselves, but I could tell something was going through baby plod's mind ('cos his face went a bit blank and he started dribbling). Obviously he's a bit green, but he knows as well as anyone that the one thing young coppers do not do is pull over their bosses. Of course, they're meant to – no one is above the law and all that shit. But clearly there's at least one lesson at Hendon School of Plod that goes, 'Don't mess with upstairs or you'll be busted down to doing school visits.' And even though I'm looking like a fucking fancy-dress nightmare, he's not a hundred per cent sure whether I'm serious about the mayor thing. So, even though he's gone, 'Have you got anything you shouldn't have in the car?' and I've said, 'Apart from the knuckledusters, guns and pills?' he's still got back in his car and waved us on. Seriously weird that, but it makes you think. Well, it made *me* think. Look how shit-scared he was of pissing off one of his superiors, even one dressed like Paul Burrell on his day off.

So that's the power of the police and I'm gonna use the freedom of speech laws we have in this country to expose them. And it's not gonna be easy, 'cos the police and the authorities aren't just thinking about now. They've got plans for the next fifty years and there's stuff happening today that some civil servant prick dreamed up decades ago. And they get away with it 'cos they run the media.

Here's an example.

What would the general public say if the police went, 'We want to bug everyone's car in England so we can find out where anyone is in England through a tracking device.' We'd all go, 'Fuck off.' That's a proper fucking liberty, that one. So what they do is they change the name of the fucking thing and call it an 'anti-theft device'. Clever, innit? So they stick it on your motor before you buy the thing and, whenever the police computer says it's stolen, they can turn it on and find out where your car is. But the thing is, you don't have to have your car stolen. They can turn the thing on any time. And in a year's time they're going to say they've saved so much money on insurance, they're going to make one part of the MOT, so then you have to have some kind of fucking camera in your car, and pay for the privilege. And that is the kind of thing they get away with.

I hear all this kind of stuff. And I make sure I pass it on. Just doing my conscientious member of society bit, like the police always encourage us.

Here's another car story to make you think. We were on our way back from Stansted airport after the *Costa Del Dosh* holiday (you've got that to look forward to in Chapter 17) and Brendan was driving, I was akip in the passenger seat and our mild-mannered chum Michael Taylor was doing fuck knows what in the back. Brendan's being a bit heavy-footed on one of the smaller roads and suddenly this anonymous-looking motor we'd just bombed past turns into a fucking spaceship, lights beaming out all over it like an in-car disco's suddenly started. And, of course, the main one is blue.

This is the weird thing, though. The undercover traffic

cop is suggesting to Brendan that, if they're doing 60 in a 50 area, they don't want to be overtaken by a cunt doing at least double that. Maybe we should all chat about this down at Chelmsford nick? Meanwhile, his mate, who's been doing that circling the car thing all coppers do – peering in the windows, checking the number plates and all that – goes, 'Who's that, then?' And he's pointing to me, Sleeping Beauty in the front seat.

Now Brendan's got a dilemma. He's already in trouble and, since Dave Courtney has never been plod pin-up of the month, things could get even worse if they learn he's one of my firm. But he's gone, 'You know who it is – it's Dave Courtney.' Talk about odd looks. These coppers couldn't get together quick enough for a little chinwag, then one of them goes, 'All right, lad, off you go and take it easier for the rest of the journey, yeah?' And that was it. No ticket, no telling off, no points.

Brendan's told me this a few minutes later – he actually woke me up, can you believe the prick? – and I've explained a few things. Number one is the authorities do not like Dave Courtney being at large (and larging it). But number two is, until he fucks up big enough for them to throw away the key, Courtney's too useful to have on the streets 'cos his house is bugged to buggery and he seems to be friends with every underworld villain going. So any traffic cop or low-ranking fuzz had better know what they're letting themselves in for if they ever think they can impress their bosses bringing in the 'criminal mastermind' Dave Courtney.

But the dreamy thing is you can proper take liberties when you know they're on your case. It happens to me so often, now I've started testing it. If I'm pulling away from the lights and a copper's there looking, I might actually jump the lights deliberately to get stopped. What happens then is, the copper goes, 'What's your name?' 'It's Dave

Courtney.' He types it in the little machine they all carry these days and this Big Brother-type message comes back, 'Move away from the assailant! Move away from the assailant!' You can see the copper looking confused and he goes, 'Why?' And he gets, 'Listen, we are spending two million quid a year following him to see who he's talking to and the last thing we want is you nicking the cunt for jumping a red light.' So he pats me on the head, says sorry and lets me go.

How sweet is that? And you know I'm gonna push that one, don't you, knowing I have to try very hard to be nicked. I bet I proper pay for saying that one . . .

Here's another example of my little love–hate relationship with the authorities. I once went for nearly three-and-a-half years without paying my phone bill. Seriously. You know, at first, I was just a bit forgetful. Then after a year I'm thinking, Surely I should have one by now? The phone still works, there's no problem there. But then I've realised what's going on: the police have gone to all this trouble to get a warrant to tap my phone, so they're not gonna let me get cut off now, are they? What fucking good is that to them? It takes a midget's height in paperwork to get a warrant for anything, so, when they've got it, like the one they need to follow me, they're gonna use it. So, because everything's controlled by Masons somewhere down the line, they've had a word. As soon as I realised this I'm phoning up Jamaica, America, Australia – I don't even know anyone there, I'm just calling wrong numbers so some cunt in Scotland Yard's got to fork out a tenner.

While we're on the subject of winding up the Old Bill, here's a little money-saving tip for you. If you've fucked up and for some reason you've got your car registered to you, do yourself a favour and buy a little strip of black electrical tape. Then you can cut off a little bit, stick it on the number plate on the back of your car and suddenly your P's an A, your L's a C, your I's a T. Change one letter then throw the tape away. This is fact: you can get as many of those flashing lights as you want, it don't matter, and they won't find you. And if the police ever do stop you and go, 'Oi, what's that?' you say, 'I don't know.' And as long as you don't have that roll of tape in your car, you cannot be arrested because someone else has stuck a bit of black tape on your motor. You can't be done for ringing it 'cos you haven't done it to the front. 'So 'cos someone else has stuck a bit of black tape on my car I'm getting nicked? Fuck off.' For any coppers out there reading, I never said that . . .

Fuck me, where was all this going? I'll tell you: the authorities have got big plans for Dave Courtney. I don't know what they are exactly, but I know it's gonna hurt. They've tried to get me banged up, that was their first bright idea, but after a dozen goes that didn't work. Plan 2 was to try and get me taken out by my own kind 'cos I'm supposedly a grass. But that didn't exactly prove too successful neither, did it? So then they've gone, 'Fuck me, let's just get rid of him ourselves – get the advanced driving mob to goose him.'

The only problem is I'm still here. Twice as large (but that's lack of exercise for you), twice as ugly and twice as fucking mad. And they know it. So what they've actually done is had to go back to the drawing board. They've got all the top police brains from around the country – and that's a meeting they could have held in a phone box, ain't it? – and they've had to come up with a new way to bring me down, 'cos just locking up or murdering don't seem to be working.

And this is what they worked out: if they can hurt me professionally, now that I'm not naughty any more, I'll either just pack up and shut up or I'll be forced back into a little bit of moonlighting with a sawn-off out of desperation and then they'll have me. Either way they win. And I have to say, that's not a bad plan, 'cos I actually see it working, bit by bit, every single day. Don't get me wrong, they're not gonna bring Dave Courtney down, I'm a bit too cute for that and there's things I've got planned that they'll never predict. But hats off to them, they set out to make things tricky for me and I've got to be honest, they're doing a blinding job.

This is how it works: everything that I've been connected with, however important or grand scale it is, you will find they don't actually allow it to make it big. Here's an example. I made this wicked little star-studded movie called *Babyjuice Express* with Nick Moran and a host of faces, people like Joe Bugner, Julian Clary, the beautiful Cleo Rocos, David Seaman, Samantha Janus, Lisa Faulkner and a bunch of the *Quadrophenia* guys. It's a real piss-take of a film, very, very funny, about a man smuggling his sperm out of prison because he has to impregnate his wife or when he dies the Old Bill get all his money. It was only shot over at the Isle of Dogs and I had to play Mr Bognor Regis, who is a complete and utter cunt. Good casting, eh? Nick Moran was in *Lock, Stock and Two Smoking Barrels* and he understands that the whole of that success was based around the story of Dave Courtney, and he just wanted a bit of that himself. It was cheap budget, I used my own Rolls-Royce in it and I supplied him all the cars and that, but it was a proper funny little film. It could have been massive.

And that's when the funny phone calls started. You know what I mean. Because they can't be seen to do these things, the authorities get other people to do them. Like I've said, that's exactly what I would do, so hats off and all that. At the end of the day, it don't matter if it's the

Inland Revenue, the headmaster at your kids' school or your bank manager – if one of them can cause a bit of mischief in your life and stop you doing something successful, they will do so. And you know who's told them to. So what's happened to *Babyjuice Express* is that everyone's pulled together, they've worked out I'm in it and there's no way they want me up for any acting awards or that, so they didn't allow it to be brought out at the pictures. They never actually banned it from being shown in cinemas, but they made it hard in other ways for it to get there. So it was kept down to video, which was the best they could have got; lesser of two evils, I suppose. But how scary is that?

Another time I did a record with Brian Harvey and Wyclef Jean. It was fucking top, this record, 'cos those two geezers are seriously good at what they do. But because I'm in the video with a load of the chaps like Joe Pyle, Dave Thurston, Mitch, Hammer, Cowboy, Dom, Seymour, Ish, Tar Can and Lou, word's put out that it must not get any airplay, it is seriously MTV-unfriendly in their opinion, so no one heard about it and no one bought it. Brian Harvey might have had better days, but Wyclef's a fucking superstar, ain't he? How could one of his records not be a hit? The prick just has to sneeze, and, as long as he can rhyme it with another one, kids will buy it.

The record we made with Tricky called 'Product of the Environment', when all the gangsters got on there and done a little thing about themselves, that was supposed to be for charity. How's that for irony: the biggest villains in the country giving money away? Who said Robin Hood never existed? Anyway, all the proceeds from that were supposed to go to Help a London Child, and a million pounds it was. But they went, 'Listen, we want the cash but we cannot be seen accepting things from people like yourselves. We cannot glamorise crime.' That made it sink in how high up this must go, even back then. To go, 'We cannot accept a million quid because we can't be seen to be saying "Thank you" to people like yourselves', that's serious intimidation from somewhere, ain't it? You don't have to be Inspector Morse to work that one out.

Because the odd thing can go wrong all on its own – mistakes do happen – a lot of people will just write off things like this as 'one of those things'. But when they're happening to you all the time, you start to see the bigger picture. And, mate, this fucking picture's so big it wouldn't even fit on the side of my house. So now I look out for it. I was in the World Cup song that they made, supporting England, with Suggsy out of Madness. Same story: because of me, it wouldn't get no airplay, and Suggs is scratching his head going, 'I don't understand.' It must be love, mate.

A few years back I made my first record with Jen called 'Who Is He?' and sold eighteen fucking thousand copies. I know this because I got paid for every one, it's all there on the royalty statement – and let's face it, no cunt's gonna pay you if you haven't earned it. But get this: it didn't make the Top 100. That many sales for any other record would have got it in the Top Ten, but it was held back somewhere. Someone conveniently forgot to fill in the odd form or tick the right box, 'cos they didn't want Dave Courtney on *Top of the Pops* with Britney. That would be a show, wouldn't it? She can hit me baby, any time she likes.

Music's potentially very big for me. It ain't hard. With all the gear they've got in studios these days, all you've got to do is fart and they can twiddle a few knobs and make it sound like Frank Sinatra. Well, Frank Sinatra farting, at least.

So I got a deal with Universal Records last year to work on a few projects. Now that's proper up there, ain't it?

Record companies don't come much bigger than that. These A&R geezers were all over me, saying how they could market me and get me in all the clubs. So I actually made this wicked record with them called 'The Ten Commandments', which is this blinding hip-hop track with me rapping out all this advice over the top. 'An eye for an eye – and a tooth for a fucking tooth'; 'It's far better to sit quietly and be thought of as a fool, than open your mouth and prove you are one'; 'The meek shall inherit the earth, but only when the strong say so' – lines like that.

Anyway, Universal just took it and they're going, 'Brilliant, Dave, brilliant! Number one in the second fucking week.' Then when it got to the bosses they've said, 'No. We can't actually have you on our label any more, we don't want to be tarnished by gangsters.' That's a fucking joke in itself, isn't it? Half the dudes in the charts these days all claim they're right bad boys from Compton, Detroit or even Peckham and the companies are lapping it up like a thirsty man in a brothel. But the difference is, they're not the real deal, are they? They're not really like that.

I made a gangsta record with Jay-Z recently. You can't not have a lot of respect for a geezer if he's got a billion zillion pounds in the bank. But what happens to these people is if you pretend to do something long enough you turn into the cunting thing. If someone was pretending to be mad and lives in a nuthouse for ten years, if I go round to pick them up one day they would actually be nutty. With these gangsta-rap people, they can't actually just do it on stage as an act, it's too hard. They have to do the gangsta bad-boy thing on stage, then when they come off there's all their fans so they have to keep it up for them. Then they do it at home as well. They have to drive the car, wear the clothes, talk the talk 24 hours a day. And because they get used to everyone tiptoeing around them, licking their arses all the time, they forget it's not because they're scary bastards but because they've got twenty million quid in the bank, thank you very much. They actually buy into the fantasy world and think, 'cos they've got minders and all that, they must be hard.

You've heard of 50 Cent? Well, I'm the real thing: I'm 49p. I know he's a good singer and all that but when they're promoting him over here they're putting it about that he's this hard geezer who's been shot nine times. Well, I can't see a fucking mark on the cunt.

When I was hanging with Snoop Dogg and he's giving it all that 'We're striving for reality, man' shit, I realised they actually believe they are these gangstas. How much are you striving for reality? Are you sure you want it? So I went, 'How real do you want, Snoop? You're singing about putting a cap in his arse, I shot a cunt in the head. Shut the fuck up.'

There's loads of other examples where they've managed to spike a little bit of success I might be able to have. They used me in the computer game called The Getaway, then weren't allowed to admit it. I was used as the model for the bald-headed geezer running around, shooting everything up – and that was fucking fun, doing all that so they could film it. But then they got this directive that they weren't allowed to mention it. Sorry if I let it slip.

I was asked to do some modelling for Pink shirts. I was the model for the year, I got paid 15G for it, and it was gonna go all over the world, with life-size cut-outs in all the stores and posters on all the tubes and buses. But then the shops were told by the police they weren't allowed to use the posters 'cos I was glamorising crime. I've just got employed by Hugo Boss to do a fucking catwalk thing in Fashion Week. Let's see how they screw that one up. I'm meant to be doing New York, Paris, Milan and London, mooching round in double-breasted top-of-the-range suits. I actually had some little faggot ring me and say, 'Don't worry, Mr Courtney. We will have someone teach you how to walk properly.' *Shut up*, you fucking sausage jockey.

I suppose I actually have to thank the police for making me multitalented. If they'd left me doing the books, I wouldn't have started making records. And if they hadn't tried to throw a spanner in that one they wouldn't be kept so busy trying to keep me off the telly. Everyone wants me on the TV programmes, every director goes, 'Yeah, Courtney, Courtney, Courtney' until someone upstairs says no. But I can cope with that. What's really upset me, though, if I'm honest is what they've done to two films I've been in. And I will never forgive them for that. But that's another story (the next one, as it happens).

to a point in my life where I'm going to start exposing what I know and start using myself as a martyr, and that's what's happening now. I've kept every bit of paperwork, every bit of mistreatment evidence, names of every woman who said, 'I'll employ you,' and then has been told by her boss she can't. Every time I do a TV programme, I keep the rushes. I've probably got a year's worth of video tape now and somehow I'm gonna make it so you can buy it. Imagine that: 'This is the hundred hours they had of Dave Courtney, and this is the hour they put on the telly.' That tells a completely different story.

Apart from burying Ronnie Kray, my life took a bit of a new direction after I bumped into this geezer called Guy Ritchie. We was at the Ministry of Sound about an eight stretch ago, and he was a bit in awe of being in my company. He left Leicester Square with his mouth hanging open that night, I promise you. It was Dave Courtney, white guys and black guys in fancy suits, telling loads of stories about crime and making it palatable because we kept it funny. And he liked that. He liked that so much he went and made a film that had white guys and black guys in fancy suits, featuring loads of stories about crime and making it palatable because he kept it funny. I never got any credit out of that, even though the Vinnie Jones character, Big Chris, was based on me. I was the one who cooked a bloke in a sun bed like he does in the film (and my boy Beau was there as a witness). I was the daft cunt who couldn't recognise two antique shooters and sawed them down an' all, but we'll forget that one. And when he come to do the TV series of Lock, Stock ... ('cos in case you hadn't worked it out, that was the name of his film), there was this bald-headed gangster with a white Rolls-Royce. Ring any bells? And it was all my mates in that as well.

The thing with Ritchie, though, is he's a good kid and

his films are top drawer. At least the gangster ones are. Have you seen *Swept Away*, that film he done with his missus? Fuck me. If ever a film was calling out for some bald-headed geezer to come in and shoot one of the main characters, that was it. And in about the first scene, an' all. Madonna, love, stop now. You'll give the rest of 'em splinters.

Like I say, Ritchie's all right and when he came to do his second one, *Snatch*, he offered me the part of this character called Bricktop. Tasty, I thought. This is a person who feeds his enemies to pigs, likes a hooky bet on the boxing and is a general cunt to be around. It might stretch me artistically, but I'll give it a go.

When it came to filling all the other parts of the various heavies and hardnuts in the movie, I roped in a load of my mates and Ritchie brought a small crew round to my place and actually did auditions in the back garden. There was Birmingham John, Ebo, Frankie Baby, Johnny the Comedian, Derek, No Neck Nick, Dean, Johnny McGee, Ian Freeman, Jeremy Bailey and loads of others. He was particularly knocked out when I introduced him to this young American geezer called Brad someone or other – Pritt? Bitt? – but he thought he had potential and gave him the star role of the mad Irish gypsy boxer. (I think that's how it went, memory's a funny thing.)

So we're all set and I'm even having a go at learning some lines. Then I get another visit from Ritchie and, as soon as I see his face, I know what it's about. The producer Matthew Vaughn has had a chat with someone who's come back and said they couldn't have Courtney in their film. Just like that. Even though I was the one who's put a load of this together with all his mates, they've said, 'If he's in the film, we take away the funding. It's him or six million quid.' Guy Ritchie's gone, 'Fucking hell, Dave, I'm sorry.' But what can he do?

I'm not annoyed at Ritchie, not really. I understand the situation he's in 'cos hundreds of people have been put in it because of knowing me. But he had the decency to come round and tell me like a man. I remember things like that.

I wish other people had half his bollocks. Not literally, not like Hitler – but you get what I mean. Vinnie Jones, on the other hand, has failed to live up to his billing a little bit in my eyes. Look, if some solicitor is saying he can't do the film if he admits he's friends with Dave Courtney the real-life murderer, 'cos you're judged by the company you keep, that's one thing. But if he's half what he's supposed to be, he could at least have rung me up in the middle of the night and said, 'Look, I'm not supposed to, but I wanted to say hello.' But he's never. He played me in a film, but he has not ever, not once, rung me, spoken to me, thanked me, or even acknowledged the fact that I fucking exist.

When I do my 'Audiences With Dave Courtney', I usually ask if anyone likes Vinnie Jones. And there's always some dopey prick who says yes. I'm just amazed there's still anyone who digs all that 'hardest man on TV' schtick. The truth is a bit different.

Vinnie Jones has grabbed Gazza's nuts, he's kicked a few people in the shin and gone 'fuck off' to the odd ref and 'bollocks' to the crowd, and he may have threatened some passengers on a plane, but he ain't a gangster, is he? He hasn't understood the gang culture, drug culture, being skint, the prison culture. He's made one film, that's all. I can show you a million interviews with Vinnie Jones on *Grandstand* before he made the film and it's a different fucking geezer. He's a nice boy, good to his mum, feeds his cat and all that. Now he's made one film and he talks all that growly, snarly hardman shite. Have you seen those Bacardi Breezer adverts he's in? I'm fucking scared, mate! If you have to pull a face to look hard – as half the people reading this book will know – then you're not. Someone who is hard genuinely just looks that way. I could smile all I like, but you know fucking well I could stick one in if I wanted to. And Vinnie Jones is not hard. He might be a hard footballer but he is not a fucking gangster and he is not a hard man on the streets, I assure you.

The thing is this. He weren't the best footballer in the world, he made a film and everyone liked the character. So when the film finished, it was 'Big Chris' that got famous, not Vinnie Jones. But Vinnie has carried on playing Big Chris in real life, you know what I mean? Well, if this Big Chris geezer he was playing was supposed to be me, then Vinnie Jones is running around pretending to be Dave Courtney. *P-rick*. Now I wouldn't challenge him to a game of headers and volleys in his back garden, and he wouldn't have a scrap with me in mine – we should both do our own thing.

From what I hear, he intends to go through his whole life without ever bumping into me. That really is his plan. When he goes to the West End I've heard he asks the doormen, 'Dave Courtney isn't in here, is he?' And all my mates on the door ring me and say, 'We told him you was here so he fucked off.' But I would happily bump into Vinnie Jones. Very hard. Another thing is, I can't help noticing Vinnie's now advertising a casino – I've had an online poker game for ages. Snoop Dogg's now mixing his music with blue films – yep, done that an' all – and he's even followed in my footsteps at the Oxford Union, so they're making a fuss of that. You never knew I was such a trendsetter did ya?

Anyway, I'm not saying I'm going to beat Vinnie up, although other people have suggested it. And I'd probably win 'cos I do cheat. You've all seen my knuckleduster by now. That is the best invention since the wheel, fire and electricity. And maybe even sliced bread an' all. Mine is solid gold with diamonds. It was actually a tiara once but I'd look like a cunt wearing that, so I had it melted down and made into this. I know everyone bumps prices up for insurance claims, but when this geezer lost this – I forget exactly how that happened! – he wrote down 27 grand. Maybe seven grand over the top, but that's ballpark, you know what I mean? Now I've melted it down and made this weapon of face destruction out of it, so as far as I'm concerned that's worth twenty grand as well. And the advantage is that anyone's gonna want to put their chin out for that, aren't they? And I look good throwing a shot with all the fucking diamonds in it, especially if the light's right. But you feel a right cunt afterwards when he's lying there, and you're trying to pick one of the gems out of his chin. I might win the fight but one punch could cost me four and a half grand. I've got a feeling Vinnie might be worth double that.

While we're on the subject, though, I'm not saying I'm the best fighter in the world, but, like I say, I cheat. It amazes me that there are so many different types of fighting in different people's heads. For boxing you've gotta be mentally tuned into it. 'Cos if someone started punching me in the face as a sport and at the end of it I'm expected to shake his hand and go, 'The best man won' – what's all that about? I can't get my head round that. So outside the Queensberry Rules, there is nothing wrong with cheating as far as I'm concerned. What's wrong is getting caught! As you get older you struggle to do that 'fair fight' thing any more. It sounds nice on a piece of paper but it hurts. And you know me, I've been a boxer, so I've got the bruises to prove it. Like I say, I was the only boxer I know to retire with a cauliflower bum, that's how good I was. I had all the tassels on my shorts and all that bollocks, and I looked the absolute nuts at shadow boxing. But I even lost at that once. So my preference of fighting styles would be eight or nine of my mates to jump out of a Transit with balaclavas on and attack a bloke from behind. That's my idea of a good fight. I don't mind doing it with six, but my preference would be nine.

All my more memorable fights are famous for being funny rather than good. I realised very early on in my boxing career that I wasn't going to reach the top of the game. Especially once they invented something called a black geezer. Not only do they seem to hit you harder than anyone else, but they don't seem to get tired and, fuck knows why, but God's given them an extra twelve inches on each of their arms. I thought, What the fuck is all that about? You do all the training with the punchbags and the sparring, but nobody tells you your opponent's allowed to hit you back.

I started my fighting career for Millwall. I had some good fights down there, spoiled occasionally by a fucking football match breaking out. But for my first ever fight, I thought I was the nuts. In actual fact, I was the guts, as you'll see. I took all my mates down to watch me at Katharine Docks. I got there and this geezer in charge says my fight's been cancelled – my opponent's got this carbuncle or boil thing. Not to worry, my mates are there and we hit the bar. So there's thirteen of us, we're watching the other fights, having a few drinks, a few bags of peanuts, hotdogs, another few drinks, then the interval came and so we're fucking crashing away proper at the bar. Then about two fights from the end this official comes down and says, 'Dave, you're in luck – we've burst the boil and you're next on.' I thought, Fuck, I've had about eight pints. And that's a lot of brandy. If it weren't for the fact I was in front of all my mates, I'd have told him to fuck off. Anyway I've wobbled out there and, you guessed it, it's one of those black guys. I got in the ring and I'm wobbling about all over the place just trying not to get hit. It didn't help that I was seeing three of the fuckers. Eventually one of them has smacked me so hard in the stomach that I've thrown up like something from *The Exorcist*. *Blaaaah*! It's bits of hotdog, peanuts, yesterday's breakfast, and my opponent's screaming like it's acid 'cos it's all down his face and front. I thought the only thing missing was if I spun my head round and said to him, 'Your mother sucks cocks in hell!' Anyway I lost that one on a *pints* decision.

The thing about boxing is this. Say you get knackered in tennis and you can't be bothered running, the worst that happens is the ball goes over the net and you lose a point. When you get fucked at football and you can't catch them up, they score a goal. You get fucked at boxing and some cunt breaks your jaw. It's like cheating. That ring is really, really tiny when you're trying to run away from somebody, and many's the time I've been in there thinking that half a decent shot will actually knock me out. Once, I thought the only way out was to get disqualified rather than knocked out. So I've give him the best round and a half that you can possibly imagine. I've given it my all for as long as I could, and by the end of the second round I'm in my corner panting like a bull mastiff on heat. My trainer said, 'You're doing well, he's hardly touching you.' The shit your corner comes out with. I said, 'Someone keep an eye on the ref – that bloke with the gloves on keeps hitting me in the head.' But because I would rather get chucked out than carried out on a stretcher – a half-decent fart in the right direction would have knocked me over – as soon as my opponent came within grabbing distance I clung round his neck and nut, nut, nut – I'm happily disqualified.

Everyone likes seeing loads of blood, don't they? A load of claret pouring out the nose and the mouth looks great. When I started out, my corner man would go, 'Look, you're on colour telly so aim for his face.' That's all well

Above On the mend in hospital (and after
my haircut), with Seymour, Micky Goldtooth,
Jamie, Steve Sadler, The Amazing Mark
and Steve Whale

Right My little bit of car trouble!
(www.knuckleduster.org)

Left Me and Bill Murray
the *Hell to Pay* film set

Below Hell to Pay: the
fantastic cast and crew,
with me and Caesar and
Jeremy Bailey

Bottom left Me as an ac
– on the set of *Daddy Fo*
with Steven Pinder

Bottom right 'In the nar
of the Father' – in the filr
Demonic

ht Me and Bruce
~~~nolds in Milan at a
~~~ference on behalf of
~~~gland

ht With Johnny, Vicky
~~~rk, Joey Pyle, Wilf Pine,
~~~y Lambrianou and Lee
~~~he Horn of Plenty, with
~~~ndan and Paul

ht Me and Steve Sadler
~~~arding Ronnie Kray's
~~~nting

ow Me and Gordy and
~~~d Pete at the Outlaws'
~~~ce

Above left Taz (right) an my Bev

Above right Me and Taz

Left Me and Jodie Marsh the front garden. What a lucky boy!

Left With Storm and Jam Hewitt

right Me and Mum, luv ya Mum

right With my son Beau in studio

below left Me and Courtney. I miss her *(Jocelyn Bain Hogg/Ashley Woods Promotion)*

below right An Englishman's home is his castle ... but mine really is Camelot Castle. At home with Jamie and Gary

Above My back garden:
Mad Pete, Tony Maloney,
Seymour, Kevin Courtney,
Lou, Matt, Chico, Ben
Sheffield, Gary, Terry Tu...
Owen, Mr Brendan, Ma...
Georgio, Eamonn O'Kee...
Adam Saint, Bulldog, D...
Lageno, Nick, Rudy and
Gary *(Jocelyn Bain
Hogg/Ashley Woods
Promotion)*

Left Nick Bateman (Na...
Nick), Brendan (no cha...
there then!), Jo Guest a...
Seymour

Left Me and my lady S...

Right Diamond knuckle duster *(Jocelyn Bain Hogg/Ashley Woods Promotion)*

Below Me at the Oxford union in the photo that Jay-Z adapted for the cover of his album *The Blueprint (Jocelyn Bain Hogg/Ashley Woods Promotion)*

The Fallen Angel by Pierre Anstis

and good if you're in the business of entertainment, but the worst shot in the world to be on the end of is the one in the stomach. It makes you look, for want of a better word, like a right cunt. I got hit in the stomach once and it felt like someone had stolen all the fucking air from the room. Now this was bad news 'cos I was meant to win this one. *Supposed* to win this one, know what I mean? (Think of that Brad Wotsit's pikey in *Snatch*.) The guy I was up against was frightened to hit me in the head in case he hurt me, if you get my meaning, so he's gone for the belly and – thwack – I'm doubled up and forgetting to breathe. I'm just about to pass out and the corner man's saying, 'Stay down till nine. Stay down till nine.' I said, 'Fuck – what time is it now!' It brought the house down, but not quick enough.

If I'm honest, what really went wrong with me and boxing is I thought I was going to be a contender. Maybe in our house I could have been, although my mum packs a mean punch. But once wine, women and song, and the odd bit of drugs and all that, got hold of me, it was never going to happen. Like I say, I like a little bit of whizz and it's always been like that ever since I first discovered it. And you know I'm more likely to put in a new kitchen on that stuff than do anything useful. So I didn't want to do the training 'cos I was down the pub, but then, if I got the other guy in a clinch and I've had a bit of whizz, I just wanted to have a chat with the geezer. 'How're you going? Did I ever tell you about the time I met Tyson?' So I decided to get out. Now I've taken up synchronised swimming with my pal Mad Pete. It gives us an excuse for taking all those body bags out to sea.

Speaking of Tyson, though, I've got loads of boxing stories. In fact, I've got one 'ear. So stop me if you've heard this one. I bought, would you believe, a training session with the boxer Ricky Hatton at an auction once.

It seemed like such a fantastic idea at the time, and everyone thought I was the bee's for digging deep for charity. But the actual day came and I couldn't believe that I actually paid one and a half for some little cunt to twat me in the face for half an hour. I could get that off my missus for nothing.

So we've worked out that I weren't much cop as a pugilist, to use an Open fucking University word. (It basically means a bloke that gets hit a lot.) And I'm looking forward to giving a diamond or two to Vinnie Jones, courtesy of the real Big Chris. But the main point of this chapter was me telling you how I got proper shafted when it came to being in Guy Ritchie's films. (You do remember that bit, right? Stop sidetracking me, would you?)

The day that Guy Ritchie had to come back and tell me, 'Sorry, we've got to fuck you off' was the day I decided to make my own film. The authorities might be able to stop me appearing in someone else's movie, but if I'm the boss, if I'm the producer, if it's my fucking money going in, who can they tell not to hire me? Silly prick, how naive was that?

I made *Hell to Pay* three years ago. I had no trouble making it, it was fucking easy, all off the top of my head. I don't need to have a script to tell me how to rob banks. I rob banks. If I was gonna ask you (yes, you mate) to be in my film, I'd get you to play yourself. Same clothes, same haircut, same accent. You don't need a script, I just say, 'This is the story, you've got to do that.' You can only get lines wrong if you've got any. Acting's a piece of piss, we all do it all the time, and we think these soap stars are so clever when they're not. Example: if I knocked on your door in the middle of the night and said, 'Do me a favour, tell my missus I was with you last night' – and you told her that, then you'd be acting. You'd save my marriage, just by saying, 'Yeah, he was here, there's where the cunt threw up.' Appearing in court, trying to convince twelve people you didn't do something when you did – that's acting. See what I mean? So everyone in the film is real. I play Dave. The prostitute is a prostitute, the doorman is a doorman, the barman is a barman, the cab driver is a cab driver. It's my gun, my house, my car, my clothes. I'm just telling a story; it's like a fucking documentary. And because I'm a control freak – I've heard too many horror stories from other people – I'm also the director, costume-maker, accountant and tea lady.

And let's face it, I make a pretty fucking good Dave. You don't need any footballers to do the role anyway, let's put it that way. And when you think about it, who's better qualified at directing some of the naughty things in *Hell to Pay*? I mean, how the hell are Guy Ritchie or Martin Scorsese going to tell me how to look pointing a gun at someone? They've never done it. Whereas I also know how to behave if someone else is pointing the gun at you. Do they? Only on the big screen do you go, 'Take your best shot, kid.'

Because I had been involved in every part of the film industry when I'd been on other films – the security, finding locations, finding actors, having a good enough name that people would lend me cameras and equipment – I was able to call in a few favours and save on the budget. I had a film camera crew living with me for a year, and one of them said he'd be a cameraman for my film. I had my own locations, I had my actors, I had my script in my head – let's crack on. I took it to Cannes and won Best of Group. Get that from the Bermondsey boy!

Everything was set up for release in England, then the authorities got word it was out there and things became difficult for me. They sabotaged me every way they could.

And in the end they took some very drastic action that left me in bits on the central reservation.

In the police's ideal world, I would never release *Hell to Pay*. And from where the Old Bill are sitting now, the world must look pretty near perfect. The truth of the matter is I'm at an all-time low financially because every penny I had was invested in the film. Which would have been fine and dandy if I didn't happen to disappear into Elvis Land in that coma for six months. So because of the car accident, I'm now two years late in bringing it out, and in that time the authorities have proper got their stories straight.

Not only did I spend every penny I had, I borrowed money I shouldn't have done on a film that was put on hold for two years by me nearly dying. And I'm not talking about a few quid from the small-loans man at Barclays. A few investors on my project are seriously not to be crossed. They all know I ain't robbed them, and they know they'll be repaid, but to be fair it is two years late. It's like, 'I know you was in a coma, so I'll give you some time.' But at the moment, I admit I am financially in trouble. It's very hard for me to get out of the hole that I'm in without a major injection of money, but the good news is it is on its way because the film is sold.

So this is the upside: at its worst, if the film does as bad as it can, I still get £750,000 just through Blockbusters having it. On top of that, I've learned how to sell it to different territories throughout the world, how to make a soundtrack album, everything. It's normally one man, one job; I've done the fucking lot. I know the people to ring in America, I know how to sell it abroad, I know how to do the editing, I know how to make a soundtrack, how to get it licensed. I've learned it all. And that all means extra pound notes in Dave's pocket.

So I can live with being skint for a bit, knowing it's just around the corner. Jenny found that a little bit hard, I think, because it's a bit fake, you're pretending. I never normally say anything, but the normal perception is that Dave Courtney's loaded. People go, 'But he hasn't got a job. He's not on benefits. Where does his money come from?' I can understand what they're thinking. But go and have a look in my fridge. Empty. Or in the gas meter. See how many pennies I've got in there. Or check the petrol gauge in my car. Jenny just got a little fucked off with it all. She'd go, 'Dave, you've gambled every penny we had on this fucking film. You've sold everything, my car. For *what*?'

When I saw the advertising campaign needed to actually promote your film in Cannes I knew that, for every note I'd borrowed to make the thing, it weren't enough to sell it. Spielberg's spending 35 grand on each poster, all made of different oils, so when the sun came up in the morning it changed colours. It was a grand a second to get anything plugged on television and I thought, I can't fucking compete with that. So I got about 45 of my mates to go to Cannes with me. We put the 'star' into Eurostar that weekend, I tell you. As instructed, the chaps turned up all wearing black suits, and I accidentally wore a white one. *Cunt.* But the photos look the absolute fucking bollocks. So we're swanning around Cannes and everyone is thinking, Who the hell is that? Proper showing off. And Cannes is the best place in the world for that. It's got the biggest boats, the biggest diamonds, everyone's got a million-pound film, and all that. No wonder Russell Crowe couldn't help wandering over.

I've got a lot of time for the old Aussie hell-raiser and all that 'commander of the armies of the north' bollocks, but I didn't recognise who he was when I bumped into him in Cannes. Without a leather skirt, a sword in each hand and a few dead Christians lying around, he just looked like a normal geezer in a T-shirt. There was all this paparazzi round him, and as we all pulled up mob-handed (and mob-everything-else), all the chaps in black suits and yours truly in his white tux, the press just all left him and ran over to us. They're like vultures, the paparazzi, they're just looking for the next thing to feed on, so they've dumped him 'cos they've seen me turn up 45-handed, sitting on a Harley Davidson with a diamond-studded knuckleduster in my hand. So they're taking photographs of me and he's an all-right geezer, so Russell Crowe comes across and says, 'Who's this fella?' and then he's come up to me and gone, 'Hello Mr Courtney, good luck with your film in Cannes.' Then he's held out this programme and gone, 'Would you mind putting your moniker on this?' In Australian, obviously. Well, I didn't know who he was, did I? I wasn't being rude. So I went, 'To anyone in particular?' and he went 'ha ha' and I went, 'Well, how do you spell "ha ha"?' All my mates are trying to put me straight and I've finally twigged. I said, 'Look, Russell, I didn't mean to disrespect you. I thought *Gladiator* was the bollocks. But all them people made you look good, and now you've come out here to get your acclaim and your accolades you've come on your own.' I said, 'I've brought my gladiators with me, and that's why the press are out here taking pictures of us.' And when I said that, all my mates just grew. They were scary to start with but now they're all puffed up hearing me talk to this film star about them. They actually grew in front of him. It was like, 'I'm Spartacus!' 'No, I'm Spartacus!' Real fist-on-chest stuff.

So what's the delay then, if *Hell to Pay* was ready for Cannes? Well, first of all, we had the small matter of a confiscated film. When we were over on the French Riviera I wasn't actually able to see my own screening 'cos I was arrested for carrying fake guns on the way in.

They had 'Woolies' stamped on the bottom and they only fired water, so what fucking threat they thought I was I don't know – unless they worried I was going to water-bomb the premiere of *Crouching Tiger, Hidden Dragon*. And they just so happened to stick me in a French nick where no fucker spoke English. And when someone I could understand did turn up, they said they'd be going to the screening room to get the cut of the film we'd brought. Of all the hundreds of movies there that week, they just happened to pick on mine. Wow. A coincidence, or do you think possibly Scotland Yard had been on the blower to Interplod? The upshot was when we left Cannes the only fucking edit of the film stayed behind.

In hindsight, that weren't the end of the world 'cos we've come up with a new edit and it's blinding. And that's what I've been trying to get distributed in the last few months. But guess what? If the powers that be don't want me to appear on the *Big Breakfast* with the cast of *Babyjuice Express*, there's no fucking way they want Dave on at the Odeon Leicester Square. But I didn't realise that. Every single cinema in the country wanted to show my film. Who wouldn't want Dave Courtney playing Dave Courtney with real gangsters? And then all in the same week, without me getting in touch with any of them, they all came back – the Odeon, Warner's, every fucking chain – and said they didn't want to be associated with the film. And two cinema chains that I didn't even ask rang me and said they couldn't put it on. It's like this round robin of everybody suddenly went round the industry and I'm left holding the phone in disbelief. As usual, they've all gone and given me different excuses. But I know and they know the only reason I've been given the old Spanish archer is 'cos they've had the call from the authorities. 'You're gonna find it tricky getting an entertainment licence next year if you show that cunt's film.' You get the idea.

To be honest, I've been in conversations with several distributors and they've all got so far. And then they've come to see me with the excuse. The last mob to let me down had the worst excuse yet. These two guys just tried to play each other off. 'I'd love to do it with you, Dave, but he won't let me' – phone calls like that, when I know they're in the same fucking room. This guy was like, 'I've got TV companies, there are documentaries you can do. You can edit your film at my editing suite.' It took a year and a half, they were arguing about all sorts, but it was soon very clear they were looking for an excuse to back out. It was as if they were trying to start an argument, but I'm not an arguing person. Dave Courtney don't give you a reason not to like him. Most people don't like me before they've met me so I try my fucking hardest in the flesh. The only stipulation I had with this pair was that the film was meant to be a showreel for me. It was a vehicle for myself and I was trying to get everyone else famous at the same time. I want to help get my records out, promote my mate's club and all that.

So one of the first things they do is come up with this edit that has chopped out all the music I'd promised other people would be in it. The record I did with Tricky, the one the charity wouldn't take a million pounds for, I wanted that in it, but it's gone because of the gangster associations. And *Hell to Pay*, the actual theme record by Steve Whale's mob, The Business, they wanted to take that out as well because he's too much of a punk rocker. But the biggest fuck-up was their decision to take out all the songs by Rancid, and that's when I knew they'd been nobbled, 'cos Rancid was the film's entry point into the American market.

Rancid actually have a record on their last album called 'Dave Courtney: England's Robin Hood'. You haven't heard it? Get with the programme, mate. That all came about 'cos I met their main man Lars Frederiksen in the car park of the Viper Rooms in Hollywood. He wasn't looking his best at the time, I have to be honest. I was over there promoting one of my little porn projects, so I had all these porn stars with me for a night out, and we were just leaving the club. Skinheads and punks are quite related, so, when I saw this geezer getting a kicking in the car park, I ended up running over and helping out. The porn stars loved that, didn't they. Proper wank material for them, that was, and I helped more than one of them rehearse a few scenes, I kid you not. So I've yanked this bloke clear and sorted out his attackers, and we've got talking. It just so happened he was Lars, the lead guy in Rancid, and he was a good mate of Steve Whale's. So now he comes over to stay at my house when he's in England, I've been on their record and he even had me on stage with them at the Apollo. Lars went, 'You want anti-Establishment? Here's Mr Anti-Establishment!' Wicked. I want to be a pop star now, don't I!

Anyway, someone at the distributors has decided that these Rancid tracks have to come out, and I'm like, 'Those songs are guaranteeing us coverage in America, you prick.' And then I realise: That's the fucking point. I did warn the two distributors there'd be pressure put on them not to work with me and they said it would be fine, and now look. I know someone's got to them but they're not going to admit it. All I know is, it's another few months gone without the film coming out.

There's loads of stuff in the film that the authorities don't want to be seen, and one of them is this scene where I'm holding a piece of paper that says 'The Jack Straw Bundle'. That is actually something I genuinely sent to Jack Straw when he was home secretary, so how powerful is that? It was delivered by the *Sunday People*, so I know he got it. And a copy of all 22 pages of it was sent to the prime minister, the editors of the papers, and I got no reply. It was startling stuff. In fact, if anyone can prove one lie in there, call me a liar. I've not had a reply in two years so, if I can embarrass them in my little film, you'll have to forgive me.

One of the worst things about all these delays is that, of course, this has been the thing the press have been allowed to report. 'It's about Courtney, it's negative, so obviously we can run it. If it were any good, we'd have to run that story about the singing frog again instead.' So you might have read that I've had fallings out with Brendan over the edit, and that's sort of true. He wants the Dave Courtney story out there as much as anyone, but I know it's got to be perfect before I unleash it in its glory. This is my chance at taking on the upper echelons of society and I've waited this long. Another few months won't kill me – 'cos they certainly haven't been able to.

Anyway, you know I'm a thinker, I like to work out answers before the questions come up, so I foresaw these problems with distribution. And obviously I've come up with a few little solutions.

The first one was to have this series of small premieres in advance of the mainstream launch, just so a few thousand people could see the thing and vouch for it. If anything happened to me, I wanted as many people as possible to be able to go, 'Yeah, I saw it, it was a funny film.' I knew full well the showings wouldn't get reported – it wouldn't matter if Robbie Williams came to my premiere 'cos his dad's in the film; they still wouldn't say I had one. And as I believe Garry Bushell was sacked from the *Sun* partly 'cos he had a role in the film as well and they didn't want me to have a voice-piece in a major fucking tabloid, I do know how serious they're going to get about it.

The second thing I'm doing is this: I intend to make a DVD documentary of a live 'Audience With . . .' and in the middle of that Audience I show the *Hell to Pay* film. It's not exactly pirating my own film, but it's making sure it exists in case anything happens to me. So if I bring that out for £9.99, you not only get the film but you also get 'An Audience With Dave Courtney'. And I can do it legally.

And the other thing: where the cinemas are actually going to give me grief for putting it on, I've decided to buy a company for 180 quid, then change the name like you're allowed to do. This happens a dozen times a day. So it could be Billy Bong's whatever. But I'll change it to something with 'Sports' in the title. That company then rings up pay-per-view TV and books a two-hour slot from eight till ten on Saturday night. Everything on telly has to have the right licence and rating, and as I've worked in all these industries I now know how they operate. As long as you pay up half beforehand and you have the receipt, they cannot cancel it. Three months down the line and ITV and all that will want to know what you're showing and, when you say it's a film, they can't actually go 'No'. They've been paid, it's a genuine company and it's an 18-certificate film. You can sell the adverts in the middle of it to make money; all of the promotion will be paid by the people who buy the adverts, so you'll get all these posters up and down the country. It'll be just like a Tyson fight. I reckon every pub and club in the country would want to have that on their screens. Tyson earned fucking £12 million last time he fought live on telly. Now I'm not saying I'm as popular as Iron Mike, but I reckon I'm at least a quarter as popular as he is, don't you? If I'm right about that, I'll get £3 million, and then it goes to Blockbusters. Talk about a gold run. I'll have an E please, Bob.

The biggest of my mini-premieres was at the Circus Tavern, owned by a very good friend of mine, Paul, home of the darts world championships and more totty than you can shake a dick at. That's a serious venue in its own way, and it showed that this wasn't a film that was gonna be brushed under the carpet, even though no fucker would report it. But it wasn't a premiere as the major West End premiere's going to be in the future; it was a showing of an unfinished version that hadn't been edited. But this particular night was the biggest premiere to date and I just happened to have along a documentary crew who were recording a new DVD for me.

We had a full house down there just off the A13, a proper mix of naughty boys and celebrities. The comedian Adrian Doughty was on that night; there was Tony Lambrianou, the darts player and now actor Bobby George, Falklands hero Simon Weston, my porn-star mate Bev Cox, and loads, loads more. The documentary boys couldn't get enough of what went on. They had my mate Wolfie going, 'Dave's a nice bloke with a massive todger. I know 'cos the last time I asked him to do a PR shot he leaped on the dinner table and got Taz to give him a blow job. Funnily enough, nobody would print those pictures.' Nice one, Wolfie. They also got some great shots of all these birds, led by Bev Cox, it has to be said, getting their tits out and generally being very friendly. Women were flashing their tits and groping my old boy. It was wild. Imagine what they'd have done if the cameras weren't there! (The proof's all on Dave's Dodgy DVD.)

The first half of the show has taken the form of 'An Audience With Dave Courtney', where I've done my usual spiel and welcomed all the various villains to my humble presentation. The jokes were flying, including this one: did you hear about the Palestinian bloke who went to a sex shop and bought a blow-up doll? It blew up on the bus on the way home. Classic, yet tasteful. But then halfway through the night, 'cos it's meant to be the premiere of the film, I get Mal, the technical brains behind the Courtney operation, to slip *Hell to Pay* into the DVD player and then sit back and watch as a thousand mates gape open-mouthed at my film. Talk about goose pimples on the back of your neck. If it's possible to multiple premature ejaculate, I was up for it. These were some of the most serious bruisers and best-connected players in the country, and they were loving it. Dreamy, there's no other word for it.

Unfortunately I didn't get to watch the film all the way through on that occasion, 'cos I had a little maintenance matter to attend to in the car park. When everyone was arriving at the Circus Tavern, an annoying little shit of a man decided to heckle them, saying that I'm a poof, a paedophile, a wife-beater and that I'm not very nice to sick animals. Something tells me he doesn't like me. The truth of the matter is I knew full well who the geezer was and, as I told the audience that night, he's not the sort of person worth worrying about. He was actually trying to challenge me to a dust-up out there in public, yelling through this fucking megaphone for me to come out and sort it out like a man. Of course I'd like to tear his arms and legs off and feed them to Vanessa Feltz, of course I'd like to batter the cunt. But how stupid does he think I am? I'm wearing a white suit, the car park is fully CCTV'd up, the place is crawling with press, and I've spent years trying to convince the world 'I'm not like that no more'. Am I really likely to go out there and take him on with all that going on?

The answer, I'm afraid, is yes. As soon as everyone had settled back to watch *Hell to Pay*, I slipped out the back door and walked up to this geezer. He's still bellowing into his megaphone, he's trying to give his own books away, he's wearing a too-tight T-shirt with his name on it – do I have to go on? Anyway, I regret to inform you that I strolled up to him and slipped my duster on my right hand. You've got to love the duster at times like that. I never leave home without one. It's the best tool in the world to stop someone. If you hit them with this, they stop. Dead. If you stab someone, it feels like a pinch. You go, 'Wassat?' then carry on hitting for thirty seconds before you collapse in a bloody heap. What you want if you're in trouble is something to go 'Boom' and see him hit the floor. Not stab him and watch him bleed to death for half an hour, or gas him and watch him roll around scratching his eyes. I could beat any fucker in the world if you let me use a duster. Tarzan, anyone. One shot going that way and you've won. Even if he covers his face, you'll break his fucking arm. Any shot on the chest puts the cunt on the floor. And if you're caught with it, the most you'll get is three years. I can handle risking three years. I have done.

So anyway, this geezer's foghorning that 'Courtney's a wanker', 'Courtney's a coward', 'Courtney tried to kill me', 'Courtney gets others to do his dirty work', 'Courtney tried to get me stabbed', and I walked over to him, held out my hand to shake his and went, 'Look, surely me and you could . . .' And as he got closer I went 'biff' and chinned him – knocked him clean out. CCTV or no CCTV, press or no press. The man's a prick. And at that moment, he was a prick sparked out on the floor with a hole in his chin.

I went back in and carried on with the show. He's now woke up, there's television cameras there and he's got an orange chin, so he's going, 'I've got an invalid card, you wife-beater' and all this. And he's still banging on that I get other people to do all my dirty work for me, even though I've just gone out there and knocked him out myself. On my own, with a knuckleduster. And he's got a big hole in his chin to prove it.

If you want to know the history of all this, you have to understand the concept of 'Courtneysteins'. Pretty freaky, ain't it? They're basically fans who've taken it a bit too far, if you know what I mean, and start thinking they're something they're not. They start dressing like me with all the gold collar tips and the suits, acting like me, and thinking they are like me. And I'm afraid this geezer was one of the worst. He got a sniff at fame when he was on the front cover of this *Hard Bastards* book, 'cos he was the only bloke who would hold a piece of wood and go 'grrrr' like a prick. The thing is, he weren't the first person they asked, but everyone else said no. Hard is hard and it's not enough to look the part, you've got to be like it mentally. Your brain has got to be a certain way if you've got the gift of hurting people. And the last thing you want to be seen doing is running around with bits of wood. You want to be seen as a diplomat. When you know you've got the gift of premier-division hurting people, you don't actually want to walk around showing people that that is your only gift, 'cos you might be the best fighter, but do people want you at their wedding or a party or an orgy? So you're humble. It's people that ain't that hard and want others to think they are that walk around like 'look at how hard I am'.

I'll tell you how seriously I take all this, 'cos I left it all in the documentary. So if you want to hear this tosser slagging me off, it's £9.99 to you. But what's fantastic is my boy Beau has put together this DVD of all this shouting and given it a hip-hop backing track, so you've got things like 'Courtney you're a wanker' to music. It's proper fucking hysterical. If I can find a way to release it I will 'cos you have got to hear this, mate. And I've covered myself 'cos the guy shooting the film says on tape, 'Do you mind us filming this?' and he's gone, 'No.' Then he says, 'Are you getting all this?' So

what I was going to talk about next. Wanking. That's right, bashing the bishop, shaking hands with the wife's best friend, the five-knuckle shuffle, whatever you want to call it. And in particular, wanking in prison.

The thing is, when you're inside, wanking is the only thing you can do that is free and nice. Everything else is shit. So there's absolutely no stigma about cracking one – or a dozen – off, nothing at all. I do it, you do and I *know* your other half does 'cos I've heard them. It's a bit awkward if you're in a bunk bed with someone 'cos, if one of you is having a toss, it rattles the whole frame. You're actually willing the guy to finish so you can get on with your own one. I was lucky in my first place 'cos the geezer above weren't exactly a marathon performer, if you know what I mean. I've had vaccinations that took longer than he did, but I'm not complaining (although I can't be sure about his bird).

They had cameras in my cell so it weren't even worth trying to pretend you weren't having one. All you had to do was pick what style to go with. Option one, the Tent Wank – fucking circus big tops in my case. The screws would see that and go, 'Ah, Courtney's having a wank.' Option two, the On The Side Wank, with your elbow up so they can't see any movement. Then they'd just go, 'Ah, Courtney's having a Side Wank.' Which only leaves the Drilling For Oil Wank, otherwise known as the Shit Wank, where you stick your bum in the air and try to pretend you're doing fuck all. So I thought, What's the point in hiding it? I'd stick it right in front of the camera and go for it. It must have looked like it was snowing to the bloke the other end. Proper Siberian weather that was.

In every prison, you can tell who's on duty by the footsteps. It's just one of those talents you pick up when you're cooped up for three years. You can't see left or right, so you just go by the sound. This woman used to creep along really quietly so you didn't hear her, then she'd fling open the door just to catch you wanking. She got off on it – and who can blame her? But one day I heard her squeaking along the other side, so I thought I'd have some fun with her. I stood on the edge of my bed, proper hard-on, the full fifteen-and-a-half inches – wide. You know what I mean? I've got my best horny face on, and everything, but she spent so long getting round that by the time she flung open the door I was sitting down with a pair of tweezers.

Apart from wanking, the other thing you do in prison that reminds you you're still alive is read and write letters. Before I first went inside I weren't the greatest letter writer in the world – I struggled with Gs, Ws and Qs mainly. But I promise you, when you're inside that wardrobe 23 hours a day, a piece of paper to or from the outside world can make the difference between you twatting a guard just to try to get shot, or knuckling down and serving your time.

I never realised this before, but if you really want to talk to someone, if you can write it down rather than say it, you'll get it all out. Whereas if you try talking to a bird, you get two lines out before she's 'Yeah, but, no but, yeah but.' By the time you get back on track, you spit another few lines out and she's interrupting again. At the end of it you're so fucking frustrated that you haven't even made your point yet, and you're probably not in the best mood anyway so it's all a disaster. She thinks she's right, and she probably is 'cos she's only heard half of what you planned to say, but, if it was a letter, she's got no choice but to read to the end. Start to finish, in that order.

So, when you're inside, you get letters from your missus thanking you for what you wrote, and they go, 'You never said all that to me when you was out.' And you reply, 'You never gave me the chance, you dozy cow.'

The other thing about being inside is this: if you haven't

got a missus when you went in, but someone starts writing to you, you can fall in love more quickly, more easily and more passionately than anyone can on the outside. You could fall in love with Nora Batty if she was writing you letters, because it's the only contact you're having with a real woman. You find yourself banging one off over her and you haven't even met her. It's mental, I'm telling you. You fall in love with letters, and with the writer, and you read it fifty million times and picture her writing it.

It works the other way though. For every letter from a stranger wanting something from you, you get one from a stranger wanting to give you something. *Hello!* When you're the poor bastard banged up, seeing that letter come with your name on it is proper dreamy. It doesn't matter that you don't know the cunt, he's taken the time to write to you and you've got a bit of a point to your day 'cos you think about writing back. And the chances are that, if someone has just announced he wants to be your friend, he'll probably be up for helping you out a little bit too.

Reggie Kray was the master of this. He was half of the most infamous firm this country has ever seen, his name's known around the world and even though he didn't set foot outside in thirty years he knew there were thousands of people who would be made up to have a piece of him. So, when he got these letters, Reggie being clever would write back knowing full well that you can go round saying you got a letter from Reggie Kray. So if his next letter said, 'Do us a favour, pal, send us a pair of trainers', you would. Without any shadow of a doubt, and if you didn't have the money you'd send your own pair. And you don't know how many of those letters were going out there to different people every day: 'Yeah, size 11, just send them to Tomlin in A wing.' Reggie gets to pay all his debts with lace-ups and you're proper smiley 'cos he's acknowledged you. If all you need to do to have that bit of respect among your crowd is post a pair of Pumas, you're laughing, ain't you?

But some geezers would get so carried away by the glamour of it all they'd get taken a little bit advantage of. I've got to be careful how I say this, 'cos it means a lot to so many people, and they genuinely would have done anything for the man, but you have to remember Reggie's got nothing to lose asking you.

Whether they're not the full HP or just genuinely concerned about geezers incarcerated all that time, you do get these people who just start writing letters to long-term lags 'cos they want to be pen pals. They are normally Samaritans who are used to being nice to people on the phone for no money, so they're just saying what they normally say to people who have no hope. But if they start writing to you, to a prisoner who's lost a little bit of reality, they might just be doing their job, but he's starting to love you more than you could know. I don't think they realise you can fall in love with someone when you're in prison, just through reading letters. It works more than someone pulling up in a Ferrari and taking you off to Monaco on your holidays, I promise you.

Then what happens is some of them on the outside think, Hang about, I didn't really mean it, I was just being nice, but no one's ever said they love me like you have and then suddenly they think they're in love too.

If I'm honest, this is what's happened with quite a lot of very famous prisoners, from the Yorkshire Ripper to old hook-hands Abu Hamza. Others have been inside for twenty years and yet they suddenly produce a wife from nowhere – and I've got mates on the outside who can't get laid, let alone married. Anyway, one of these romances happened to my mate Charlie Bronson. Now, Charlie is a strange one, yes. Very talented though, a fantastic artist and a pretty, er, imaginative writer. He lived underneath me in the Special Unit when I was on remand for a year in Belmarsh, and we used to have the odd chat. Window to window, through the floor, 'You there, Charlie?' 'Grrrr.' Every day, for a year, we spoke, but I never laid eyes on the man. He weren't allowed out once in that time. So I know him really well, but I couldn't tell you what colour his eyes were.

When I arrived in Belmarsh I was actually a known force and so was he. Fight-wise, I wouldn't put myself in the same bracket as Charlie Bronson in a million fucking years. I would last approximately the time it took him to get up and reach me before he tore a fucking lump out of me and spat me out. Maybe we would be in the same bracket if I'd been subjected to seventeen years in solitary confinement where all I did was stick my feet under a radiator and do sit-ups for ten hours a day, '2,705, 2,706 . . .' and the next day eight million press-ups.

All the pent-up anger at being inside for nearly two decades and not speaking to anyone in all that time has got to give you a slight slip in reality. You know it has. So imagine living next door to him? '*Morning*!' You'd have to have a sign at the bottom of your drive saying 'Beware of the neighbour'. This, after all, is the geezer what spent two years applying to have a budgie in his cell then the day he got it he bit its fucking head off. Who's a pretty boy, then?

The thing with Charlie is that successful men know life isn't all black and white. What counts is how you tiptoe through the grey areas. The more Neanderthal you get, the more simplistic things become. 'He's a policeman, gotta be a cunt. He's a skinhead – one of us.' We all know geezers like that. And you get that sort of character in prison, only it's magnified because of the circumstances. So he's going, 'I'm a prisoner, you're a screw, I punch you, you hit me with a stick – that's the name of the game.'

That's it. There's no 'Well, that one's all right 'cos he has a chat.' It's just 'Cunt!' for nothing. Black and white.

If I, out of nowhere, just walked up to a screw and stabbed him in the eye and broke a chair on another one's back, Charlie Bronson is the kind of guy who would run over and help me, no questions asked. You understand what I mean?

The problem he's got is there are plenty of black-and-white screws as well. If there's someone you don't get on with, as a warden you just stick an anonymous note in the governor's box saying you think so-and-so might commit suicide tonight 'cos you've heard a whisper, and now he's under official scrutiny. Because all the prisons are camera'd up now, you need a good excuse to actually go and annoy the inmates, and that's the best way. So in the middle of the night, 'cos you think he might try to top himself, you and your mate go along to a geezer's cell, bang on the door, turn on the lights and go, 'Oi, Baker, Baker, out of bed, son, let's see you're alive!' So the poor guy crawls out of the sack and they go, 'All right then, as you were.' Then fifteen minutes later, they're back. *Crash!* 'Oi, Baker, are you all right?' If you want to mess with someone, you have to plant the excuse first, but once you've done that they're fish in a barrel to the screws.

He's known as 'Britain's Most Dangerous Criminal' but I think Charlie Bronson's the bollocks. I might get chastised for this, but I love the geezer. When we went over to Brazil for Ronnie Biggs's seventieth birthday party, he gave me this letter to read out to the old convict. That blew everyone's minds, I can tell you. The fact that Charlie's still walking, talking coherent when he's been locked up and wheeled out every so often when they want to show how bad criminals are is a definite tribute to the man. But you know he's suffering, 'cos we all do, and for the same reason.

The worst thing about prison is this: the whole world is going on without you, and you know it. It drives you mental. You go, 'My missus is still going to work.' What do you expect her to do? Sit at home all day for 23 years waiting for you to stop chewing up screws and be let out? If you write to someone inside you even feel guilty telling them anything about what's going on, however shit it is, 'cos you know it'll just eat them up. But if they could do something that would get them in the papers, that's almost the same as fame, it's the same as winning an Academy Award considering they're just living in a wardrobe. Imagine you're RB739. Your wife's left you, your mates have stopped writing 'cos you kept asking for puff and there's nothing to live for. Then all of a sudden you do something and it gets in the papers and you think, Wow, a million people read my name! They know I'm here!

The problem then is you might be guilty of going, Right, what can I do to get in the papers again? If you're doing a proper bit of bird, you have a mental battle just to not go crazy. All you do every day is get up and sit in your cell for 23 hours apart from when you go for a little walk around the yard. So, when Charlie Bronson got famous, that was the first bit of adrenaline that geezer had ever had in real life. He'd never been in the papers when he was out! Remember, he actually got a five-year prison sentence and ended up doing seventeen. Work that one out.

Anyway, young Charles has got into this pen-pal relationship with a Bangladeshi bird called Saira and, before you know it, it's love. Sort of. Even his mum has stopped writing him letters, so he's been a bit cute and gone, 'Well, they can't give me parole, 'cos I've got no fixed abode. But if I was married, I'd have a proper address. Then they'd have to consider me for parole.' Er, yeah, Charlie, sure. *One more budgie for Mr B.*

So he gets a letter from someone being nice and sees his

way out. But, fuck, she's a Muslim – OK, I'm a Muslim as well now, let's do it. But talk about fucking unlucky. He got married on a Saturday, became a Muslim the day before because of his wife's religion, then on the next Tuesday Bin Laden's boys blew up that block of flats in New York and now every cunt in the world hates Muslims. He went, 'Fucking hell!' As if the world don't hate him enough already, he's only changed religion to get married and now some Saudis have driven into a couple of tower blocks, everyone's going, 'Charlie Bronson's one of them fucking Muslims.'

As for Saira, this is what she's done. She's twenty, thirty years younger than him, she's an unmarried mum and she's a minority-religion bird who no fucker has taken any notice of, ever. She weren't even born when he went in and he's never coming out, but now she's getting letters back from this famous bloke it's like, 'Hello, someone's noticing me at last.' She wasn't the prettiest thing on two legs, but the bloke's famous – 'I know he's only famous for eating budgies and all that, but that don't matter – who likes budgies anyway?' So she writes him the letters and they get married.

Because of my relationship with Charlie, I arranged his reception down at my pub, the Manhattan, all at my expense, I'll have you know. It was a funny do, 'cos the groom had no chance of putting in an appearance, which meant I had the first dance with the bride in all her traditional Sari gear. It was like dancing with a maypole. But all the chaps turned up; there was Charlie Richardson, Roy Shaw, Charlie Breaker, Davy Lane, Joe Pyle and Tony Lambrianou. But most interestingly for me was the appearance of an old geezer called Lord Longford who you might remember as the religious chap who campaigns against miscarriages of justice on the behalf of proper villains. A real straight character.

Anyway, Lord Longford goes to me, 'Ah, Mr Courtney. The fear of whatever it is they think you are, let me tell you, goes right to the very, very top.' Come again, your worship? So he did. And what he meant by that was that I'm known at the highest level, there's a file on me in the government. I'm the one who can't be arrested, I've got Old Bill to nick themselves, I stick two fingers up to the law whenever I can. My days, he wanted to assure me, are seriously numbered. I told him I knew all this, but it was the first time a bona fide member of the aristocracy had had the bottle to admit it. In a strange way, it was a huge weight off my shoulders. After all, they might be trying to fucking kill me, but at least I weren't going mad!

But back to Charlie. I know him now and we write quite a lot, 'cos I know how important a letter is. I might get one every ten months or I might get four every week, 'cos he bangs them out, and he does all these pictures, but we're in regular touch. Will he ever get out? I doubt it. Seriously, they have created a monster, and from what I can see they're doing everything they can to keep him there. The authorities' little game wouldn't work if he was out, would it?

Charlie Bronson's wedding might have been one currant short of a fruitcake, but at least it was a largely happy occasion. By contrast, one of the saddest things to happen during this time was the death of one of our great friends, Tony Lambrianou. It was one of those sudden ones that caught everyone out. We was all floored when we heard the news, especially as he'd been in such good form at Charlie's wedding.

As a member of the Kray gang, Tony had served fifteen years for his involvement in the murder of Jack 'The Hat' McVitie, so not only was he respected by a lot of important people, he was actually a figure of worship to thousands of normal people out there who'd read about him.

Tony was one of the dinosaurs of the gangster world, from that old 'stick 'em up' era before we turned them into legends. But he was a genuine gentleman, a nice bloke. I'm too young to have known him when he was naughty, but he always treated the young and up-and-coming naughty person who was supposedly stepping into his shoes with the utmost respect. It was a sad day for me, it was a sad day for everybody. In fact it was a sad day for naughtiness as a job, 'cos one of the last links to the Krays was gone. But they'll always be there. The word 'gangster' is no more, it's part of history like knights in shining armour, cowboys and pirates who were all romantic bad guys. But the gangster myth will grow bigger than even the Krays were. Everybody who is in the business that I'm in now of celebrity-ising their gangster past owes a lot to the Krays. They made it acceptable to be famous and a villain.

Tony had been very instrumental in introducing me into that little circle. Ronnie Kray asked to see me first, so I went down to see him and he wanted some bits and pieces done. And like a silly little cunt I did it 'cos it was for the Krays. Then Reggie got in touch. At the time I had a security company, raving had just come in and I had 500 doormen. No one had 500 doormen. Clubs only had three doormen, but now there's raves at the Ministry of Sound, they needed 28 doormen. What the fuck's that about? To the outside world it looked like it was 'my firm', but I weren't looking at it like that. I might as well have had 500 office cleaners to nick a bit of money off, 'cos all their actions went down to me. Any fight they had and 'it was Courtney's firm'. It weren't fuck all to do with me but you'd get 'Courtney's firm shoots so-and-so'. But with the reputation comes the glory. So if I'm accepting the blame I'm getting the glory too.

Anyway, this was one gangland funeral I didn't actually arrange, because it would have caused a problem to put Dave Courtney's name over the top of things. But I got a lot of publicity for helping out anyway. People in the industry I'm in are very fucking aware of the barriers I have to climb to do anything. The stigma that's attached to me makes me more of a threat to the police than before, 'cos now I'm telling people about it. So saying I was in charge of the funeral would have caused more problems for the Lambrianou family than it solved. Doing the Kray funerals was a double-edged thing for me. It was the making of me in one respect and the destruction of me in another.

But even though I've publicly said this, I've still helped out 'cos they still actually need things from me: the organisation, the right people to be there and the razzmatazz and that, but they daren't actually say that Dave Courtney is in charge 'cos everyone remembers the last time when I actually met Sir Paul Condon (of course you'll have read about it in *Stop the Ride*). I was cocky and humiliated him on telly. I goaded him publicly and I've never been allowed to forget it.

Tony's funeral was run by two young chaps that weren't actually criminals. One was the Geordie connection, Stevie Raith. He was a pen friend of the Krays and he actually worked in a post office. The other one was a bloke called Christian who's a bodyguard from New Zealand, and the man who actually introduced me to Phil the Outlaw. Phil's the geezer who saved my life in Holland (see *Stop The Ride* . . .) and I then introduced him to the complete UK criminal fraternity. And that gave us a secret weapon, 'cos we could use them whenever we wanted 'cos they're so fucking handy. On the other hand it gave them a little bit of respectability and they weren't just looked upon as greasy little bikers. But it's been a nice little marriage and everyone's earned a lot out of it friendship-wise. Like I say, my firm ain't all bald-headed, flat-nosed Crombie-wearing geezers. I've got bikers, Chinese, blacks, poofs, whatever.

So they was in charge, but I was doing bits and pieces for them where I could and they was coming round here asking for advice and that. I remember I had to go with Ritchie Hawsley to see a geezer who wasn't up for doing what the chaps felt he should be doing, and I was only too happy to do that. One of the other things I took it upon myself to do was make the day a bit more razzmatazzy. I'd seen Roberta Kray fail and do miserably what she should have done for Reggie's funeral. Because she was the last word on what did and didn't happen, 'cos she's legally his wife, she made a real hash of it in my opinion. Because she wanted a little quiet one 'cos she was really timid, she said he did and no one could prove otherwise. But I knew Reg: he would have wanted fireworks, cheerleaders, the fucking lot. And I definitely knew Tony would have wanted exactly what he got. And I've got emails and letters from people like his brother Chris saying that.

Anyway, for Tony's funeral, there was loads of television coverage. But as you cannot glamorise crime in this country, none of the cameras were from here. English editors have since told me they tried to run a picture but as usual it was snagged by legal. As soon as my name gets typed in, it flashes up on this computer. 'Courtney Alert! Courtney Alert! The cunt's up to something.' And the people telling me all this are pretty high profile, like all those journalists that I gave stories to when they were starting out who are now editors. One of them was actually a junior journalist on the *Maidstone Gazette* when I was visiting Reggie Kray twice a week at Maidstone. He was my friend and I was giving him all these stories to put in about the Krays and he did so many the *News of the World* bought him 'cos he had the inside track on the fucking firm. He's still a mate, they all are, and they tell me the SP.

As soon as I realised the Americans were very interested in the death of an English godfather, I was on it. 'Cos I continually go over to the States and I intend to live there eventually, I'm looking at what the Americans want from me. If they want every Englishman to live in a castle, I'll fucking live in a castle. If Vinnie Jones can get nominated for an award for pretending to be me, what the fuck am I going to get? And the deal with America is this: I'll be that for you, if you do this for me.

The Americans are fascinated with the crime lords over here more than they are their own. And it's the same the other way round. Over here we would want to watch something like the Gotti funeral 'cos that's the Mafia, that's them! Our police, of course, will always try and make sure there was no home-grown coverage for any English villain. And this is what they did. There was deliberately no police presence so there would be disorder at Tony's funeral. The English newspapers had been told how to report it, if at all, and it was the American press that were looking for the real razzmatazz, the glamour and the myth.

I had chats with the American TV companies, so I knew exactly what they wanted. I got the Harley Davidson, I got the Outlaws as outriders, and I brought 150 of my mates and my documentary crew and we met at the Blind Beggar where Ronnie Kray shot Jack 'The Hat'. You know, everything the Yank director was looking for we served up for him. There was eight blokes from Manchester, eight from Leeds, ten from Glasgow, a dozen from Birmingham, a proper national event. There was too much fucking testosterone in the air for anyone to want to disrupt the funeral or cause a riot or pickpocket or start looting. Even with no police presence, no one would start heckling, 'Murderer' or any of that. They just wouldn't do it.

Despite the press trying to keep it really low key, 'cos the authorities don't believe someone like Tony should get the big hero-worship thing, it was a fantastic turnout. Not just from fans lining the roads but premier-division mourners like Freddie Foreman, Duchy, Mickey Goldtooth, John Nash, Joe Pyle and Roy Shaw – a right A–Z of British crime if ever you saw one. The whole day was proper respectful. The flowers in the lead hearse said 'A good man', and that weren't far off the mark. The only dodgy bit was the vicar's ponytail. But just when you thought everyone was getting a bit too serious, I lightened the mood. We were about to set off from the Blind Beggar, and we heard this police siren getting closer. 'Ah, that's my cab,' I said, and it was like all the tension in the air vanished.

Once we got going, and in front of the cameras as well, I had the helmet off and gave it both barrels of showing off driving the Harley in front of the hearse with Taz hanging round me. If you've ever seen the prime minister or the Queen being driven through central London and wondered how they never seem to get caught by the lights, it's 'cos they have these police bikes squirting ahead in teams and shutting every road along the way. That way Her Majesty don't get delayed from reaching the racetrack and snipers can't get a clear shot in neither 'cos she ain't stationary long enough. You only need four or six to do a proper job, and for Tony's procession we had dozens of them, all the Outlaws riding ahead of us blocking each road so we didn't get held up. Considering we were only doing about ten miles an hour, it weren't that hard.

'Cos I knew there was a load of people in another country looking at it I thought, Whether I deserve the title or not, if I'm labelled the typical English gangster I'll fucking play the part for you. Unenviably, I have to live by 'practise what you preach' and I ain't a bad old person to pick as a mentor for that world if you have to. As a subject, I'm probably an awful lot better than a lot of other people who, if you went in depth with them, would not stand up to scrutiny. I wore the clothes, I rode the bike, I brought the people and I gave them what they wanted to look at.

We're doing all this for Tony, guaranteeing him the sort of send-off that Reggie should have had, and more American coverage in death than he ever got in life, but the police look at it and all they see is, 'Courtney is *policing* the road himself? He is riding down the middle of the road with no helmet on and shutting roads off himself?' They looked at it as a pure act of defiance and I'm doing it as a 'be proud of me, Mum' moment. That seriously messed with them.

The police's job is to investigate and not put anything into the realms of 'it might not happen'. They have to work out all possible permutations so they're always looking at the networking that goes on between players. 'Ah, he knows him, does he? So that's where he gets X from.' Meetings like Tony's funeral just blows all the computers with them. It's a headfuck trying to follow who's interacting with who, so they were filming everyone there. There were more police with cameras than press, believe me. Individuals with cameras, just walking along with instructions to get pictures of five or so targets. Snapping whoever they're talking to, even if they're just doormen, while someone else is snapping the mate from the other side. Because now we've done a lot of these funerals we can actually look out for that.

Now I didn't know what picture the press were going to use the next day. But because at the time my wife was taking me to court and thinking of dropping the charges against me, and the police seemed to be using her for their own purposes, in the picture they put in the *Sun* it's me and my new girlfriend on the back of a motorbike, obviously breaking the law by not wearing a crash helmet. In one go they single-handedly kept any feud going with Jen so she'd still take me to court. However off that sounds, that's exactly what happened. Because I had a constant flow of information from Jen's sister, I knew what was going on. So when people are coming up to me and saying, 'Didn't you look good in the paper?' I'm thinking it's actually made me Public Enemy Number One so the authorities are entitled to give me twenty years for something I should only get five for, 'cos they've put me down as a known gangster in the paper. That's exactly what they did with the Krays. They made sure they were wrote about all the time for being nasty villains, so, when they get thirty years for something that should have got fifteen, no one jumps up and says, 'Oi, that's out of order.' Because the police had spent two years brainwashing the country.

And so that picture was what fuelled Jennifer to push on and allowed them to throw all these spanners in the works in accordance with their divide and conquer rule: number one, he's a grass; number two, he's a wife-beater; and now, number three, he's nicking all the glory from his mate's funeral. When was the last time the press were ever allowed to run a picture of me? I turned up to court in a jester's outfit and it was banned from every newspaper. How could I have known they were gonna suddenly go, 'Stick his ugly mug on the front page,' this time?

Except, of course I should have. 'Cos anything the authorities can do to make it difficult for me they will do. And just so I know they're in charge, they even have little pops back that only I can possibly see so everyone I tell thinks I've lost it. How about this one, this is the absolute God's honest: I was browsing through the *Sunday Times* one weekend, like I do in between washing my car and mowing my lawn in my pipe and slippers – *shut up!* Anyway, they had this full-page piece on the education secretary Charles Clark (and what job is that for a bloke, being a secretary?); the picture they run next to it was him dressed as a jester, which I thought bore an uncanny resemblance to the pictures of me in my jester's outfit coming out of the bent-copper court case. But they wouldn't do that, would they? This big paper of the Establishment wouldn't nick my picture and not credit it? Not much. Not only was the folds round the hat identical and the cord coming out from the collar pretty similar, but he was wearing my fucking bracelet! Cheeky bastards, or what? It's just like Jay-Z's people mimicking that picture of me at the Oxford Union (which I'll explain later) – I do all the work and others use the ideas. I suppose I ought to have been flattered that the *Sunday Times* used my photo, but it's a bit of a cheek, considering that they wouldn't run the proper story about me the first time round.

15. CUNTSTABLE COURTNEY

Spitting, Scotsmen and a spell inside

I've always considered Brendan as one of my closest friends, but even I had to raise an eyebrow at this one. He had this occasional arrangement with a mate that they'd shag each other's birds when they could get both of them to agree. A little four's up. And just to make it a bit interesting he invited me along to one of these little parties. Or so he says. Unfortunately, the invitation must have got lost in the post 'cos the first thing I know about it is him cracking up telling me that, 'cos they'd promised their birds I'd be there, but Brendan and his mate didn't fancy sharing with me, he nicked one of these life-size cardboard cut-outs of me from a book shop, and stood it at the end of the bed. He thought that was hilarious, turning up with this flat-pack Courtney and saying to his bird, 'Here's Dave.' What wiped his smile off though was his bird actually asked to keep the thing and that was the last he saw of her. I'm such a great shag, I don't even have to be there.

That's not the first time we've had a bit of fun with those cut-outs, though. I once sent one to the governor of Belmarsh. Parcel Forced it right to the door and he's had to sign for it, so I know it got there. It's all wrapped up and life size, it must have looked like they was carrying a body bag in. 'Oi, mate, we don't have stiffs here, the morgue's that way.' And on the note with it I've written, 'Since I know you're so desperate to have me here, I've sent my cardboard mate so you can stick him in a cell and believe it's me. With love, Dave Courtney, OBE.'

But Brendan's solid and he's been one of the clever ones and kept on the outskirts of the criminal fraternity. The occasional cup of tea and slice of Mr Kipling at my gaff is as close as he gets, officer, although he has been a witness to people being tied up and covered in petrol, shot at and stabbed. In fact, he's been stabbed himself and you can't get a closer witness than that. But he's actually been quite a main player, although now he's retired and doing very well with his own plant hire firm.

But it's 'cos we have the same warped sense of humour, I think, that we get on, and I realised that the first time I met him. It was at the Ministry of Sound and he'd obviously been out a bit too long – about two days too long. He was living in a flat in Thamesmead at the time so I said I'd run him home. It was Sunday lunchtime by now, and when we've got near I said, 'So where exactly do you live?' And he said, 'I know it's got a blue front door.' And he's been about that useful since.

Brendan comes with me all over the country when I do these 'Audiences With . . .' and sometimes drives, but we were on our way up to a charity do in Liverpool a few years back and they'd sent a limo with a chauffeur for us. We knew it was gonna be a good night when the driver's doing 100mph on the M6 and he says to me, 'Would you mind holding the steering wheel while I roll a joint?' So we arrived on a right high. Literally.

There were loads of stars there and one of them was Ricky Tomlinson. Top bloke is Ricky. Proper working class, and that. It didn't matter to him he was at this posh function, he always takes his own beer with him. But the highlight of the trip for me was seeing Sean Connery in this bar with Bruce Forsyth and Jimmy Tarbuck. Neil Ruddock's there with Jamie Redknapp and a couple of other Liverpool players from the time (I said it was a few years ago) and we're talking and he says he's met Connery before. 'Course you have, Razor – prove it, go over and talk to him then.' So Ruddock to his credit saunters over, giving it all the cock-of-the-walk swagger, he's got us in fits before he even gets there, and he actually starts talking to them.

For some reason, and we can hear all this, the first thing Razor's asked old 007 is 'who is the dirtiest bird you've ever had?' Razor's a big bloke, but he ain't a match for a grumpy old Scot with a licence to kill, and it looked like he'd proper offended Connery 'cos he folded up his copy of *The Times*, downed the rest of his gin and tonic in one mouthful and started to walk away. Then, without even looking at Razor, he's just mentioned the name of a 1960s pop diva. '1964. Up the arse.' And he's strolled out. I can never look at that lady in the same way any more.

But it's not been all laughs for Bren and, despite keeping his nose clean for so many years, it weren't long ago that he tasted a bit of Her Majesty's hospitality. And when I tell you about it, you'll know it's 'cos he's a mate of mine. But judge for yourself.

It's a sunny Friday afternoon in Charlton and Brendan's stopped off to drop his dry-cleaning into a shop. He's no Maurice Greene but it's taken him literally less than one minute to dump his load, as it were, and get back out to the motor. And there's a traffic warden halfway through writing a ticket. At first he thought she was congratulating him, 'cos she's written 'parking fine'. But he's soon twigged the truth and pointed out that there's bugger-all traffic, no one's being held up, he's only been forty seconds and all that and she's just gone, 'You've got a ticket to teach you not to disrespect my uniform.' Brendan's gone, 'Are you having a laugh?' and she's said, 'Don't get lairy with me, love. My husband's a police officer and he'll make your life very awkward.' It's midday, nearly the weekend and Brendan's about to explode, but he holds his breath and chokes up the largest stone of phlegm he can muster and lands it square in her face. Splat! And she's just gone mental, yelling, 'That's it! That's it! I'm telling my husband,' and so Brendan's just launched another one straight between the eyes. 'That one's for him.'

He's had his moment of satisfaction, 'cos this bird did look like she got off on the power of the uniform, but now Brendan's realised things could be as sticky for him as the gob hanging off her nose and he doesn't want to pay for her dry-cleaning and all. So he's said, 'Listen, I'm not getting dragged into an argument, I'm leaving.' And off he's trotted to the police station.

Even though he's been hanging around with me for ever, and he's seen the powers that be that run this country pull some seriously underhand strokes to get their way, Brendan was still unpleasantly surprised to see just how hard it is to make an official complaint against a serving traffic warden. Woolwich plod were no use. A fat bloke behind the desk said that he could say he was married to a belly dancer but that wouldn't necessarily make it true, so Brendan shouldn't have taken this warden at face value. To which Brendan, really getting into this diplomacy thing now, says, 'Judging by what you look like, pal, with the best will in the world the only way your missus is a dancer is if she's in the Roly Polys.' So obviously he's been told to fuck off from there, but he's written an official complaint about the service and we've had a laugh imagining the investigating officer phoning down and saying, 'Who's the fat bloke on reception he's talking about?' and the copper's gonna have to go, 'It's me. I'm the fat bastard.'

Eventually he finds some complaint forms at the parking office, but while all this is going on a couple of Old Bill have turned up at his house looking for him. His sick dad who's on medication for high blood pressure gets the shock of his life, and the way the coppers have had a look round means they were only interested in intimidation.

Three months and two more unanswered complaint letters later, he was invited to an interview at Plumstead nick. And they've given him a legal-aid brief to advise him through it. That's a bit weird, don't you think, considering he was the one complaining? But it gets worse, of course it does. Tell me you didn't think they'd just say sorry and let him go home. When his solicitor has come out, Brendan recognises him as Peter Crow, a geezer who served with Austin Warnes, who Brendan just happened to have given evidence against at the Old Bailey. What a coincidence. And get this – the police officer the traffic warden is married to is Warnes's old partner.

Without letting on he's clocked him, Brendan hears Crow's advice, which is basically to deny sending the letters. 'Just say it weren't you.' Do *shut up!* They've got Brendan's handwriting on, he's signed them and he's just about to repeat the complaints verbally. Was there any chance he was trying to be seduced into lying to the law? So now he's asked the solicitor about Warnes and the geezer's nearly choked on his mints. They were Polos, as it goes, the ones with the arseholes.

In the interview room Brendan pulled out his own

Dictaphone to tape the proceedings. 'What's that about?' says Sgt Fuller, who's leading the thing.

'Well, since you conveniently stitched my dad up a few years ago by editing his interview, I'm recording my own.'

'But we'll send you an official copy straight after.'

'So then I'll have a pair. Lucky me.'

Then it all kicks off and they're proper shouting at Brendan, accusing him of saying this and calling her that, all of which the warden had just made up. But the worst bit was when he hears she's described him as 'South London accent. Mid-thirties. Going bald on top.'

'Oi, excuse me,' he's gone. 'For the benefit of the tape, I'm not fucking bald. I've got a full head of hair. Sergeant Fuller is bald but I am not.'

Then he's taken a look at the other officer and said, 'And also for the benefit of the tape, I don't know whether Officer McKim has piles or is actually trying to intimidate me with that contorted face but I think he looks completely stupid whatever it is.'

Even though one of them's supposed to be on his side, it's obvious to Brendan that all three coppers in that room were probably Masons. 'Cos, as Lord Longford says, where Dave Courtney and his firm is concerned, the planning goes on right at the very top levels. And here's another little gem of proof for good measure. The motor Brendan got the ticket for in October, he'd sold by the end of the year. The new owner rang him in January to say this police Mercedes Sprinter van had pulled him over for no reason whatsoever and searched the vehicle top to bottom. Two non-uniform and four uniform just stood round the car like a Ferrari pit stop, basically intimidating the guy. Even before they pulled him over they knew it was registered to Brendan. And the fact the owner saw the coppers heading in the opposite direction earlier, which means they must have spotted him from the other side of the road and swung back, just gave him the creeps. 'Brendan, it's like they were actually looking for you, mate.' And that's fucking scary.

It's hurt me as much as him to see Brendan being carved up by the authorities like I have been for so long, so obviously I pulled out all the stops to provide a few distractions, Courtney style. The London Marathon passes near our manor in Woolwich so we went down there and stood near one of the drink stations. All these sweaty cunts are staggering round the course but there's a few tasty ones up the front. They're all holding their hands out like Oliver Twist for a drink as they go past, so I've held out these cups and watched the first poor bastard take one. Unfortunately for him, it's not water. The cup is completely filled with vodka, but the runner's just chucked it all down his throat then literally stopped dead in his tracks. 'Uggggggggggg!' I think is what he said, which was pretty ungrateful, I thought. That was proper Grey Goose, none of your shit.

Another time this big bodybuilder geezer came up to us in a club. He's obviously a bit in awe of the Dave Courtney image and he wants to ask my advice on his love life. Do me a favour. Do I look like Dear fucking Deidre? So he's gone, 'I'm really in love with my bird, I think she's the one for me and I just want to make sure it all works out.'

Brendan's waiting for whatever crap comes out of my mouth so I try not to disappoint. 'Look,' I say, 'the moment you have a row, you've got to kick the living daylights out of her. Got that? The first argument, just batter her.'

And steroid boy has looked at me and you can see him trying to process the information at the speed of steam, which is blinding fast for him. 'Why's that then, Dave?'

''Cos after that, if you have a row and you punch her in the mouth she'll think she's had a fucking result.'

We let the poor bastard ponder that one for a while before we told him it was a joke. But the worrying thing is I'm not sure he believed me. If you're reading this and you were his missus, I'm sorry, all right?

Almost a year after the original gobbing incident, Brendan was invited to take the stand at Greenwich Magistrates' Court. Right from the off, you knew the judge didn't take a shine to him. As soon as he found out Brendan had a Land Rover Discovery it was all, 'So you're obviously a wealthy young man, then,' and you could almost see an X going next to his name. Apparently Judge Cooper has a bit of a rep for treating the accused like shit. Rumour has it some villains he'd sent down once attacked his family.

There was all sorts of fucking with Brendan's mind before the thing got to trial, and for starters they didn't even tell him about the various hearings. Letters never arrived, his copy of the interview tape included (there's a coincidence), and all the police would say was, 'We sent them.' But that's an old trick, like the anonymous phone call, fucking with the mail and that. If there's an element of doubt, the police will always get the benefit. They play that a lot and they always get away with it, you know what I mean? They send you letters saying things like, 'We wrote to you saying you had 28 days to respond or we confiscate your licence and you ignored it' – how do you answer that? You know full well they never sent it. The other one is they don't send you your court date so you don't turn up, so then there's a warrant out for your arrest and you don't even know it. The bastards probably haven't even sent it and suddenly you're a marked man. They don't send it, wait till you've missed your date then have a word with their mate at another station and say, 'Keep an eye out for him, will you?' – how simple is that?

When it's kicked off, Brendan's not been allowed to call

any witnesses or nothing like that, and the traffic warden has not mentioned in any of her interviews that her old man is a copper. Considering this is the whole point of the threat she made against him, Brendan mentions this in court. And, of course, the judge calls him a liar and says he guessed she was married to a man of the law. So now he's Mystic Meg. 'I see pigs playing a large part in your life . . .'

The upshot was Brendan was sentenced to 42 days in Belmarsh for common assault. For spitting at an annoying little bully in a uniform. It was his first ever offence but he's Dave Courtney's number two. What does that tell you about the playing field we're on? Six weeks for a bit of mucus.

I've always tried to keep it light where my boys are concerned. I never want anyone to be scared on my behalf, so I'm all about morale-boosting. When they stuck me in Belmarsh, I've come out saying, 'That was great. Everyone should try it,' just so my lads aren't worried about me. And even though they've had a TV camera in my cell 24 hours a day, I never let that stop me wanking or taking a shit. I love an audience, so as soon as I saw it was there I was giving them a full-on show all the time. And you know the screws monitoring it are tearing their hair out going, 'For fuck's sake, Courtney, you're not meant to enjoy it!'

So I tried to prepare Brendan as best I could and to be fair he got through it great. For those of you who haven't had the pleasure, imagine Guantanamo Bay without the lovely orange jumpsuits. You get taken first to a holding cell, you're strip-searched completely naked and made to squat over this mirror. That's what I fucking call foreseeing your own end. Then they do a spot check for tattoos and that and throw your clothes back.

The first night he was told not to get too comfortable in his cell 'cos he'd be moving in the morning. So he's woke up and stripped his bed and got his kit ready to be transferred when a screw tells him there's been a change of plan and he's staying. So in between a couple of introductory wanks, he's made his bed up again and settled down for the next few weeks. Then, in true fucking piss-taking fashion, another screw turns up and says, 'Why haven't you got your gear packed? You're moving, you cunt.'

Apparently he met some good sorts in there, a geezer called Indian who'd cut the boys' hair, and Ritchie Childs, who he shared a cell with. I did my bit by giving out his prisoner number so he got loads of letters from all over the country. Our pal Mark Fish sent a four-foot magic ladder with instructions to stand it in a bowl of water and it would grow to the height of the wall. In a way, this has cocked things up for Brendan, 'cos he's come back to his cell and it's been given a proper going over. 'Ask your friend why,' a screw says. Anyway, when Fish writes later, 'Did you get the ladder?' it's all become clear. The pricks only believed it was real, didn't they? They're just pissed off it weren't magic beans for the beanstalk.

When it's come to the end of Brendan's stay, that's when we've really decided to have a bit of fun. We've got Charlie Breaker and Johnny Jacket in a limo, Outlaw Phil and some of his boys are giving us the outriders bit – and we're all dressed as coppers. Even yours truly, complete with a stupid bunch of keys on my belt and a bobby's tit hat on my head. (It's got this wicked sticker on it: Fuck the helmet law.) I looked a right cuntstable.

While the others go in the limo, I decided to add a bit of class to the proceedings and take the Harley out. Who am I kidding? If I'm making a prick of myself dressed as a boy in blue, I want as many people to see it as possible! And seeing as I was wearing all this clobber anyway,

I couldn't resist getting off the bike and doing a bit of arm-waving at a box junction. It was gridlock in about thirty seconds before anyone's realised I'm actually just doing some Bruce Lee moves. It's amazing how people respect a man in uniform.

The funniest part of it was, we drove past some real coppers who'd pulled over a Transit driver. Obviously I slowed right down and gave them the old salute. The look on their faces. You could see them wondering how they're driving a Ford Focus and there's some beat bobby on a fucking Harley smoking a stogy the size of a baby's arm! *Touch!*

So we all pitched up at Belmarsh dressed in police gear. I had my truncheon out, I was flashing all my medals and I promoted myself to a flat-cap inspector while Taz got her hands on my helmet. You can fill your own joke in there . . .

Johnny Jacket had this bugle and so we're blowing it outside the gate trying to get someone's attention. And it's worked. The last thing they wanted to see was us lot poking fun at them outside, so, faced with all these blokes, they sent a bird out to sort us out. She realised she couldn't do us for waiting for our mate, so she had a go at the documentary crew that was following us for having a camera. 'I'm gonna have to ask you to give me the film that's in there,' she says. Our cameraman's gone, 'We don't have any film in it,' which would make him a pretty shit cameraman if that was true. The funny thing is you can see all this argument on Dodgy Dave's DVD, so we put up a fair struggle.

Meanwhile, indoors, one of the screws has gone, 'Which one of you is Courtney's mate?' And Brendan's stepped forwards, this soppy Cheshire Cat grin on his face. 'Well, he's outside making a fucking exhibition of himself as usual.'

'I'd expect nothing else,' Brendan's gone. 'I'm just amazed he's on time.'

But for that bit of cheek they had to play more games, didn't they? Brendan was told it was his turn to go, he got right up to the gate and then he was called back 'cos there'd been a 'miscount'. Mis-cunt, more like. It was another half-hour before the pricks got their sums right, and Brendan's come out to see us lot and a few of the security types sniffing round the limo. The decanters on the back window ledge might have made them jealous, but there was nothing they could do about it, except circle the car about sixty times. When Brendan finally came out we stuck a jester's hat on him (for old times' sake) and poured him a glass of bubbly back in the limo. How the poor lad suffered. 'I've done a three stretch,' he said, all serious. 'Three weeks.' Then he's picked up Johnny Jacket's bugle and gone, 'I've really got the horn.' At least the experience hadn't knocked the stuffing out of him.

Once everyone was ready to go, I thought I'd push my luck and try to get the film back. It was annoying that they'd took it, but it's also a compliment really 'cos they've realised it's Dave Courtney. Them taking their time letting Brendan out just 'cos he's a friend of mine, that's another sign we're under their skin. 'Mr Courtney's mate? You can stay in another hour.' So I went over to the front desk.

'Can I help you, Mr Courtney?' one of them said.

'I'd like my film back, please,' I said, all airs and graces and pretty fucking pleases. And the copper goes away and only comes back with it. What a wanker. *Touch*.

From there it was all back to Charlie's pub, The Old Mill in Plumstead, for a bit of a celebration. And 'cos we're still dressed as the filth, you can imagine the looks when we've gone in. 'Right, this is a raid. You're all under arrest, you pricks. Now give us a fucking drink.'

To celebrate being a free man again, Brendan's left the pub and got himself a brass with the discharge money he'd got from the prison. He's a very shrewd and selective investor is Brendan. As he said, it was either that or I had to dress up. He says he didn't get it up the arse while he was in there, except from the screw who fingered him when he went in – and that bastard had a long fingernail. I just hope it's the one he stirs his coffee with.

Like me, Brendan came out of Belmarsh completely the same in spirit as he went in. In fact, we might both have been even more upbeat on the way out, which is the last thing the authorities want to do to you. That old saying, what don't kill you makes you stronger – it's proper true. And the thing is this: there's always different people to meet and stuff to learn inside. After three weeks, Brendan had progressed to three wanks a night and 28 games of computer Solitaire a day. Me, for my eight-month stretch on remand, I perfected the rare art of playing one-handed pool. I was the association orderly, and the place's leisure facilities left something to be desired, put it that way. With half of a pool table and half of the balls and half of a cue, I sat there for eight months eight hours a day just knocking them away with one hand. When I came home and played on a proper table, I've since won the All London One-Handed Pool championships two years running. So it actually paid dividends for me.

I never found out why it was in such a bad state, but it's not hard to work out. Pool tables are an argument-maker in prison, anything that gets a bit of competition going always has potential to start a fight, and when you're in prison you're not necessarily in the best mood to start with. But you could find a reason to argue about absolutely anything inside if you wanted to. Sure, pool tables are danger-ous. Course they are, but so is a toothbrush in the wrong hands. Especially if it's one of Esther Rantzen's.

16. MAD, SAD AND DANGEROUS TO KNOW

Ronnie, Reggie and Frightened Frankie Fraser

Here's one for you. Hitler turns up in Heaven. He goes up to the door and St Peter says, 'What are you doing here? Fuck off.' But Hitler goes, 'Just let me come in here for one day and have a look.' St Peter says, 'No mate, you killed six million Jews. Go away.' Then Hitler sees Jesus walking in the background and he calls him over. 'Let me in for a day, will you?' he says, but Jesus tells him to fuck off as well. So Hitler goes, 'Look, if you let me in for one day, I'll give you the top German medal, the Iron Cross.' Jesus takes a look at it and says, 'This is fucking proper, this is. Wait a minute – I'll go and ask the old man.' He goes inside and says, 'Dad – Hitler's outside.' His old man goes, 'Whoah – no way. Tell him to fuck off. He's bad news, just get rid of the cunt.' So Jesus goes, 'But, Dad, if I let him in for one day he's going to give me the Iron Cross.' God says, 'What good's that for you? You couldn't carry a wooden one.'

I like that one. What's it got to do with this chapter? Fuck all, unless you think it's a bit disrespectful to talk about Him like that, 'cos that's what missing in the modern gangster business: respect.

Young people today are inquisitive about the likes of Tony Lambrianou and Freddie Foreman because they're talking about a time they want to know about. The youngsters today look at Tony, Joe Pyle, Roy Shaw and the rest because it's history to them and there's a lot of respect for what they've done. But because these young-sters are actually living on the street they know that them sort of people can never evolve again because the world isn't like that any more.

Because the old-fashioned gangster and villain came from the war era, they were actually ex-soldiers. Roy Shaw, the Krays, the Richardsons and Freddie Foreman were all army boys so they still actually had an awful lot of respect and honour and comradeship around them and their men, 'cos those were the sort of qualities instilled in them. That was the way they'd been brought up, so it was natural that their business was run almost like the military. Today we're a bit unruly. We're multicultural, we have a very real drug culture as a nation, and respect does not come into modern criminals' vocabulary, which is a real shame.

Where the modern criminal fraternity is concerned, respect is a past-tense word. If you want, you can say, 'Well, everybody always thinks that the era they lived in was the best.' If you lived when Glenn Miller was alive you still say, 'Oh, music was better in the Glenn Miller era.' Or it was better when rock'n'roll was around or it was better when I was a kid. But this is true: crime was a much more respectable, honourable way of making a living than it is now. And the reason can be summed up in two words: drug money. Respect and honour among thieves goes out the window when greed enters the frame. And it does enter the frame where drugs is concerned because we're talking about millions and millions of pounds.

I like to think of myself as someone who sits right on the middle of the fence – and that's painful with the splinters and that. I'm in between the old-school gangsters and the new era, even though I'm not active no more. But the thing I miss most is the genuine comradeship, honour among thieves. You know, you don't grass anyone up, you stand with your friend and die rather than run away. It is sad to see it go.

And with it has gone the gangster. We no longer go, 'Draw!' we no longer go, 'Right, you cad' or 'Shiver me timbers' and we no longer have any respect for each other. I'm really sorry about this, but it's the truth. Lack of respect was the downfall of the British crime lord. That's what's made it all messy and unsightly.

But even with all the respect in the world, even in the good old bad old days, there's still got to be times when you have to respect yourself a little bit more than someone else. And that's where the balance has gone all wrong, 'cos you can respect someone but if he does something wrong, something that doesn't warrant your respect, you can shoot him. Respect that – *bang*. In all honesty, the fact that someone's got an awesome reputation and the people he hangs around with are murderers shouldn't give him the right to disrespect you. Because an awful lot of people who got shot make you think, Well, why did he do that? How could he dare say something to that bloke, Dave Courtney, or whoever? But if I was actually rude to you, you are entitled to argue back, of course you are. But a lot of people won't because they know I've got a lot of mates with me and they know I'm supposed to be a killer so you just sit there and take it and take it while I'm being a cocky bastard. It's not out of respect. Because not every criminal is into respect and hand on the heart swearing allegiance any more, that's not real life.

I would hate to think a bloke wouldn't stick up for himself because of all the people around me. If someone disrespected me or my missus, I wouldn't give a monkey's who he was, he could be King Kong, Ronnie or Reggie Kray, 'cos I would completely forget his reputation and not hesitate to put it right that minute. And that's actually what happens. If you hear a geezer actually go to your wife, 'Well, get rid of him, I want to sleep with you,' do you pretend it's never happened because he's got a reputation or do you go over and punch his teeth out? Me personally, I'd go and punch his teeth out. Bullies like that can only do it to so many people before one of them goes, Woah – me being one of them. I don't care what the papers say about you, you ain't talking about me like that. Take that, bang bang, if you're so tough.

Here's one of them sod's law moments, though. Being known as a really tough, good fighter is normally proper handy in those situations. But it actually has two effects. One is it makes 99 per cent of people go, 'Ooh, better not have a row with him, he's tasty.' But the other one per cent it makes think, You can't fight him, he's too good – better shoot the cunt. So the fact you're such a tasty bastard, there's no option but the bullet, and rightly so. It makes sense, don't it? I'm normally not a fan of the gun. I think you shouldn't have them hanging around you 'cos you can pick them up too easily. You have an argument with your missus over breakfast and there's a shooter on the table, you could actually kill her just for burning the toast, you know what I mean? But there are certain situations where people do deserve one in the nut. And I'd probably say, 'Get them.' And if you do have to go that far, we've now learned the trick of 'no body, no murderer'. Who needs bodies on the floor so people go round and investigate it, when you could just get it took away? Remember that Mr Wolf in *Pulp Fiction*? There are people who provide that service. Another one for the missing-persons list, thank you very much.

Just to prove I'm not some misty-eyed cunt who thinks black-and-white films and all that were the best 'cos that's just what I remember, how about this for a few home truths. Yes, the gangsters of the 50s and 60s had more honour and knew the meaning of respect, even if they couldn't spell it. But it weren't all sugar and spice. You've all heard the one about 'it was different then 'cos gangsters only hurt their own' – but the truth ain't quite so romantic, 'cos in reality it's more a case of 'gangsters only mingled with their own'. So if there was any trouble, the chances are it would be with someone you knew. It's obvious, innit? Because you daren't socialise too much with anyone else because you're doing something illegal, you end up just knocking about with other people in the same position. So, yes, naughty boys normally only hit other naughty boys, but that was a bit of coincidence, 'cos they didn't have the widest circle of friends.

I don't want to ruin anyone's wank material, but that's the truth of it. And here's another one that's a bit hard to say just 'cos of how many people don't want to hear it, but you know me, honest Dave. Among the general public, the Kray twins have still got this 'lovely fella' mythical reputation. And I say mythical because 99.9 per cent of the people who think that didn't know them or never met them or anyone who knew them. But anyone who did actually know them would disagree very much with what lovely fellas they were and how romantically nice they were. But that doesn't stop you admiring what they done or giving them respect for the way the authorities went after them.

But the thing is this, Ronnie and Reggie Kray ran their empire on fear. Once the actual fear has been taken away, and that happened when they were put in prison, then people would grass them up. They'd been too frightened before but now they're banged up already and it will keep them away for thirty years, it's a win–win for the grass. Once they went to prison, the threat of the Krays was no more, so everyone sort of turned coat and grassed them up. And that's where I personally think they got it all wrong, 'cos the more clever thing to do is run your empire on being nice. People do an awful lot more for you if they like you than they would if they were frightened of you.

So, knowing all that, my motto is 'it's nice to be important but it's important to be nice', but to be honest, to the modern criminal that's actually looked on as a weakness. It's like this other old saying we used to live by, of 'treat them how you'd like to be treated'. That's gone out the window too. The mix of different nationalities in England all chasing this drug money now means that's all lost, there's no unity and standards are different. These days, the colder you are and the quicker you would resort to violence is why they respect you, which ain't pleasant 'cos you never know where you are with people. You need rules to play any game, even this game, and that's what we haven't got any more. It's all gone arse about face.

Speaking of arses . . .

Just 'cos it's all bad now don't mean it was all good then, and there's at least one person from the old days who I wouldn't piss on if he was on fire. He's a nasty piece of work now and I imagine he was then, although 'cos of the era he's come from it took me a while to work that out. So don't accuse me of looking at the world through rose-tinted glasses. (Talking of glasses, I was in Specsavers the other day and guess who I bumped into? Every fucker there. *Shut up!*)

It can be a fucking burden having knowledge. But I know all about Frankie Fraser. I know what's in books, I know what the rest of the world thinks of him, I know what the majority of people believe he's done.

And I know the truth.

Believe me, there's no fucking comparison. I know the people, I've met the men, met the wives and been to the places, so I know what the rest of the world believes is a complete myth. When I realised this I was like, Wow. But if I actually came out and said, 'Nah, it's not like that,' I'd look disrespectful so I try to shut up. 'Cos at the end of the day, he's from that generation of gangsters that's hero-worshipped, and you don't want to fuck with people's dreams of history, the romance of it. But he's been a bit naughty where I'm concerned, so fair's fair. But I'll get to that in a minute.

Frank was known as 'The Dentist', right? 'Cos of his own brand of root canal surgery. Cheaper than the NHS, but then he never bothered with anaesthetic, did he? But interview or talk to him now and he will admit, 'Well, I never really pulled anyone's teeth out with pliers' – which is what his whole notoriety/fame thing was based on. Like all the other chaps, when I got to meet Frankie the first time, yes, I was excited to meet the person – you know, hat off to you and all that 'cos I'm only a whippersnapper – but then you get to know him a bit and it was like, you ain't actually *that*, are you? Lovely guy and everything, but not what it says in the books. (And it didn't take me much longer to work out he weren't even a lovely guy.)

Recently there's been a glut of books. Anyone who can even spell 'Kray' seems to have written their life story. But what some of these characters have done is realise how these books are written and that some of it doesn't have to be real; it's a façade. It's like we think we know what happened in the war. But you go talk to a soldier and they go, 'No, it weren't like that.' So these geezers work out what looks good, and then spend a couple of years planning it. So they're seen in the right places – here's me at Ronnie Kray's funeral, here's me at a load of boxing dos with Frankie Fraser, here's me with Roy Shaw and Joey Pyle – and then they go off and write the book. And who's gonna not believe they didn't do the things they claim, 'cos here's the pictures. You know, 'I was working with Lennie McLean, I did stuff with Tony Lambrianou' – and it's all made up.

The thing with Frank's book is that anyone who might know the truth is dead and the rest are too young to remember. He's such a fucking arsehole. I'd love the privilege of writing a book about things forty years ago that no one can remember. But now it's all coming out. The Richardsons even made a film called *Charlie* and in that they said, 'We didn't actually pull anyone's teeth out with pliers. It's not true, they were lies to put us away.' It was just the police adding bits to get them banged up. And now Frank's even made a video saying he's never done any dentistry in his life – but in the same breath he's said he's shot forty-odd people when he was a member of the French mafia. And he was a great mate of Reggie Kray.

So because he hasn't got any big hero stories to say, we've actually got to hero-worship him because he's done the forty-odd years. Fair play to him, anyone who has done 47 years in prison and is still coherent deserves a clap. But it's not the same as doing it in one go. There was a three, a nine, a life, a seven, an eight, and so on, which means he was banged up a load of separate times. And I can't find it in me to hero-worship a man who got caught at everything he ever fucking done.

But the next generation comes along and they don't actually know these fibs, and the one after that knows even less. And I was like, Wow. I never thought for one second I'd be on a par with all these so-called celebrity gangsters and what they're famous for. Like everyone else, I had built my opinions on what I thought these people were by what they said they were in their books. But of course, you don't necessarily know a geezer by what he says in his books, 'cos he wrote them himself. I didn't realise that till I wrote one! My books are proper straight up, you know that, 'cos I've got the stories and there's enough people around today to back them up. But I've read half a dozen books about the Krays so I think I know them, forgetting they wrote them themselves, you prick! I mean Ronnie's written five books about himself and in not one has he happened to mention he's a cocksucker!

The real story of Frankie Fraser is he hung around with a known gang and was happy or stupid enough to take the blame for things he hadn't done. He was living in a breaker's yard free – he wasn't given no wages – just so he could say he was with the firm. So once the gang gave this geezer a good fucking hiding with a sack over his head, no one wanted him to see who'd done it, so they got Frank to take the sack off. At the time you weren't taped during police interviews. It was just written down so you could easily be verballed up. So they'd jog witnesses' memories and write down things like, 'Yeah, he pulled my teeth out with pliers, he did this, he did that' just to help put the geezer away. Frank had never actually done it. But when he got nicked for it, he's only a little tiny midget, it suited everyone that that's what came out in the papers, all this stuff about how violent he is.

So he's in prison on his own and no one beat him up 'cos he had this reputation as a torturer. The gang didn't have to have him hanging around any more but it suited them to have the world think they had a torturer on the books. So he weren't going, 'No, I never' 'cos it was keeping him alive in there, and the gang kept quiet. But then, when the Krays were put inside, all of them together, the whole firm on one day, he suddenly went, 'I want to go into solitary confinement.' You've got to give him some credit for this. He didn't say, 'I'm the only one of the rival firm here and the whole Kray firm has just come into prison and I'm going to get about 25 bellybuttons in a minute, can I run off and hide?' Had I been him I would have done exactly the fucking same and locked myself up voluntarily in solitary confinement for three years. So the screws have said, 'What do you want to go in solitary confinement for, Frank?' He just said he wanted to, he fancied it. But 'cos it was just bread and water in there at the time, they said, 'You're fucking mad.' And Mad Frankie Fraser was born. Not Frightened Frankie Fraser. But, and this is quite cute as well, he's worked out how it might look with him hiding himself away, so as a publicity stunt he's smacked the governor of the prison in the mouth. He goes 'whack', the governor can't hit back so it's 'put him in the stock', it all gets out and now you have the legend of Mad Frankie Fraser.

I got to know Frankie – the real Frankie. I was actually the one who initiated the meeting in Maidstone of Reggie, Charlie Kray, Charlie Richardson and Frankie Fraser – and yours truly, of course. I set the meeting up, brought them all together and sat with them in there. No one had ever seen anything like that before. A high-powered gangster meeting taking place in the visiting room of a prison? Do me a favour. That had never been done before, and I pulled it off. 'Cos each prisoner, even if he didn't have a visitor coming that day, would say he had so he could be in the same room, they all came in themselves with minders. We all sat round this big table and there was the so-called hierarchy of British crime meeting for the first time in a British prison. Eventually a fucking screw runs over and says, 'What the fuck you doing?' It was mental, a real goose-pimple moment. Proper history in the making.

I drove Frankie there and back, in a gold-plated 5.8 XJS convertible in graphite black. Everything on it that was chrome had been gold-plated. The knobs on the radio, the pedals, handbrake, wing mirrors, bumpers. The jaguar on the front had two holes drilled in it and diamonds put in for eyes. It was out of this world, with a light-beige interior. It was the most beautiful car I've ever seen in my life and I actually owned it. This bloke who made it for me was called Les Moore. He used to have a shop called Just Jags in Rochester and it took him eight months. I ended up actually buying the golding machine off him 'cos he said, 'I'm never gold-plating another thing in my life. That has just fucked me off!'

So at the time I got to know Frankie Fraser very well, and his wife. Then his wife and my wife made a documentary called *Gangsters' Molls*, so we were quite close. But it was then I started seeing the disloyalty in him, the preying on the weak, all the stuff that wasn't true. But the worst thing of all was this: at the time I set up the prison meeting, he didn't know me from fucking Adam. I've just watched him in the prison room with tears in his eyes, holding Reg's hands saying, 'If only we'd known they were actually manipulating us to fight each other, the police saying things in the paper to make us have goes at each other. If we'd stuck together . . .' But as I was driving him away, he's going, 'Reggie Kray, fucking cunt, dirty little cocksucker' and all that. He just weren't real. I still took my hat off to him at the time, 'cos everyone else did. But it weren't fear no more. And it weren't respect.

Anyway, a few years ago there was this exhibition called 'From Cons to Icons' at the Tardis Gallery in Clerkenwell, where Nick Reynolds, Bruce Reynolds' son, made sculptures of all these gangsters' heads. There was me, Ronnie Biggs, Bruce Reynolds, Frankie Fraser, the usual suspects ('cos we normally were). And some bastard actually nicked the bust of me – and then had the cheek to return it, saying he was actually after Ronnie Biggs! I don't know what's worse? Being mistaken for a geezer who's twice my age and half my height or not being nickable in the first place.

We had a bit of a giggle at that, but the smiles proper vanished when Frank actually went, 'I'm not being in the same exhibition as Courtney.' Whoa, there, Frankie boy, are you having a laugh? But no, he wasn't. Then he rung the others individually and sealed his coffin down one nail at a time. I would never have had the confidence to go, 'It's him or me' because of his history, even though I knew how much of it was true. And apart from that, it's the same fucking gang. Even if we don't get on, we keep it in house. Don't split ranks and all that. But he actually rung up Freddie Foreman and the others and went, 'It's Dave or me,' and they've all gone: 'Dave.' One at a time he crucified himself and split him up from everyone else.

The reason he gave all the chaps for throwing his toys out of the pram was this: he said I was a grass. There was Austin Warnes saying he paid me for information, and there's me saying he was bent and on my books, and guess which one of us Frankie believes? In his wisdom, and having done 47 years in prison because of the police, he actually went, 'I believe the copper. Courtney's a grass.' And everyone went, 'Frankie, shut up.'

So all right, Frankie, who did I grass up? It's the same question I ask anyone who believes that shit. It's simple, if Dave's a grass, who did he grass up? And Frankie goes, 'I don't know, he just is.'

The funny thing was, when his little phone-around against me looked like it weren't working, he started saying Freddie Foreman's a grass as well! Then Fred sees him out one day and beat him up – that got in all the papers. It happened while I was in hospital. A member of Freddie's family rung me up and said, 'You'll be pleased to know . . .' And that cheered me up no end.

Like I said, that's the reason he gave the chaps but he'd had a downer on me for a little while and I suppose the fact that his missus got a bit too friendly with someone I knew didn't exactly win me brownie points with him. But Frank's not gonna take on Dave Courtney on his own, he's gonna need a little bit of help. And unlucky for me, he had it with knobs on.

For the eight months that Austin Warnes was pleading Not Guilty, the papers were going 'grass, grass, grass' anyway and soppy Frankie Fraser fell for it. He was always gonna be an easy touch, but stone me! Out of 100,000 sperm can you believe he was ever the fastest? Put it this way, if you lent Frank twenty quid and you never saw him again, it would be money well spent. (Here's a tip: only borrow money from depressed people – they don't expect to get it back.)

With Frank, it all boiled down to him thinking I knew his wife was sneaking down the club to see someone. He's also been pissed off at me since we done that record 'Product of the Environment' and I got the front-page photo. It was a story about all of us but they used my picture and he just freaked out one day down the phone. So I wouldn't be his phone-a-friend on *Who Wants to be a Millionaire*, but to actually go around and repeat the words the police have given you, do me a favour.

In his defence, the police used Frank like they used Jenny. I never saw coming what she did neither. He was actually being turned by the authorities. The people advising him were advised by the police. They'd go, 'Say this 'cos Courtney's gonna get put away, you'll be proved right.' And he did. They actually had Frankie saying, 'I think Courtney's a grass.' So that's your weak link and your divide and conquer in one go. All in one soppy bastard.

When all this was coming out, what the police didn't realise was how many of the main players I'd actually helped out with these bent coppers. Roy Shaw is still wearing one of Austin Warnes' bulletproof jackets, do you know what I mean? Everyone in the business knows what went on, they knew what I was up to running these coppers. Everyone was benefiting from it, it weren't just me.

Because he's listened to by an awful lot of people who are not in the know, and because he's been ostracised by the big boys, Frankie don't get invited anywhere or nothing like that. He's skint, he lives on the fifth floor in a bedsit with a Casio watch and holes in his shoes. 'Cos even though he ain't in prison no more, he's never been able to make any money. He'd just do the old prison trick of asking favours based on who he was. And now he's been doing these open-top bus tours to try and live off the reputation a bit more. That's when you know he's Old Bill friendly, 'cos the media coverage for that little stunt was fucking huge. Like he'd won the fucking FA Cup. When have you heard of any other gangster being allowed to get publicity for what they're doing, ever?

Anyway, it works and the first few weeks the bus is packed with silly Northerners come down to Bethnal Green to see where all these historical gangland murders and that took place. But because he's getting old he forgets things and he's actually going, 'That's where I killed so-and-so' – and the place has only been built a year. So the bus went down to a Transit. And now he does it in his mate's Jag, just one at a time. A one-on-one guided tour with the Dentist. He should call himself Sad Frankie Fraser while he's at it.

You can't help feeling a bit sorry for him, though, 'cos he was once one of them to me and I would never be disrespectful enough to think I would win a popularity contest against him. (Yeah, all right, I know I already did. *Shut up!*) But what people don't seem to realise is that the celebrity gangsters we're hero-worshipping now aren't actually gangsters any more. What we're actually worshipping is retired gangsters. They're all wandering round writing books, but you couldn't actually do that when you was at it. When you're actually at it you can't have a flashy car, better get a Mondeo. You can't wear a Rolex, might stick out. It's only when you've retired you get a bit flashier and people start being interested in you. So I've now realised that what I actually wanted to be all along was a retired gangster before I was a gangster. It was them I was looking at. And I hear the pension plan's quite good. People are going into the boxing dos, birds and tomfoolery hanging off their arms, and that's what gave me a hard-on as a kid, 'cos I never saw the real villains in action. I was really impressed by them, but I was too young to realise they'd retired.

Even when you're retired, the rules among the criminal fraternity are pretty simple and the first one is 'keep your problems in house'. You know, we might not get on with each other, but against the police we are one, Three Musketeers and all that. Like with a wife, we don't have a go at each other in public, we wait till we get home and give each other hell. So Frankie, the silly sod, actually broke the fucking rules when he had a pop at me. He could have got me killed, he's lost all his mates and he's a joke as far as the industry is concerned. And where's it got him? It's like the inflatable kid who trips up taking a needle into his inflatable school to show his inflatable classmates. The inflatable teacher smacks his inflatable arse and goes, 'You've let the school down, you've let me down, you've let your friends down, but most of all you've let yourself down.'

So it's fair to say me and Frankie don't see eye to eye – but that's 'cos it hurts my back to bend down to his height.

I can't let the subject of letdowns go without mentioning a geezer called Bernard O'Mahoney. I'd love to keep him anonymous like Gaffer, but as he's spent so many pages of his books volleying me off, it only seems fair to share his name with you. He's more famously known as the grass from the Leah Betts ecstasy case. Even though he had nothing to do with it, he was also the one who disappeared sharpish when his bosses at Raquel's in Basildon – three tasty bastards called Tucker, Tate and Rolfe – ended up splattered inside a Range Rover in the Rettendon murders. He got smacked in the mouth at the premiere of his own film and Tony Lambrianou once threatened to kill him with a hammer – and I know Tony was a good judge of character. Are you getting a picture?

Bernie's one of these people what's made a career out of telling stories about how he was best mates with all these chaps who are conveniently too dead to deny it. Ronnie and Reggie Kray were his closest chums, apparently, and Tucker, Tate and Rolfe looked at him as an equal even though he was just their doorman-cum-human shield. I first noticed his sort when Lennie McLean died and all these people claimed they was tight with him. But now I've written a few books I know how easy it is to say, 'I was bitching to John Lennon one day about

Freddie Mercury, then Elvis Presley fucked off, I beat up Lennie McLean and then Buddy Holly and me gave a spit-roast to Jill Dando.' And that can be printed and no one can contest it 'cos they're all dead. So that's his career for you. For the record, the people I write about are still alive.

17. A BENT OLD AUSTIN

Micky, Marbella and Jodie Marsh

I've been stitched up big time by the papers over the years, but it's never the journalists who are the problem, 'cos they're all mates of mine. It's the suits upstairs. They're the ones who get the instructions from the authorities and send the message down the food chain: 'If you can't say anything nasty about the cunt, say nothing.' One of them could show some fucking spine once in a while and actually say to the police, 'I'm printing a nice story about Courtney, now stick your Masonic trowel up your arse and have a nice day.' That wank from the Pope's looking more likely by the minute compared to this.

So I had a little smile on my face the day Robert Maxwell decided to do a Natalie Wood and do a bit of late-night swimming. But the funniest thing of all was something that never got written. One of my mates on the *Daily Mirror* said they wanted to run this front-page headline: MAXWELL LOST AT SEA: FEARED ALIVE. That's how popular he was, even before they knew he'd nicked their pensions.

But there's one media mogul I've got a bit of time for and that's old cork hat, 'cos without the Murdoch empire this country wouldn't have satellite television, and without that my right arm would have fuck all to do on a Saturday night, you understand what I mean? But apart from all them great porn channels, the other reason Sky's just dreamy for me is 'cos it's the one place the authorities haven't really been able to stop me appearing. 'Courtney on national TV? *Stop it!*' The worrying thing is it's not just the fucking BBC who I think the police have got in their pocket (just next to the coke they're gonna plant in some poor sod's flat). Channel 4 went all wobbly all of a sudden recently when someone in charge realised that their booking people had invited me to appear in the audience for *Big Brother*. I've still got the tickets. *Unused.* Some poor bird's had to phone up and say there's been a change of format for that evening so they're doing without the live audience thing. Who are they kidding? For one of their eviction nights, I don't think so. I watched the programme on telly and it was packed as usual. Well, apart from four empty seats at the front. Someone didn't want me there, did they, that much would be obvious to anyone. Someone didn't want me anywhere near a live TV broadcast, being interviewed by Davina McCall. But there's a million different satellite channels and, for every one they manage to stop me going on with all their intimidation tactics, there's loads more waiting for a bit of Dave Courtney.

One of the best ones for me is the Jodie Marsh show, which I've been doing a lot of recently. They had me on there the other week as the guest she has a chat with on the bed. Fuck me, that brought back a few memories. The bed bit, that is. Oh, yeah, and the 'fuck me' bit an' all. Television X? It could have been XXX, 'cos Jodie and I have had our moments over the years. We've known each other for a very long time and she's someone I'd describe as a very, very good friend of mine, we're extremely close. And whenever we can help each other out, we do. She's always up for coming round my house to pose naked on the Harley with me for some magazine shots, and all that. You can hear the neighbours' curtains twitching from Romford on them days, and it's not just the Old Bill showing interest now. You'd have to have a look, wouldn't you, if Jodie fucking Marsh was naked in the garden opposite. *Shut up!*

We have the odd bonk now and then. As nice as it is to be able to say we've been intimate, it's because we've been close on and off all our lives. I knew her when she was just a club girl, a raver, when she was partying out of her head. I knew her before she was 'Jodie Marsh'. It's been amazing what's happened to her. She became famous overnight on that *Essex Girls* programme, where she kept getting her tits out, and everyone went, of course, 'Ain't she lovely?' Two minutes later, her very next job was lifting her top up on the front page of the *Sunday Sport* and her next job was Page 3 of the *Sun*. That's the way to start your modelling career, ain't it?

And she's a natural on this TV show when she's allowed to be herself but, believe me, she's even better in real life. Giving her all that scripted stuff ain't really her, 'cos the real Jodie Marsh is really funny, really relaxed. For this show, I think she just gets a collection of her naughty friends along for a laugh. Trust me, she's been given a million fucking geezers' numbers to choose from since she was propelled into stardom. The last time, I was on there with Ben Dover, the porn star bloke, and Linsey Dawn McKenzie who, I don't mind telling you, is another close friend of mine. And there was 'Royal love rat' James Hewitt as well, who actually went out with Jodie for a bit. And I bet he got a bit, an' all. It was in the papers 'cos she was following in Diana's fanny-steps. I asked her if she'd learned anything about the Princess. 'Apart from that she took it up the royal arse, no.' *Shut up!*

She's a good girl, Jodie, quite a down-to-earth sort of bird, and she knows what she is and what she ain't. She doesn't actually believe she's the prettiest girl in the world. She's a little better than average in her mind. But she's a proper horny little girl, her body's fucking near-on perfect, and she don't mind going, 'Here, have you seen the pictures on my phone? Here's one of me with spunk on my forehead. Guess what pop star!' So she's a funny cunt, too. Jordan's now trying to do the whiter-than-white, 'I like pink and I never took drugs in my life', and all that shit, but that's a hard one to keep up, isn't it? Even if you're Mother Teresa. Which she ain't. Whereas if you say, 'I like cock, I like going out eight nights a week and I'll take anything I can to keep me up *nine* nights a week,' that's fucking easier to live up to, isn't it?

But Jodie's a very clever girl. Personally I think the thing between her and Jordan is a little bit of fun. But she's said in a couple of her interviews that it would take at least a million quid to get a photograph of her lying naked on top of Jordan. She's actually planted the seed and, eventually, someone somewhere will go, 'That will be a blinding picture. Here's a million quid.' And she's already put the price out there; for one click, a million quid. *Bosh*. So she keeps the row going. It's all hype, isn't it? And it keeps them both in the headlines, which means papers keep printing wank material of them, so we're all happy, ain't we?

I've spent some lovely times with Jodie's family as well. We had a wicked fireworks party round at hers, 'cos I'm a good friend of her mum, her dad and her brother Jordan and they've all had the pleasure of hearing me sing 'Blueberry Hill' once the rockets had all gone up.

Jodie's definitely got her head screwed on right, and she's making hay while the sun shines out of her arse. She was on that celebrity sports programme, and she's quickly wrote her autobiography before her popularity runs out, she's got her own show and she's got all these phone numbers of friends she can invite on. And now she's announced she's becoming a proper novelist. Forget Jackie Collins, this is Mills & Boobs. I'm getting a hard-back just thinking about it . . .

Bravo's a good channel too, and the boys down there have been good to me as well, so I was happy to return the favour a little while ago. What happened was some TV work-experience kid thought it would be a hoot to make a programme called *Costa Del Dosh*, about all the naughty boys hiding over on the Spanish Riviera. So they schlep over there with their cameras and that and discover that no bastard will talk to them, and the rest are either nicked or on holiday. And so I get the call: 'Dave, bring a couple of mates over, will you? We'll stick you in a top hotel for a fortnight in exchange for you lot acting the cunt for the camera.' Hmm, let me think about that one for a second.

So obviously Brendan's gotta come with me, and we've also asked this geezer Michael Taylor as well. Now, Michael is a house-trained Neanderthal. He's a top bloke, very funny, very strong and very humble. He's a star. But the animal in Michael is nearer the surface than in most people and it definitely is in his sex drive and the size of his cock. Cock? It's a fucking rooster. He's a bit of a Jekyll-and-Hyde where narcotics or alcohol are concerned, though, and you could get a wrong reading off

Michael if you met him under the influence of one of those things. And here's a few stories to prove it.

A few years ago I was entertaining Chris Penn, giving him the guided tour to Dave's London. Chris is the brother of Sean Penn and he was in *Reservoir Dogs*. I forget which colour he was, Mr Dulux Apple White, or something. But he was over to talk about possible film work together 'cos he's really into the Dave Courtney thing and so I'm rolling out the red carpet a little bit as far as showing him a good time's concerned. Well, that ever so slightly backfired when I invited Brendan to meet us down at Pop nightclub, 'cos he brought along Micky Taylor and they'd both been out for two days solid already.

Chris had pulled this bird earlier in the night but, while I'm sitting there with him, she's gone off with Brendan. Now there are two certainties in this life. One is you'll die (although I'm working on that one). The other is Brendan will get a shag. I just didn't expect it to be with my fucking guest's bird. Luckily Chris was all right with that, by which I mean he never noticed, and so we've all piled off to this garage club for a bit of serious music. Outside there's some geezer getting hit, and he falls on the floor and accidentally lands on a bit of broken glass, so now he's screaming, 'I've been stabbed! I've been stabbed!' which of course he ain't. Micky Taylor's got this glint in his eye, he's finding it hysterical, yelling, 'I used to carry a knife and now I carry a mouth organ' – don't ask – and this mad bird starts screaming, 'I want to make a snuff movie out of my mum!' Now that's proper real, that is, but Chris Penn is all, 'You know what, guys, let's jump in the car and go some fucking place else.' Funnily enough, I never heard from him again.

But that weren't the end of the evening, 'cos now Michael's got the smell of pussy and, let's be honest, this bird seems a bit of a kindred spirit really, so he's taken her home. But he's got no money so he hails this night bus and has a word with the driver. I don't think scared would be the right word. Fucking scared might be closer, 'cos this driver has actually spun his double-decker round and flat-pedalled it to Sidcup from the West End, stopping for no fucker on the way. A bit of an eye-opener for all them goths on the top deck ringing the bell for Camden.

Two days later, Brendan gets a call from this bird. 'Will you come and get me?' He speaks to Michael: 'I'm not really doing anything wrong, it's just like having a pet. I keep stroking her.' Er, yeah, Michael. So Brendan's gone round and released her back into the wild (and Sidcup's pretty fucking wild) and she's another one, funnily enough, who never rung back. Some people are so picky.

Another time Brendan's been Brendan and he's driving to Ministry with this bird he's just pulled at the Aquarium, and Michael's in the back. Brendan's giving it all the blarney to his lady, but when he does his mirror, signal, manoeuvre bit all he can see is Michael's ugly mug behind him mouthing, 'Threesome?' Next time he looks, Michael's actually got his cock out and, trust me, he could strangle her with that thing. But the bird don't notice and Brendan thinks he's got away with it, till they get out the car and Michael says, 'So have you asked her about the two's up yet?'

'Not really, Michael,' Brendan says. 'I thought I'd try to get her name first.'

I think you're getting a picture of the man, ain't you? The thing is, all this is when Michael's sober. Give him a drink and then he's really nutty. We got him a job on the door in Tenerife once and told the guv'nor, 'Whatever you do, do not let Michael drink. Do not let him drink.' Did they listen? The next thing I know we get a call saying, 'What the fuck have you sent us?' Turns out Michael had

had a few drinks after work, got right off his nut, and gone back to the place about ten the next morning for a few more jars. Trouble is, it's one of them clubs that only does food during the day, breakfasts and that, so when he's asked for a drink the geezer behind the bar says, 'We're not serving till tonight.' The next thing this geezer knows is he's being planted, head first, in a flowerbed outside and Michael, still in all his bouncer's clobber, is helping himself behind the bar.

So we've told the guv'nor it's just teething troubles, it could happen to anyone, and generally to calm down. Then Michael himself has called. 'I've just beaten up two Libyans as part of the timeshare war,' he says. Timeshare war – he's lucky he didn't start the next Gulf War. So we've gone, 'OK, Michael, time to come home.'

'Nah, fuck 'em.'

Two days later we receive the *I'm a Celebrity, Get Me Out of Here* call: 'I'm on the next plane home – there's fifty Arabs outside my room and they're not looking for oil!'

So anyway, you can see why we thought Michael might be the man to 'act the cunt' on this *Costa Del Dosh* thing. Of course, some of the funniest things never made it to the screen. On our first night the camera crew went out and bought us loads of food, so we're sitting there getting stoned when it becomes apparent that Michael has managed to have a drink without anyone noticing. From out of nowhere he's standing on the table going, 'I'll fight anyone for three quid – two for a fiver!'

We tried to calm him down with a bit of whizz and sent him off to his room, and the crew have started filming a 'Dave's first night' type thing. But out of sight, Michael has necked a couple of Viagra that we'd told him to save for when he got a brass. The next thing we know, he's walked into where we're filming, stark bollock naked apart from a pair of Hush Puppy boots, with an erection that looks like Tower Bridge being raised, and he's gone, 'Do these boots make my bum look big?' You could see the cameramen thinking, What the fuck have we let ourselves into here?

I don't mind a bit of fresh air where my Jacobs are concerned either – I'm like, it's nice out tonight – I think I'll leave it out. You with me? So when they've asked me to dress up in the gangster suit and all that for an interview, I've strolled out of my bedroom naked from the waist down. Course, they think they're clever just filming me above the belt, so to make it interesting I started moving about just to see the cameraman squirm, 'cos if my cock gets in the shot he has to start again.

As for the programme itself, I liked the idea of showing how British villains have been going over there for years to 'stash their cash and blow their dough', as they put it. It's a bit of history in its own way. And the way they did it was like one of those Hollywood tours that bus you round all the stars' houses. Except instead of showing you where Nicole Kidman, Russell Crowe and Tom Cruise all live, it's a guided tour of naughty haunts like Wyn's Bar. All the chaps used to go there and play backgammon for £500 a shot, and have a drink and all that – before the extradition laws started fucking it up for everyone. And they showed all the homes up in the mountains of geezers like Ronnie Knight. Ronnie only lasted ten years, spunked it all, then went back and done his bit of bird. His ex-missus, Barbara Windsor, is a mate of mine as well, and she's got a few stories. It was Ronnie and a few friends who were behind Britain's biggest cash robbery (before the Irish mob did over the Northern Bank in 2004). Six million quid they got, which in 1983 was proper money, but it weren't pretty. They poured a gallon of four-star over the security guard's bollocks, rattled a box of Swan Vestas in his ear and said,

'Open the door.' There's no choice, is there? – not unless he wants to make his own version of 'Great Balls of Fire'.

Then they showed where this villain called Stuart Hutchinson lived. He's the bloke who chopped up his wife into 35 pieces and dumped the bits in bins up and down the coast. One of the maids recognised the smell of burned flesh and that's how he got twenty-our years, although he only did six. But it's all those tramps I feel sorry for, fishing out bits of barbecued bird when they're rooting for something to eat. You want fries with that, mate?

And of course they had to show where the Undertaker himself, Freddie Foreman, hid out. He was deported in 1987 for just being nasty, which is a bit of a joke. He hadn't done anything wrong specifically, but having Jack 'The Hat' McVitie's body on your CV was good enough for El Filth.

But like I said, the best ones don't live there no more and the ones what do don't want to be announcing their whereabouts to a TV camera, do they? Which is where Dave and his couple of performing cunts come in (and that's a show I'd pay to see).

We were a wet dream for the film crew right from the time we arrived at Malaga airport. This gives you some idea how the Spanish think (and I'm not one to let a dago by), 'cos they managed to lose Brendan's case – but let through the one carrying all the guns and shit we'd brought over for the filming. You've heard of 'Que Sera Sera' – this was case tara tara. Ah well, with guns you can always get more clothes.

So at least some of my more interesting props got through customs. They were filming the other lads in our room at one point, and I've come out wearing this pig facemask that's got an Old Bill tit hat built into it. If you see the programme, the camera starts shaking at this point 'cos the camera guy is crying with laughter, especially when I've gone, 'One of us is undercover Old Bill – and I intend to find out who!'

For the purposes of the programme the other two introduce themselves at this point, and that's pretty funny in itself 'cos how Michael and Brendan met is fucking hysterical. Looking right into the camera, straight face and everything, Michael just said, 'He owed some money and I had to go and get it. I thought I'd have to kill him.' Just like that, and it's all true. About ten years back, Micky turned up looking to do a bit of damage to Brendan. This drug deal had gone tits up and for some reason Brendan was getting the blame. There was a twenty-grand hit out on him, or else. Michael, being a local Woolwich boy, nipped round to Bren's and offered not to give him a slap in exchange for handing over the money, although he weren't that fussed. Somehow Brendan talked his way out of it and they've been sharing birds ever since.

That's not to say they won't stab each other in the back if they can get away with it. Their motto is if one falls down, the other one carries on. I'll give you an example. When Michael was staying at Brendan's once, he could hear all this row coming from Brendan's room, and he thought he was having it away with a bird. In actual fact, he was being screwed but not like that, 'cos he was being attacked with a Phillips by this bloke in a Father Christmas hat. Eventually Michael's turned up to see if he can join in, naked already of course, seen the screwdriver sticking out of Brendan's foot, snarled a bit and Santa's legged it back up the chimney. So they go to the hospital but then it all gets a bit tricky, especially as Brendan's got ten grand on him. 'So, Mr McGirr,' one of the nurses says, 'you come in here saying allegedly you've cut your foot on glass, but we can't find any glass in the wound, it looks like a stab injury and you happen to have £10,000 on you.' Blimey, Doc, say what you see.

So that's when they turn up at my house. I've got a lot of gear in my place but anaesthetic and a wound-stitching kit ain't two of them. But 'cos I'm Mr fucking Do It Yourself, ain't I, I've got superglue. If it can stick a bloke to an aeroplane over the Thames, I'm thinking, it should be able to knit two bloody bits of flesh back together. It's obvious.

Mate, you've never seen a raspberry move so quick. I'm squirting from this tube and Brendan's doing his one-legged Tarzan bit hopping over to the front door. 'Cheers, Dave, I think I'll give the hospital one more try.' So he goes back down there, they decide to keep him in all night – and Michael fucks off in his motor for the Christmas holidays. 'You won't be needing this for a few days then, Bren!' *Touch!*

For our first night out on *Costa Del Dosh*, obviously the producers want to see some real gangster chic, so I've got out the flash suit, the cigars and all that. Brendan's got some shitty T-shirt on and we're just grateful Michael's dressed at all. He's already streaked through the hotel restaurant going 'wooooo', so you're never sure. (One old girl pointed him out to the waitress and said, 'I thought you weren't serving sausage?' Dirty old cunt.) But he's made an effort, and checked he's got everything: 'Hash, cash, coke, keys.' And then we've hit the bars. Brendan's like a ferret up a drainpipe, of course, and manages to get these two birds back with him. Jesus, there's a sight when I wake him up the next morning. Talk about looking for love, he's looking for new diseases. Next to him were two of the most hideous creatures you ever saw. Spielberg would be proud of him: Jurassic Minge. It was like he was trying for some kind of prize: 'But I did it, though, didn't I? I did it.' I said he always got laid. I didn't say he always got quality.

Yours truly, of course, only talks to the finest-looking

tarts and I was proper cracking on to this right tasty bit of skirt – and then she gave me a price. Fuck me, I didn't see that coming. You get a better type of brass in Marbella. She had a whole menu worked out. Starters, main course, dessert. Kids' portions an' all. I said, 'Do I look like the kind of geezer what has to pay for it? I'm proper offended by that.' That fucking put her in her place ... Still, best thirty quid I spent all holiday.

Somehow Michael manages to go the whole trip without a shag. But one morning when we wake up, the cameramen show us this film they'd took at four in the morning of Michael, naked of course, standing at the fridge stuffing his face with ham. And he's a vegetarian. So that's a turn-up for the books, 'cos I bet he didn't expect to have more meat down him than up anyone else.

One of the little 'events' the film guys wanted to see us do is firing a few shooters, so we've all piled down to the Marbella Gun & Country Club, all tooled up, ready for action. Just like any Saturday night in Peckham. This geezer Andy who runs the club tells us that they get loads of English characters up there, people like Mike Reid and some of the more colourful ex-pats who are maybe keeping their hand in. Andy's all right, but he does win Dave's 'Stupidest Cunting Question of the Holiday' award 'cos he took one look at us and said, 'Have you all done this before?' *Prick*.

But he's got a point 'cos we're not allowed to play with guns much at home, not in daylight, and not without a balaclava and a load of shouting. When we got there I hadn't held a gun for – let me see – about three or four days. For me, the only thing that compares to holding a nice gun is lying in bed holding your cock. It's exactly the same. And they can both be a bit messy and get you in trouble. So this was dreamy for me, and I've definitely never shot anywhere as picturesque as that. Peckham it ain't.

Also there that day were some nice people from Essex called Steve and Dawn and their little boy. A right milky bar kid he was. Every clay that went up, he brought down. I don't think I've ever seen prouder parents. It brought a tear to the eye. Steve and Dawn have a funny relationship and at one point she pretends to shoot him with a handgun, which he finds quite funny. And then she decides she'll have a go at the shooting. 'It's the only bang I'm gonna get on this holiday so I might as well do it myself.'

Talk about tasty. She made the rest of us look right wankers. But obviously I couldn't let a woman win our little competition. For some reason the camera didn't pick this up, but on the deciding clay I got the fucker. Honest. If I'd lost I wouldn't be telling you lot now, would I?

Another thing they wanted to film us doing was see this fortune-teller to find out if we'd always been naughty in our past lives. I've played it straight and said to the geezer that I was interested in learning about my history, so he went all Mystic Meg and said I'd been a freedom-fighter in the Middle Ages, a Roman centurion and a nurse with Florence Nightingale. A real fucking player, in other words. *Touch*. Michael's been told he was a black sex-slave girl in Egyptian times, a lion-tamer and a witch-burner, which to be honest got him a little bit excited. But Brendan weren't having any of it, even for the cameras, and when the geezer's asked him why he's there he's gone, ''Cos I've got to live with the other two and I'm stuck in the car with them.' That wasn't the smartest thing he's ever said, 'cos the clairvoyant's took one look at him and said he was a prostitute in Jack the Ripper's time and a poetry-writing poof from Edwardian days. We only reminded him of that every other minute for the rest of the day.

There are loads of other funny little moments on the finished programme and here's a couple. One of them is when they film the others coming out a supermarket looking like shit with a trolley full of booze and grub. Brendan looks at the camera and says, 'Michael here is the new *Supermarket Sweep* champion, and it is now the evening's job to find some tart to cook this lot.' I think we ate out that night.

Then there's them two staggering back in the early hours and they're asked if they've been naughty. 'No, we're showing zero tolerance for drug abuse,' Bren says. When what he means is no fucking money to buy any. And it's been a slow night on the pulling front, an' all. 'Yeah,' Brendan says, 'we're just looking forward to a bowl of cornflakes and a glimpse of snatch.'

But for me the funniest thing was this hard man geezer Michael, who's shown himself to be a bit of a nutter so far, lighting up a Marlboro and shitting himself when he notices the camera there. 'Oi, I don't want me mum to see me smoking on telly,' he says. 'She'll fucking kill me.' Classic.

Another programme we did for Bravo was called *Car Sharks*. This was dreamy for us 'cos we got the chance to stitch up the Old Bill on telly and there was fuck all they could do about it. Except try not to laugh.

The idea of the show was cops versus robbers, so at least that bit was realistic. There were two teams, us and them, and we had to take a battered old Sierra each, do it up for as little money as possible, then see which is worth more when they're auctioned. How could we not be any good at that?

There's no doubt the police are doing everything in

their power not to be made to look like mugs on this one, so day one and the four officers from Swanley nick turn up in full fucking SWAT gear to meet us at nine. Except we're not there because the night before Michael has had a drink and is nowhere to be found. By the time he arrives at midday, he's absolutely rotten, still reeking of booze and off his face, but a spoonful of whizz later and he's as fresh as a daisy. A daisy from the Addams' Family courtyard.

We've done all the introductions and then the cameras start rolling so it's time to play up a bit. While the fuzz are opening the bonnet on their motor, we've popped up the boot in ours and taken a look in there. 'Jump in, Michael, let's see what it's like for kidnapping.' I think that's when they realised they was in for some fun for the next few days.

We had five hundred quid to do our Laurence Llewelyn Bowen bit on the car, and Brendan gave Michael three hundred of it to get some parts. This was not a good idea. Unfortunately the only parts he got was about sixty empties, 'cos we never saw him for two days and by then he'd spunked the lot. So with only two hundred left, we took the Sierra to Bedford to one of my mates, Ricky, who works on a car magazine. I'll tell you what, two hundred quid goes a lot further in Bedford than in London. Ricky and his boys stuck £1,700-worth of new wheels on the motor, had it lowered, blacked out the windows and had a wicked sound system put in for good measure. Then we went to Twickenham where another mate called Stuart built a Rolls-Royce grille to go on the front, and then took it down to see Les from Just Jags in Rochester. He put two sign-writers on the job and we spent fourteen hours hand-painting the car.

By the time all that had been done it looked proper tasty, especially the front grille, so we christened it the

'Northerner's Roller'. Half Sierra, half Rolls-Royce! It looked like a Volvo Bentley and anyone who saw it would have thought it was going through a serious identity crisis. Smart car? This one was fucking mental.

But then we heard from the camera crew that was nipping backwards and forwards between the Cops and the Robbers that the other team was getting their car signed by loads of celebrities to push up the value at the auction, and that's given me a brainwave. You know how I do like a picture of myself? Well, we stuck a giant poster of yours truly and friends on the roof, and just to make a point, it was the picture of me in the court jester's outfit on the day I took Austin Warnes to the cleaners. We painted a giant gold knuckleduster on the boot, and next to that put slogans like 'who polices the police who police the police', 'Dave Courtney – 1, CIB – 0', 'there is such a thing as good baddies and bad goodies' and 'what happens when the law-makers are the law-breakers'. But my little moment of genius was this one: 'this car is a dead straight Ford, not a bent old Austin'. Who's ever heard of a car telling a story? That should get the point across to the Cops.

The rest of the car we covered in signatures of the chaps and loads of pictures and posters from *Hell to Pay*, and inside we filled it with guns and uniforms. In other words it was just a walking – sorry, driving – commercial for the film. I was just waiting for some clever bugger to call it a Hell Coupé.

The only problem now was the auction: the car looked so bloody amazing we didn't want to part with it. Luckily I had another little light bulb above the head moment. You see these quite a bit now, but at the time I'd never heard of an auction that sold to the lowest bidder before, so that's what we done. We had the thing in Charlie Breaker's Belvedere pub in Nunhead

Grove, with about thirty of the chaps all waiting to make a bid. Aquarium Lou was there, Seymour was there, Dave Archibald, Kevin, all the gang. Without telling the camera crew, the plan was to kick the thing off at twenty grand, then bid downwards till we was virtually giving the car away. Everyone knew what they had to do, and I said to Aquarium Lou, 'When I've got it down to fifty quid, you offer a tenner.' Unfortunately Lou had had what could be described as a good weekend, and he weren't the most with-it on this Monday morning.

So we started the auction at twenty grand, and immediately Lou sticks his hand up and goes, 'I'll give you a tenner.' Everyone laughed and I've gone, 'Not yet, Lou, not yet', like one of them theatrical whispers, in other words something every other cunt could hear. But every time we got the number down another grand or two, up would jump Lou: 'Tenner'. This goes on and on until we actually get down to fifty quid. I looked over at Lou and he's just smiling back. For fuck's sake! All he's got to do is say 'tenner' like he's been doing all morning, and I'm going, 'Over to you then, is it, Lou?' and he's just all Cheshire Cat in the corner. So I said, 'Any other offers?' and Charlie Breaker bought the car for a pound. The camera crew thought it was a right carve-up, and they were right. But they still shit themselves laughing and couldn't wait to tell the Cops.

For the big finale, both cars had to drive down to Gravesend promenade, so I spotted another opportunity for a bit of plod-bashing here. They're already waiting when we arrive, and when we pile out of the car we've all got knuckledusters, machine guns and pistols and we've said to the Cops, 'Any chance of a picture of all of us?' So there's this great shot of four active-duty coppers and us lot all posing with guns and looking the bomb in our gangster suits. Michael's got a tit hat on his head, I'm wearing a traffic hat and Brendan has a SWAT baseball cap, and we're all armed to the teeth, but the classic line actually came from one of the coppers who looked at Johnny Jacket who was holding this Super Soaker, and said, 'I'm not happy about that water pistol.' Nice one, sarge.

You won't be surprised to hear we won that little competition, and what a lovely headfuck it must have been for the four Cops to actually have to stand and applaud us lot? Not just them, though, 'cos to be fair they were all right and actually a couple of them asked me for autographs. But their bosses back at the station and the suits upstairs must have been proper cheesed off. I had to smile when one of them took a look at the car, which was basically just a promotional tool for Dave Courtney Enterprises, and said, 'It's almost as if you've done this deliberately.' 'Us?' I said. 'We're criminals, we'd never be that clever.' But he knew the truth. Then when the Cops looked at the fact that they'd raised more than two grand and we'd earned one pound, they thought we must have cheated 'cos our car looked the bollocks. It didn't exactly bring a smile to their faces when I said, 'Well, to be honest, we had a lot of help from people for free, 'cos let's face it, everyone wants to see the Old Bill lose. At everything.'

Maybe now's the time to mention why it's called *Car Sharks*. Actually, I still do not have a fucking clue. But the prizes were given out by a geezer in a shark costume. Well, that was the theory anyway, but it turned out Bravo didn't actually have anyone to wear the shark costume. Luckily one of our mates, Dave Archibald, is a good sport, so he put it on. At least he tried to. Steve's six-foot plus, and that suit was made for Ronnie Corbett's smaller brother by the look of it. So we actually got our prize from the fattest-looking shark in the world. That's what I call being up for any 'fin'.

There's a postscript to this story. Micky Taylor has recently got Guilty for chopping his wife up into Chicken McNuggets and has just accepted 25 years in prison. Who could have predicted that one?!

18. LAST WON'T AND TESTAMENT

Belfast, briefs and bananas

I said at the end of my last book that, because of the route my life was taking, the authorities would have no option but to take me out. And you've seen them have one go already. I've got taped evidence of 27 bent coppers and when I was doing it I knew that I was giving the authorities a reason to not want me around. They couldn't care less about the 27 policeman, they know there's fucking loads more bent ones than that, but, because I had it on tape, they knew I would publicise it. And what they care about most of all is the great British public having confidence in its boys in blue. If I go around saying that I happen to know 27 bent ones, and that's just the ones I've got on the tape, so there must be thousands more out there, no fucker's going to take the law-and-order mob seriously any more. 'Pay my speeding fine? What, so you can spend it on drugs, copper?' So they would rather I returned to a life of crime rather than a life of showing off. But a death works for them just as well. I'm not worried about it 'cos, in it actually happening, it dotcoms everything I've been fucking saying and predicting. Thousands of people will know I was right and they'll start to look at the police a bit more closely. Even in dying, I win.

I've made a will anyway which says that Beau gets full authority on use of my future video, DVD, record and film releases. He's the last word where that's concerned. And Stormylicious is in charge of the rest. She'll see all my kids right and give them what they need.

It's a bit macabre talking about dying, don't you think? I mean, I always thought I'd live forever – and so far I'm doing pretty good. So fuck my last will, I've called it my last *won't* and testament – that's how much I intend to die.

The only reason I've done it is 'cos I've seen so many bad things happen when people haven't made a will. Like Reggie Kray marrying Roberta and her thinking he wants a tiny little no-cameras send-off when he goes. Fucking hell! You really think a geezer banged up for 31 years wants to slip away unnoticed when he saw how much grief his brother's funeral caused the authorities? I've seen people leave their missus of forty years to shack up with an eighteen-year-old barmaid, and then died. So it's his new bird who picks whether he's buried, burned or eaten, she picks what to have on the tombstone and she chooses the records he gets at the service. I'm really sure some 63-year-old bloke wants to be sent to the other side by DJ Giant Bonez ft. Miss Terry W'man and Danzefloor Classix 38. *Shut the fuck up!*

By the way, did you hear about the guys who stop near a gravestone on the road. One of them starts scratching the moss away from the stone and says, 'I want to be like this geezer, 'cos he lived till he was 188.'

'Fucking hell, that's great. What's his name?'

'Miles, from London!'

What I'd actually like to be done by the closest person to me when I'm finally dead is for them to put a mobile phone in my inside pocket while I'm in the coffin. A fully charged one, mind, not some kiddie toy. And just as they go to lower me in the hole, I want them to ring it, so, while the vicar's throwing dirt on me, you can hear it – the 'diddle er duh diddle er duh diddle er duh duh'. I know that will fuck a load of people up, that will.

And if you can't sing along to that, the records I'd like are 'You'll Never Walk Alone', 'The Laughing Policeman' and Elvis Presley's version of 'Blueberry Hill'. So I'll see you all there!

Speaking of funerals, I'm sorry to say my good friend and solicitor Ralph Haeems passed away this year and I had to go and pay my respects to him and his family. He'd had a triple bypass recently and never really recovered and he's a great loss to thousands of people. So many people owe him so much – I personally owe him fourteen Not Guiltys' worth of love and respect over the last 25 years. Most recently he sorted out the case with me and Jennifer. So in his last year he had her in court going, 'I lied on the telly, I lied on all those documentaries, I lied in the books.' He was a great man.

Because he was the Krays' brief and he saw how they was stitched up by the authorities, Ralph was actually very aware of the situation with me and the bent policemen and Austin Warnes, and he has actually looked after the tapes I had of the 27 bent coppers. He's the one I've actually sent all the bugging devices I found to, he was a very security-conscious man; he always thought his place was bugged and he lived accordingly. He was a very clever man. With him dies one of the important weapons I could always fall back on in proving my accusation of what they're trying to do to me.

I'll tell you how good Ralph was – he weren't even

meant to be doing my Jennifer case 'cos he's more of a criminal lawyer and, despite what they were trying to do with it, that was more of a domestic, weren't it? So I had this fantastic lawyer called Tokes on the case until he was knobbled by the police. They said to him, 'You'll never have another legal-aid job come through you if you keep in with Courtney,' and 'cos that's how he made his living he had to do it. Unfortunately he's in prison on another dodgy charge himself, but we're thinking of you, Tokes.

Someone said to me the other day, 'Dave, how did you find prison?' And I had to say, 'Mate, I didn't have to – some Group 4 cunt drove me there in his van.'

Because I've tasted the inside of a prison, I feel for Tokes, I really do, 'cos if you visit Wormwood Scrubs or Strangeways, you'd see that only half of the people in there are actually criminals. The other half are just people who done the wrong thing on the wrong day. Fact: you do not need to be a criminal to go to prison.

If I'm honest, I found prison very character-building, and I'll let you decide if you like the character it fucking built. I sometimes think everyone should do a small stretch just to understand it. But would I want to go back there? *Shut up!* But then I never had any intention of going in the first place. The trouble is everybody does not know how close they are to going to prison, right?

I know thousands of people who you'd think have no chance of going to prison: just a lovely geezer, works nine to five, has a couple of kids. But he goes down the pub one night, a geezer picks on him so he defends himself with a punch in the mouth, breaks a few teeth and suddenly it's GBH and three years. So now he's lost his job, can't pay the mortgage, lost his house, comes out and the wife's gone off with his mate. If you'd said to him earlier on, 'Do you think you'll ever go to prison?' he'd have laughed at you. But you can accidentally bump the back of someone's car, have him jump out, drag you out of your car and start beating you up and, if you actually win that fight, you get done for GBH. Straight to jail, do not pass Go, do not collect £200.

So there's an awful lot of people in there who, yes, they should be there because they've done the crime. But no, they're not your typical criminal. And if you ask me if I'm going to go to prison again, no, I've no intention of going, but I'm too intelligent to say, 'No, I will never go again.' I'm only a gnat's gonads away. All of us are only that much away. Especially with the new laws the police are bringing out about aiding and conspiracy. You could come round and visit me a few times for a cup of tea, have a couple of pictures taken with me, ring the house and, because they've got pictures of you coming and going, they'll just drag you in as part of my firm.

This might come as a bit of a shock to some of you, but in reality, the gangster world is not all full of colourful characters. In the media it might look that way, but the real workings of the gangster world have got an awful lot of everyday stuff about them, and there's a lot of nine-to-fivers. And a lot of them aren't even gangsters at all, so work that one out. When he was alive, the police would label Ralph Haeems as a gangster, for example. Because he only looks after premier-division clients, the police look at him as a villain, as one of us. Jim my mechanic, he gets the same treatment. Because he repairs all the chaps' cars, the police give him grief as a mob-run garage. Can you believe that?

But that's the way it works. You need someone to proper look after your cars, you need a mechanic who ain't gonna ring the police up if he finds a bullet under the carpet or a squashed-up paddy in the wheel arch. You need someone who's actually going to shut up about it.

You need a dry-cleaner who ain't gonna squeal, 'Wow, I found three geezers' blood on the back pocket of his trousers, I'll ring the police.' You need people around you who know what's what.

The knock-on effect of living in the criminal world, and what's nice about it too, is you cannot sit around and chitter-chatter business like you can if you're a bricklayer, a plumber or whatever. My missus can't go down the school to pick the kids up and have a natter with the other wives about what they're doing, 'cos what's she gonna say back? 'So anyway, I says to Reggie Kray, "Get that fucking shooter out of my kitchen."' So you can only talk to people like yourself for safety reasons. It makes you 'us and them', a nice little unit. It's very nice if everyone is playing by the same rules, but every now and then you get the odd spanner in the works who mucks it up. And that's when the shit really hits.

But 'cos I want to help all of you reading this to stay out of the clink for as long as possible, here's a little tip that could actually mean the difference between ten years and a 'honey, I'm home'. And the advice is this: don't ever worry about witnesses. Say for instance your job is this. You're being given five grand to go into that pub to give this geezer a hiding. Here's what you do: do it for four grand and bring your own witnesses. Four of your mates, two couples, all happen to be drinking in the pub. You walk in, do the business and leave. By the time the police get there, no cunt wants to be a witness. The only witnesses they have of this event are yours. And they're going, 'This tall ginger black geezer left by horse and went that way.' The geezer who's had the hiding is going, 'Nah, nah, it weren't like that.' And the witnesses are like, 'What do you know? You were under the table getting kicked while we saw it.'

If for some fucking reason you did get caught, make

sure the four blokes who come to pick you out of the line-up are your mates. So bring your own witnesses. Don't look on that as another little joke. That's a proper tip for you.

What you might have realised by now is that, mentioning that little titbit of information, I've actually wound up the Old Bill even more. It's one thing telling a few mates, 'cos chances are they probably know it all. But when you've got 100,000 people buying your books, that's a hell of a lot of people learning about how to rent a witness. And that's what the authorities can't cope with, 'cos I'm making the truth palatable to people, however fucking un-nice the cunting thing tastes. That is the art or gift of communication. And this is why the Old Bill aren't fans. They know what I'm really saying, and they see people lapping it up and they go, 'He's taking the piss.' But of course I am. Communication – and that's what I believe I'm fucking exceptional at – is about how much of a disguise you can put on what something really is, the different agenda, a bit of sugar with the medicine. And for every one of you laughing at this book, that's another person the police have got to get worked up about. That's another one lost to the system.

And you know that I love fucking up the system. When I was in the Special Unit at Belmarsh, I soon realised that 'cos the screws were ordered to scrutinise every bit of my post and look for hidden messages of Dave's latest plan for world domination (I'm not even joking) I could have some fun. So I started ordering holiday brochures, tax forms, even the manual from a 1937 Singer sewing machine, which I was delighted to discover was fucking eight inches thick, just to give them something to read.

I know what you're thinking, though – so *stop* it, you'll go blind.

But am I being a bit selfish and using up more of the

authorities' time than I should? No I'm not, 'cos I can prove other people benefited from my little games as well. One day while I was inside I got a letter from the missus saying, 'Dave, I want to plant the lettuces this year – tell me when's a good time.'

Quick as a flash I wrote back: 'Whatever you do, *do not* touch the back garden. That's where you-know-what's hidden.'

About a week went by and she wrote back saying, 'The funniest thing happened – all these policemen turned up with shovels and dug the whole garden up. It looks like we've been Ground Forced by Alan Titchmarsh.'

So I said, '*Now's* a good time to plant the lettuces.'

All right, I admit I made that last bit up. It was actually *tomatoes*. (Speaking of vegetables, though, if God had meant us to be vegetarian, why are animals made of meat?)

But you can see how I'm not gonna let anything, not even that lot, get me down, can't you? And I admire that sort of spirit in other people, too.

My mum is top of the list where fighting spirit is concerned. I don't see her as often as I should, but she was there for me every day when I was in hospital and she knows I love her to bits. One of the happiest days of my life was when I went round to hers the other day and she'd had her hip operation. She couldn't wait for the post to come so she could fucking run over and grab it, just 'cos she could! I think she must have been chopping onions that day 'cos I do remember being a bit tearful. Love ya, Mum.

Here's another super trooper. I went over to Belfast with my mate Stuart as a guest of Roy Emberson's Emberson-Yamaha moto-cross team recently, and unfortunately Roy ended up in hospital. His team, Gordon Crockard, Glenn Phillips, Jordan Rose, Tom Church and the rest, is one of the leading motorbike teams in Europe, so when they won the UK Super Cross event at the Odyssey we went out to celebrate. Belfast's a blinding place but they're a bit highly strung where religion's concerned and another mate, Eddie, got into a bit of heated discussion with this local in the hotel foyer.

The end product was this geezer came back to the hotel with a gun and a knife. They'd been killing each other all day on these motorbikes, and now over a religious argument you've got a geezer with a knife in one hand and a shooter in the other trying to kill my mates. Before I could do anything, he's stabbed Roy in the stomach as he'd tried to grab the gun, and only didn't shoot him 'cos he had 25 geezers putting their drinks down to batter him. So the rest of the vacation was spent visiting Roy in hospital, which was something else. He's about sixty and doesn't give a fuck about anything – 'Oh well, I've got another bellybutton.' Top, top man.

I visit Belfast two or three times a year. I've got some very good friends over there. The Beast, young Davey and family, loads of others, and even though it makes Beirut look like a quiet holiday destination, you're guaranteed a fucking wicked time as soon as you get there.

I introduced Roy to Mark, Hahhan and Bob at Dock Gate in Southampton and he went in and bought three brand-new Harley Davidsons, just like that. One of them, this Harley Juice, he's only done 120 miles on, and he's had it a year. He calls it a thug bike. Harley are actually going to be sponsors of mine and we're doing a documentary called 'Bad Boys on Fat Boys'. Course, I won't be showing the bit where we went down there to buy the Juice. As I drove home on my bike it pissed down with rain and there's me with no socks, just shorts and T-shirt.

Roller Danny, so named 'cos he's the guy I buy my

Rolls-Royces from, is another mate of mine who manages to raise a smile in the face of adversity. That's not all he raises, neither!

'Cos my house is fucking full of writers, film-makers, editors and all that, there's always stuff going on. We were filming a new Dave Courtney documentary the other day when someone rang and said Danny was in hospital with a heart attack. It just so happened we'd been filming a lovely young lady friend of mine called Gemma when the call came, so we decided to pile up to the cardiac arrest ward and cheer old Danny up.

So we all drove up there dressed as policemen as usual. (No jokes about cardiac arrests, all right?) There was Big Tits Bev, Gemma who part-owns the Aquarium with Lou, Seymour, Steve Whale, Beau, No Neck Nick, Chris the cameraman, Chris the market trader, TJ, Al the head doorman from Mermaids, I Love You Ricky from Belfast, Jay, Alistair the mercenary and, most importantly, Gemma. She's a dancer and glamour model and a right beautiful young girl, and fortunately for us she's wearing one of her new stage outfits under her long black coat. As soon as she sees Danny, she just jumped out, dropped her coat and started kissing him. If he didn't have heart trouble before, he felt a tremor then, I promise you!

The more he tried not to look, the harder Gemma tried to distract him. He's showing us this scar on his stomach that's like a fucking oil slick, and she's lying down on the bed next to him and having a little play with herself. Halfway through her performance, Gemma said, 'How's your heart, babe? Is it working?' which I thought was very funny. But nowhere near as hysterical as Danny's face when I passed Gemma a banana to help with her act. He's gone, 'Oh no, not the fruit.' Order your DVD now . . .

Phillips, who will stand up to the shit the authorities can pass their way by associating with Dave Courtney, to make me know I'm on the right path. And don't ever think I don't have a fucking fantastic time being Dave Courtney, 'cos I do, 24/7. Or if the clocks have gone back, 25/7.

And if I can possibly help out anyone who's getting it from the law, I'm there. My mate Steve Clark down in Portsmouth is a godly man who does his work for the church, and he helps out the local kids. He's got hold of a bit of land and he was gonna build a church, which I was gonna help him with. It ended up that the land he took weren't his to have, and it went to court, so who do you think he asked to come and represent him? Since I've spent more hours in court than Rumpole, I think I know my way round a legal argument.

On the way there I hit a traffic jam on the M25. I couldn't be late getting to Portsmouth so I drove junctions one to eight on the hard shoulder at an average speed of 120 miles an hour. This copper pulled me just as I got to the end and he's pissing himself that someone would actually do that. He's said to me, 'They've got you on the camera, Dave, so I can't let you off. I'll just do you for speeding, I won't throw the book at you.' So I went, 'Lovely,' and I went over to my car, signed a copy of *Stop the Ride* ... and chucked it in his direction. 'I'll throw the book at you instead, then, pal.' And off he went.

I threw a little fetish party down in Fareham in Steve's neck of the woods and so I invited him. I said everyone's all dressing up in fancy gear, but he didn't twig what I meant, so he's arrived done up like a sea captain. He went down a treat, strangely enough. 'Have you met Seaman Staines?' *Stop it!* But speaking in court on behalf of him was a laugh for me. You could see the geezers there not knowing whether to take me seriously when I walked in, but then I opened my gob and they realised they had some work on their hands. And we got it adjourned.

I've just taken the new doorman licence exam – a complete waste of time – which I passed with what the examiner said was the highest marks that he has ever give.

No one actually needs this course – I know I fucking don't – but it works like this. Like the police find a way to bug everyone's car and they call it an anti-theft device, or they say they're after speeders so that's why we need cameras everywhere except certain stretches of a certain road when Dave Courtney's driving along it, they say you have to have a licence to be a doorman because they want total control over everything. And get this: by saying you can't pass this course if you've had a criminal record, that actually wipes out anyone who genuinely is a hardnut, don't it? They're now in a job where, if they do hit someone once, they get sacked. How the hell are you meant to be a good fighter if you're not allowed to fight? The very first time you clump someone you get put in prison for it.

The more the police control, the easier they can punish you. They can move little bits around the chessboard and stop you doing this job or stop you living there or stop you getting that for your kids if you've got a criminal record. But what I think they're actually doing is safeguarding their future employment. They are making it impossible for ex-offenders to wipe the slate clean and get on with their life. They might have only done three months in prison for not paying their telly licence, but they're punished every day after that with their prison record. And if they can't do this, that or the other 'cos of their record, what's left? Fucking crime, that's all!

Anyway, I did the test just to see if I could and now it's down to the police to see if they will give me a licence. It's down to their discretion. And if they do say no, I'd like to know what for 'cos I actually got higher marks than anyone ever has. The teacher actually asked me to be a fucking instructor.

Storm did it 'cos she's sort of my right hand and I thought it would be useful. There's lots of times that she's been left in charge of a load of money, like when I've done raves or she's been the manager of certain little events, and if you're in charge of people it's best to have come through the ranks and know what you're talking about. So she can say, I've done the test, I've passed it. The best owner of a nightclub is someone who used to be a potman, and all that.

The course was four days. It's common sense really. The emphasis is on how to do everything without using any physical contact at all. Which, even though I was teacher's fucking pet and I got 101 per cent, is totally impossible. I promise you, it will not fucking work. There are people out there in the nightclub world for whom a good smack in the mouth is the only way they will do as they're told. If they know beforehand that you're not allowed to hit them and you ask them to leave, they'll go, 'No. So fuck yourself, prick. If you touch me I'll batter you 'cos I won't be nicked and lose my job but you will. I stamp on people's heads all day long for fun but you don't 'cos you're one of these untouchable new doormen.' They know that if you lay a finger on them you'll lose your job, so there can be as many of you as you like but they're in the box seat, ain't they? But the authorities have now tied all this up with the pub owners and managers, so if there's any trouble they get it taken into account when their licence comes up, so suddenly they're in the police's pockets an' all. The owner of the pub can only employ someone who's passed this test, but they only let you take the test if the police have vetted you.

Day one in the classroom and I felt sorry for the guy at the front who had to teach Dave Courtney how to be a doorman. He felt quite overawed by it all, 'cos in his class there was also Dave who runs the Blind Beggar, which has a little bit of history. There was me, who's been a doorman longer than he's been alive. There's Lou who owns the Aquarium nightclub. There was Seymour Young and Frankie Baby who've both been doormen for twenty years. And he knew that. I felt for him 'cos I'm sure most of the people he teaches will have been doormen before and they're only doing the course for the qualification. And that poor guy has to justify these new tactics of door work with a form of sincerity when he knew it was absolute bollocks.

Did he recognise me? Course he did, and, just in case, I had a film crew with me and we filmed the whole thing for my next documentary.

But while you mull over whether you think it's right a doorman with 20 years' experience and 3,000 clumps under his belt should take exams to do the thing he's best at, have a think about this. The leader of the Tory Party thought he'd try and win an election by coming out with this idea of banning people like me from making money from their illicit pasts. OK, it might stop my mate Jeffrey Archer banging out a novel every other minute, but think about it: what are they really up to?

I'll tell you. They're saying we're not allowed to own a pub. We're not allowed to be doormen. We're not allowed to go to America. And now we're not allowed to write books. Every natural legal avenue of employment is being shut off to ex-offenders, so they're actually forcing you into a life of crime. What fucking choice do you have? Tell me this isn't part of the plan?

The other thing they're doing to screw people like me is

this 'double-jeopardy' law. We used to have a system in England that, if you got tried for one crime, you couldn't be tried for it again except in really, really special circumstances. Even if you came out afterwards and said, 'I did it.' Now that's changed. So I'm fucked, aren't I?

Actually, not really. Sorry, Mr Plod. I've seen this coming for a while so I've been a bit cute on the amount of things I've said. There are no lies in any of my books – I leave more stories out of my books than other geezers put in theirs (and we know who they are). But I am very clever in not mentioning certain facts that could come back to hurt me, or I make sure I cover myself. I was actually pulled in over the shooting in Holland that I told you about in *Stop the Ride* ... They had pictures of me leaving the country with Dougie and coming back alone, and there's my book telling you what happened in the middle. So, as he was on a missing-persons list they thought a little investigation might be in order. But without a murder weapon and without a witness and without a body, there's not a lot they can do about it.

But they are slowly changing the laws to shut up these loopholes. They've got a five-year plan, so a little law change here, another one next year and they've got you banged up within a few years for something that weren't illegal when you did it. They can't do it in one go 'cos the human-rights brigade would kick up and go 'too much nanny state' and all that, so they adjust little sections of laws that already exist so they now cover a lot more than they used to. They don't actually mind if someone gets Not Guilty 'cos they learn of a new loophole then spend a bit of time planning how to shut that one down. They're in no hurry, they'll get you for something else while they're waiting.

But the worst thing about the double-jeopardy law is it's made more people who are writing books talk absolute bollocks, 'cos they daren't write anything that'll get them nicked. Freddie Foreman has actually been a victim of trying to open something that was considered closed. Then, as soon as people got a bit too interested in that little confession, he had to go, 'It's only a book, I made it up.' For the rest of them, it might have 'autobiography' written on the front, but some people will say what they have to to make it sellable.

I don't need to make nothing up to sell books. If anything, I tone things down to protect the innocent and their owners. Every day of my life could be a new chapter of a book. So here's another average day in the life of Dave Courtney.

A guaranteed good night for me every year is the Brit Awards, 'cos they always lay on a table up the VIP end for me, Stormylicious and a load of my mates. I seem to remember this year the music was pretty good, which is always a bonus, 'cos it's the parties afterwards that usually stand out.

This year we went to the ceremony, drove back to Jodie's to do one of her TV shows, then went on to the after-show party at the Penthouse on Leicester Square. I was hanging with Snoop Dogg, Pharrell, Jennifer Ellison, Goldie, Michelle from *Big Brother*, Stuart from *Big Brother*, in fact every fucking nonentity from *Big Brother*. What was nice for me was that every single one of them I've actually met before, so introductions weren't necessary, we're just old friends. So it was good for me, walking into a little room and all these stars going, 'All right, Dave, come over here.' The only ones I hadn't met before were Javine (the Eurovision tit-tape bird) and the So Solid Twins, who are actually being managed by a friend of mine. But they all came up for a chat as well.

You probably saw in the papers that Goldie had a bit

of bother trying to get into the after-show gig and ended up lamping some doorman. I have to confess, I may have had something to do with that, but I'll come to that in a minute. Before all that kicked off, there was another little dust-up involving one of his mates, which was pretty fucking hysterical, actually.

I was standing there in front of all the advertising boards giving my interview to the cameras, like you do, and while I'm yapping, this geezer behind me gave a smack to someone else and he went flying past the back of me. I've seen the film, my mate Liam got it all on camera. What happened was one of Goldie's friends was at the bar and, as he was leaning forwards, his trousers have come away from his shirt and this geezer behind has tipped a drink down for a laugh. He's legged it and Goldie's mate has chased him into the interview room where he thinks he'll be safe. Guess again. *Bang!* I make Goldie's mate right, to be honest. I make him fucking full on, but I would have been a bit more slippery than that. I would have followed him around until he went to the toilet or something like that and then prescribed a bit of Dr Dave's diamond-encrusted medicine. But he certainly would have got it that night, no doubt about that, cheeky cunt. 'My bird saw you do it and, if I don't do something about it, I look like a fucking prick' – so *whack*.

The night before the Brits, which just happened to be my birthday, Simon Ward and his partner at Spearmint Rhino, Peter, invited me down to spend as much money as I possibly could on their behalf, and write a little thing afterwards about what I thought of the place. It's a hard life being a journalist. They sent the Spearmint Rhino limo down to pick me up and take me to the club, so there was loads of attention the second I stepped out of the motor. Fuck, in all that commotion I nearly lost my journalist's spiral-bound notepad. (If you must know, I thought the place was fucking excellent. The food was fantastic, it's a beautiful restaurant, and the swordfish was out of this world.)

But that's not what you want to hear about, is it? At the end of the evening I managed to grab one of the girls and bring her home with me. Her name was Nicebody. She was a fucking wicked shag, and she stayed with me until morning, and so did the Spearmint Rhino limo which was parked outside. Then it drove me around all day. So it took me to Jodie Marsh's show, and drove me to the Brits and it was fucking fantastic. We had Storm with us, and Tia who runs a company that hires out pole-dancers, and Emma, who dances but is actually a nurse. Tia is a stunna. She was on the Jodie Marsh show the first time I went there – she was getting marshmallows licked off her tits by Ben Dover. More of that on the BBC and no one would dodge their licence fee.

We've come out of the Brits party, and in front of us was Jennifer Ellison and all that, and this is where we actually caused the commotion that prompted the fight between Goldie and the bouncers. As he was walking in, this big black limo pulled up to pick us up and everyone was going, 'That's Dave Courtney the gangster,' and all the paparazzi were going, 'Dave, Dave, Dave.' Because Tia's a stripper, I know she hasn't got any knickers on, so I've said to the snappers, 'Don't take a picture of me, take a picture of this,' and I've lifted up her skirt and shown her bare bum. Well, it just went absolutely fucking mental. Paparazzi in that mood are like flies round shit.

While all this is going on, there's loads of jostling, loads of people getting shoved around, and this has kicked off the Goldie thing with the bouncers. I'm proper sorry about that 'cos Goldie is a good mate, and I thought I was gonna have to help him pick up his 24-carat teeth.

While Goldie's getting the 'you're not on the list'

treatment over there, the photographers on the red carpet are still on it. They've gone, 'Dave, Dave, put your hand on her bum again!' 'Over here, Dave, point her arse this way.' Fucking disrespectful, if you ask me, but what wicked pictures. They even had their hands inside the limo, just shooting off film in the dark. It was mental.

Back at the house a few hours later I got a call from the features editor of a major newspaper who said, 'Dave, I hope your night was as good as it looks in these pictures we've got in front of us!' I said it might have been, yes. Then he went, 'You know, we're not allowed to actually use them, don't you? They're the best pictures of the Brits. There's the black limo, the Spearmint Rhino thing, the gangster, a bird with her arse out and a thousand flash-bulbs going off – but we can't glamorise crime. I can't put it in and I just want you to know I think that is all bollocks.'

But getting back to that double-jeopardy thing ... I'm a naughty boy, I've always been a naughty boy and, despite what I might say in a courtroom, you name it and I've probably done it. See, I don't mind admitting the things I done. But not everyone's like that. I did an after-dinner speech a while back with that Nick Leeson guy and he severely pissed me off. 'Cos he'd nicked a load of money from Barings Bank, the organisers thought we'd make a good team. Fuck that. I've never heard anyone ever be so apologetic about their whole life. You know, 'I never really stole anything, I was just fiddling on the computer, I never nicked anything, I was just the fall guy, I got caught and I went to prison and I got cancer and my wife left me.' Fucking hell!

When he eventually shut the fuck up and the spotlight swung round to yours truly, I got up and said, 'I don't know about you lot, but that bloke has fucked me right off.' And that got their attention. I said, 'If you think I'm anything like that, leave now 'cos I'm not sorry for anything I done. Anything I was accused of I did. Whether I got away with it or not is different. But I fucking ain't that.' And you should have heard them clap. They was standing on chairs, wolf whistling, cheering, the full fucking nine yards. Not bad for a Women's Institute meet. And this Leeson is just sinking into his chair next to me. Why some twat ever thought his story would make a good film I don't know. He gives villains a bad name.

20. ALL THE QUEEN'S MEN

Pete, parliament and the police

You know when people die in clubs because of drugs and the *Daily Mail* sticks it on the front page and everyone says, 'Drugs are evil – she only took one E tablet and she died.' It's always that headline, isn't it? Well I've worked out the best way not to die of ecstasy: take *two*, not one. You never read of anyone dying 'cos they took two Es, do you? So that's what I do, take two all the time.

Look at that, I just saved your life there. How nice am I?

While I'm being all educational, here's a thought for you: without people like me, the country would fall apart. It would actually cease to function properly if there weren't any criminals. Why's that, Dave, I hear you ask? Because the biggest employer in this country is the legal system: the police, the law courts, traffic wardens, social workers and the rest. So if there weren't naughty boys running round at all levels, half the country would be unemployed. The whole of the UK would be like living in Liverpool! (What do you call a Scouser in a suit? The accused.) If people didn't throw rubbish on the streets, there wouldn't be road sweepers. If people didn't drive too fast, there'd be no speed cameras.

You need good and bad in this life. I'm not actually pro-devil, but without Satan would God have anything to do? Which reminds me: Jesus walks into a hotel and drops four nails on to the reception desk. He goes, 'Can you put me up for the night?'

Satan came up to one of my mates the other day and said, 'Go and shoot this bloke for me or you'll burn in the fiery pits of hell for eternity.' My mate goes, 'Fuck off, beardy.' Satan's all confused and says, 'Aren't you scared of me?' and my mate goes, 'Nah, I've been married to your sister for twenty years.'

What I'm saying is, you need a mix of characters. It's all very well watching Man United thrash Peckham United every week, but it wouldn't mean anything. You've got to see them come up against someone a bit special, like hammering Bayern Munich 8–0, and then you can appreciate it and go, Wow.

But since there is good and bad on this planet, even if some of them are good baddies and bad goodies, it keeps things interesting locking horns against the other lot from time to time, don't it? I'm permanently in a battle with the authorities and, to be honest, they've been getting the upper hand of late. Bastards. So when I have the odd chance to wind them up in a small way, you know I'm going to take it.

A few weeks ago I was invited to dinner in the Houses of Parliament by the wife of one of the Spearmint Rhino partners. She happens to be the head chef there, 'cos she's a very independent woman and her hubby Keith ain't the typical nightclub bloke either. He'd much rather be at home having a game of chess. But it's a money-spinner.

Anyway, she's given me the invite and handed over this pass and it only says 'Access All Areas'. Me, Dave Courtney, scourge of the British justice system given triple-A licence to roam anywhere I fucking like in the highest court of the land. *Touch!*

The only problem was I had to get in first. As we get to the entrance, there's this small private army of Old Bill searching everyone. There's dogs, machine guns, dogs *with* machine guns, and they're making everyone walk through this metal detector like you do at airports. Shit, I'm thinking. You *know* what I've got in my pocket. As I'm getting nearer I'm trying to work it out. Fucking hell. What's more embarrassing, getting caught with it or taking it out now in front of all these people and getting it over with? I can't chuck it 'cos of the diamonds and the car's a million miles away. Basically, I'm screwed.

My best gift is the spur of the moment stuff. Ad-libbing and all that. When you're under arrest, what you've got to immediately do is spin them one. So as I walked towards this fucking scanner thing, I was watching this copper staring at me like he'd seen a ghost. Here we go, I thought. The thing is, all footballers know David Beckham, all chefs know Jamie Oliver and all coppers know Dave Courtney. He's tapped his mate on the shoulder and said, 'Look who's here.' I gave them my best grin, bobbed down a little bit and went, 'Evening all.' And he said, 'Piss off, Courtney, we're too young to remember all that.' How to make a bloke feel old. *Pricks*.

I reached the machine and decided to bluff it out but, as soon as I walked through, this air-raid siren's gone off and I thought, Fuck, there goes my twenty-grand duster. But half a second later, Keith's missus walked through and it went off for her as well, and as she didn't look back, like it happens all the time, neither did I. Result! This cook has just walked an armed criminal through the security of one of the most guarded buildings in England, the alarm's started singing its head off and no one even looks up. Fucking *touch!*

As we walked down the corridor there were loads more coppers lining the walls, and you could hear their radios crackling as we approached each one. The airwaves were fucking alive with 'breaker, breaker, one, Courtney's heading southwest by north-northeast'. I think they were trying to say he's just going past the gents ... When we got to the restaurant, five or six MI6 geezers came in on their own and then they all sat within firing range of, and directly in line with, anyone of importance. The cameras in there are inside the chandeliers, giving whoever's monitoring them an aerial view of the room. So they work out that, if a bloke sitting there wants to shoot him over there, then we'll get Bob to sit over here. And if Lord Thingy looks a bit of a target, we'll stick Steve in the way over there. So I walked in for a bite to eat and went, 'I'll have a bread roll' and they was immediately all on me. I was like, Wow, what a headfuck it must be for them. I had this circle jerk of six geezers just surrounding me, like plainclothes Ring-a-Ring-a-Roses, and they're all thinking, What's the cunt up to? Who's he after? Oh yes, happy days.

You know that joke – what's the difference between the Houses of Parliament and a hedgehog? The hedgehog has its pricks on the outside. After a day at the place I can actually say ... it's totally true. But there were one or two straight-up good blokes there. One in particular came over and gave me the full guided tour of the building. I have never seen anything more beautiful in my life – and the building weren't bad either. Seriously, it's a fucking amazing place, no expense spared on anything. I'd hate to see our tax money pissed away on inferior luxury goods. And this Lord was so cool he even stood in front of me while I slipped one of Her Majesty's government cups and saucers in my pocket. Proper, he was.

One of the reasons that little escapade felt good was because a few years ago the government's security forces proper stitched me up. I wouldn't have minded, but I was actually waiting for some real stitches at the time.

They actually threw me out of hospital just because the Queen was due to put in an appearance. I was booked in for five days, 'cos they had to give me tests before they did an operation on my leg, and the Queen was coming to open a new wing that week. I'm having the operation on Friday but on Wednesday the place is filled with all her security. They're looking around for where snipers might stand, who looks a bit suspicious, has anyone joined the staff in the last few weeks who might be a bit dodgy? All that, and to make sure as well the place smells as much as possible of fresh emulsion (have you ever thought that she must think all buildings stink of new paint?).

The reason Her Majesty's Secret Servicemen are so twitchy is that Ronnie Biggs was in there at the same time and they considered him an active risk to the head of state. But since he was in a coma – *and* handcuffed to a bed – unless he's going to mount an assassination attempt by ESP they're probably over-reacting a little bit.

'Cos I'm up all hours and I have thousands of people visiting, the night security people all know me. I'm signing stuff and giving away books and that, willy-nilly. So all the Queen's men have gone to the night porter, 'Where's that mob of skinheads off to?' And he's said, 'Going to visit Dave Courtney.'

Picture, if you will, half a dozen large blokes in suits'

jaws dropping. 'Dave Courtney's in *here*? We can't have that. We've got the fucking Queen coming Friday!'

So anyway, the next morning the head surgeon of the hospital comes into my room and says, 'I'm sorry, Mr Courtney. We can't do the operation till Monday, so because we need the bed space you'll have to go home this afternoon and come back after the weekend.' I was like, Fucking hell, 'cos I had bits hanging out where they were only halfway through the tests.

I looked at him and said, 'I've heard different.'

'What have you heard then, Mr Courtney?'

'Is the Queen swinging by tomorrow by any chance?' Now this doctor doesn't know the night porter's told me the truth, so the look on his face was one I treasured for, ooh, about six seconds.

Obviously there's gonna be a bit of a stink now, 'cos you can't go chucking sick patients on the streets just so the Queen can avoid a load of bald blokes, so they've actually paid for me to go private at a clinic in Blackheath. Fourteen grand, just like that, just to get me out of the way of Her Majesty. Somehow the newspapers found out (I wonder who could have told them?) and when they came to interview me I went, 'Listen, I sit at home with a fucking Union Jack flying outside my house. I big up this country whenever I'm abroad. I fucking sing the praises of the Royal Family and the armed forces all over the world. I do free shows for our boys and I fucking sponsor their football team, and *she* won't come in the hospital until I've gone? Send her victorious? I wouldn't send her yours.' (Just kidding, Yer Maj, and thanks for the OBE.)

She has no say in all that, though, does she? I can't blame her. But she's got the police doing her security and you know the scariest thing about them is their imaginations. They've seen all the gangster movies so they're looking out for old ladies stabbing you with poisonous umbrellas. They just go right over the top. You give enough things for them to work out and they go into overdrive. And yet they don't notice little things like me legitimately sponsoring the British Army football team for a year. That was one of my best coups, that was, having 'Dave Courtney' written all over the back of the government's deadliest fighting machine. It was like my own private army, but with more hair.

The problem with the police – all right, *one* of them – is they've got this fucking great blind spot when it comes to predicting the behaviour of their opponents. They might be able to work out all the permutations a villain might come up with in any situation, but what they never do is consider that a villain might actually think like a copper. And if you can do that, you've got them chasing their tails already.

I know how to do the psychology stuff that they specialise in, 'cos it's my job as well as theirs. I know how people work, how they think, how they act. You take an Avon lady. She might be trudging through the wind and snow, freezing her tits off, but when she gets to your house she's giving it full-beam Carole Smillie and 'Hello!' It's a work face, nothing more. And I do a fucking good 'Oi' face when I want to, but there's a time and a place. Recently I had a good chance to use it, and it was against the Old Bill.

The bird who gets shagged in the Jacuzzi in my film is actually a working girl. I let them work in all my clubs and I don't charge a percentage or any of that. But considering that's what they do for a living, I do expect, if I've got some people over who could do with a shag, that they'll pop over for a house visit free of charge. Scratch your back time, innit? And I might throw in a bit of debt-collecting for them on the way home, 'cos I know they're frightened of some bloke. We all do our own thing, square peg, square hole.

Anyway, this bird come up to me and said, 'One of the blokes who's shagging me at the moment is a copper and his sole job is, for 24 months, to get as close to Dave Courtney and associates as possible.' She knew he was the fuzz 'cos he's selling drugs so cheap he must be making a loss on them. He's trying too hard to fit in, you know what I mean? And this was their first port of call 'cos they knew I ran that club and was there all the time.

So I said to her, 'You make him fall in love with you. Head over fucking heels, proper full-on romance.' And she did. He's thinking he's had a result, 'cos not only is he getting premier-division shagging, but she's just so happening to spill all this information about Dave Courtney. The only problem for him is it's all bollocks. I'm feeding her all the lines, aren't I, just laughing at what they must be thinking down at the nick. 'Courtney's going after the Crown Jewels? Courtney's mob are gonna steal the FA Cup and melt it down into knuckledusters.' Crack on.

I was having a great laugh thinking of all this, but then it started to get a bit serious 'cos two coppers were starting to get to know people through hanging out with my girl. I didn't want anyone else getting caught up in it, so I decided to nip it in the bud.

Because the way the police operate has become a bit of a *Mastermind* subject for me, and I've started so I'll finish, I know that if I were to go up to these blokes and say, 'I know you're coppers,' they'd have to sit through this massive debrief back at the Yard. Everything I say and do will be gone over with a fine-tooth comb, so I'm not gonna say nothing or do nothing, except tell them I know. And that's when I've been able to have a bit of fun.

So on my instruction, this girl, Kerry, has invited the

two Old Bill round to my gaff for a bit of a knees-up. They've turned up and gone, 'Where's the party then?' and she's said, 'In the other room.' So off they've trotted, and as they get to the other room I hear one of them saying, 'Anyone thought about some music? Like a fucking morgue in here.'

In them days, the back room was done out a lot more Humphrey Bogarty, a lot more like a gangster's castle. It's matured a bit now, thanks to a bit of smart handiwork from Coffin Steve. Steve used to make a nice living from manufacturing compressed cardboard coffins and sending them out to Iraq. That was before we fucking invaded. Suddenly there's a war out there and they now want a million of the things and he's a millionaire. Just through these cardboard coffins. But he's a carpenter by trade so he made me a little baby wooden coffin, which I've got in the front room, as well as coming in handy for all my DIY repairs. (How great is it to have someone in my firm called 'Coffin Steve'? The police think he's some kind of hitman. Another one is Gavin the Gatemaker. He's actually responsible for making the gates on the front of my house – which is why they've got big gaps in them. But people hear his name and think he's gonna hurt them. It doesn't occur to people that he might actually make gates.)

Anyway, back then there was this massive table in there, a proper King Arthur's round table (well, it is Camelot Castle) and it's got loads of gangsters sitting round it. Proper, proper hardnuts. Mad Pete, Welsh Bernie, Seymour and the rest. So Kerry and these two have come in, and I'm standing at the door. Before anything else, I know I've got to get the bird out of trouble, so I've said, 'I'm really sorry, darling, I've lied to you, there is no party, here,' and as I've shut the door, they can suddenly see these nine gorillas behind me.

On debriefing at the station, a copper can only say

what he sees and what happens. I know what's going on in their heads 'cos I've been there, I know they're shitting themselves being in a room where everyone hates them, but they've got to carry on the bluff. So I said, 'Kerry, I'm really sorry, I don't know what they've told you, but these two are actually policemen. They're on a fucking job here and they've used you. And through the Old Bill who are still on my payroll, I've learned this. Go home, and I'll talk to you later.'

Now these two are in bits. They're shitting themselves, but they still haven't got anything to arrest me for.

I said to them, 'Before you say anything, I just want you to know you're in no danger of being hurt by me. But the minute you lie to me, I'll be personally offended. Before we get into this conversation, I just want you to know that.'

And then I just waited. And before I could open my mouth again, one of them's just started blabbing, 'Pleasedon'thurtusit'sjustanintelligencegathering-operationitdon'tmeannothinwe'rejustwatchingyouwe-didn'thurtthegirli'mnotwiredi'mnotwiredipromisei'm-notwired.' Fucking Niagara Falls of information, we couldn't shut the prick up. The other one was looking at him as if to go, 'What the *fuck* are you doing!?' But as the first one gets into it he can't stop and he's virtually crying, telling us all this stuff. You can see him thinking, I'm in front of Dave Courtney and a bunch of his mates and he's told me I can't lie. It's like when you're at a funeral and you start sniffling. When you're in the flow, you can't stop it. It just takes over.

I didn't say anything and he just carried on. Every time he stopped, I kept schtum and then he'd start up again. 'I'm telling the truth!' I'm just standing there, but inside I'm doing cartwheels 'cos I know that they will now have to go back and undertake a full debrief about this evening, and all this has got to come out. You know when you're in court, the arresting officer reads out from his little notebook every grunt and 'erm' and 'I dunno' that you've said. So, when you've had that a few times, you know they have to do the same to themselves. That's why they give them a bit of paper to read, so they don't cock it up.

So I'm imagining the debrief already. It has to go like this: 'So what happened?'

'Well, Courtney said there wasn't a party and suggested to the bird to go home.'

'And then what did he do?'

'Well, he had a bit of a chat. He walked round the table slowly, no one threatened us, he said he wouldn't hurt us but he knew we were police.'

You know he can't admit he's told the bird, so he also has to confirm what I said, that some copper must have tipped me off – and that just fucks their heads up. They have got to keep investigating now, ain't they? So then they have to admit all the crying from the other one.

So when it comes to the one who didn't lose it, even he's got a story to tell. 'Cos while Tiny Tears next to him is blubbing away, he's gone, 'I'm not wired.'

And I've said, 'I don't mind if you are.'

So then he's said, 'I'm not armed.'

And I've gone, 'I never asked if you were.' So, while he's scratching his head, I've walked round and said, 'All I want you to do is go back to your boss, whoever put you up to this, and tell him the same message he would have got on his school reports: Must. Try. Harder.' And then I've chucked them out.

The first one gets to the front door then he literally ran. He leaped over the side wall and had no idea there was a nine-foot drop the other side. A few seconds later we heard him land – head first. Back at the nick it's 'What did you say?' 'I said this.' 'What did he say?' 'Well, he said . . .'

I've done fuck all, they can't pin anything on me, and I've fucked up his entire career. How wicked is that!

When it comes to coppers, if I'm honest I would say that 95 per cent of them are good blokes. They're just like you and me, well maybe you, and they just happen to have shitty jobs like the rest of us (definitely just you this time). I've seen enough coppers reading my books round swimming pools on holiday or heard enough reports of mates being given a let-off when the arresting plod has seen my book in the car to know there's a few good ones out there. It's like I always say, there is such a thing as a good baddy and a bad goody. Now if the suits pulling the strings only realised that, the world would go round a lot more smoothly.

The thing is, if the top bananas in the police force aren't prepared to see there's something else out there apart from black and white, they can't be surprised when the odd villain takes the same view. And as far as the police are concerned, my dear old friend Mad Pete takes a very single-minded view indeed.

Mad Pete is a doorman friend of mine of from Margate. He's a very connected man and he's not called 'Mad' Pete unjustly. He is one of my Spartacuses. He spent a lot of time in the merchant navy. He does a bit of gym work and all that, but he's one of those people who takes bravery to new levels, do you know what I mean? There are times when things happen and you like to think you'd be courageous enough to get involved – well, Pete does. Then there are times when you go, 'Fuck no, that's suicide.' And Pete does them an' all! He's different class. Five blokes outside fancy a fight with you and you've got a good pair of shoes on, you might fancy it – that's brave. Ten blokes outside and they've all got an Uzi and you fancy that – then you're name's Pete. I'm proud to say he's a very fine friend of mine. We've been all round the world together, he's come to my shows, he's defended me, he's come to the court cases with me and looked after me when I was in hospital. He slept at my house when someone tried to machete his head off when he lived in Great Yarmouth and we nursed him back together again after he signed himself out of hospital. That was an interesting one, him turning up here with his head virtually under his arm.

It's never a dull moment with Pete and it's minimum dull when there's an Old Bill involved. You know when you talk to a copper you normally have an air of 'better listen to the fucking nine-stone ginger weakling 'cos he is a policeman after all' so you go, 'Yeah, officer, no, officer.' Well, Pete can't do that. He is absolutely incapable of playing that game, which makes for some very interesting scenes. 'Do you know how fast you were going, young man?' this copper said to him when I was sitting in the car.

I think I actually heard the switch go in his head. *Flick*.

'What the fucking hell's it got to do with you?' So Pete's out the car, snarling, and the copper's thinking, Fuck, I pulled the wrong motor here.

'What the fuck's it got to do with you, cunt? No, I *don't* fucking know how fast I was going.'

'You were, er, going too fast.'

'Well, tell someone that fucking cares then.'

And that's the point the geezer looks round to see if anyone's watching. If he can back out of that one without getting in trouble, he's off. And running.

Fantastic. Proper fucking off the cake. But then Pete goes, 'They all like me, Dave, 'cos when they see me they smile.' And I thought, I'll fucking bet they do! I'll bet the geezers are probably buying him sweets, candyfloss and Kiss Me Quick hats.

Margate doormen, in fact most seaside doormen, are better in the summer than they are in the winter 'cos they have more practice than anyone else. Margate has big coachloads of men on a beano, 56-seater coaches driving to Margate *to get pissed*, and then come home. And there's fifty coaches coming from all over England to Margate for that day. Every day. So those men in the summer are fucking right on it. They are the best doormen in the world. But in the winter, what's happening down at the seaside? Fuck all, so they've got no one to fight. They're just talking to seagulls.

Fighting's like any other sport in the world. If you don't do it often, you don't get good at it. If you don't spar, you'll be shit on the night. If you haven't played snooker for six months, when you have a game you ain't as good. If you haven't kicked a ball for a year, you'll be crap when you do. A doorman who is big rarely has a fight. People always leave when he's big, so he don't have a fight for a fucking year. But if he asks somebody to leave and the geezer starts spitting blood and screaming, 'Or *what*?' then if he hasn't done it since last summer he's in fucking trouble.

So that's Mad Pete. Another character I know is Bernie Lee. He's a bit of a pikey, but a lovely man. His wife's name is actually Brenda. Brenda Lee, can you believe that? She's my favourite singer. Bernie talks as if he's got a mouthful of gravel from a tropical fish tank. Proper low. 'All right, Dave, how's it going?' He's an explosives man and he's still got all his own legs and arms, so I suppose he's a good one. He's a very colourful character, and that colour is mostly gold. He's got more rings than he has fingers. In fact, he said to me one day, 'Where can I get a new finger? 'Cos I've seen a blinding ring I want to buy and I've got no room for it.' And knowing Bernie, he most probably meant it.

I'll tell you another thing I can't get over. Very high walls – especially if they've got barbed wire on. *Stop it!*

But I've just done a film with a couple of familiar fun-nymen off the telly, John Thompson from *Cold Feet* and *The Fast Show*, and Craig Charles, the Scouse geezer from *Red Dwarf*. Oh, and I play Dave. I never said I was the best actor in the world but I play a fucking not-bad Dave. The film is called *The Dealer*, and it was made by a friend of mine called Lee Phillips. What I like about Lee is he's fully aware of the penalty people pay having me in their projects and he takes that risk. He's also used Dave Legano and Mickey Goldtooth, and it's a fucking fantas-tic plot about a gangster who gets a letter sent to himself from himself in the future. 'If you don't believe this letter, look out the window and this bloke will fall over' – and he does. And he says, 'Your daughter is marrying the wrong bloke and you need to invest in these stocks and shares.'

John Thompson was actually going through a bit of a kicking in the press at the time, but he's a top guy, really helpful if you're trying to get on. Like a lot of them profes-sionals, he's a really serious guy and can turn on the funny when he wants it.

Like I did on *Hell to Pay*, Lee's learned the technique of getting real people in where he can. Don't pay an actor to be 99 per cent the perfect tramp, when you can get a real one in. 'Don't lie in that doorway, mate, lie in this one, I'll point a camera at you and give you a hundred quid.' You're not going to beat that. And that makes everyone look like fantastic actors.

Lee pulled in a lot of favours for this one, borrowed cars and boats. We filmed all these murders and there was one that got in the papers 'cos some witnesses thought this body we chucked off a speedboat was a real one. Actually, it was, but that's another story. So they've phoned the police who've shut down Rochester River.

To be honest, I've not had the best of luck with boats

recently. Or rather, the owner ain't. A few weeks ago I borrowed a boat from a pal of mine, Johnny, and then I lent it to another pal of mine – who fucked it up. He picked up a rope and got it caught round the propeller and the prop shaft and caused a bit of damage. So I've had to go back to my mate and say it was me who's done it, ain't I? I have enough trouble admitting something was me when it *was* fucking me, so taking the blame for something I didn't do does not taste nice. But that boat was still broken when I've gone back to borrow another one, which I merrily took for a trip down the Norfolk Broads – and promptly smashed the roof off on a low bridge. Who puts those fuckers there, anyway?

When my mate Johnny first called up and told me I could have a holiday as his treat, I weren't exactly that excited. My missus had taken the message and I've misread it on the paper. I thought, Who the fuck wants to have a trip round the Norfolk B Roads? There's enough round my way I haven't got round to visiting yet.

Anyway, just when Cap'n Courtney thinks he's cracked it, I realised we was surrounded by all these other little boats. You know when the QE2 pulls into those Caribbean islands and all the locals come out in their tiny fishing boats to wave her in? It was like that. And they're all going the opposite way to me, bouncing off the front of us like flies on a windscreen. (What's the last thing that goes through an insect's mind when it hits your front window? Its arse.) What I didn't realise was I was in the middle of a regatta. How the fuck was I meant to know? We don't get many of them down Peckham. I think we actually got third prize (only two other boats finished).

So we got the roof of the boat missing like that bit where James Bond converts a double-decker to a single-decker in *Live and Let Die*. We got fifteen upside-down silly little boats splashing around us. And worst of all, I dropped my fucking mobile in the river. There's a fish down there with some very tasty phone numbers at his disposal.

In case you haven't worked it out, I'm more of a naughty man than a nautical one. I saw on telly the other day that we're all about 95 per cent water. Shouldn't we have drowned by now? But, Johnny, if you're reading this, mate, I'm sorry. (And I hope you found the boat where we left it.)

Anyway, where was I? Oh yeah, sitting over here . . .

The other thing I was impressed by in this *Dealer* movie was the fact Lee had actually hired Rochester Cathedral. I don't know how much that would cost if money were involved but, because you know who you know, he can get it.

Another film I've just done that comes out soon is *Six Bend Trap*. It's set in Middlesbrough and it's like a northern *Lock, Stock* . . . and when you consider most of the country is up North, it's gonna be a big hit. It's about a London bloke who owns a dog track, hence the title. Gordy Metcalfe is the name of my character. There's a great scene in it where I've got all these naughty geezers who owe me money, they're naked in the dog track and there's a midget sitting on the rabbit with a shotgun aimed at their dicks. You got a mental picture of that? Then the midget's shouted 'Go!' and they have to race round the track. The last one gets shot. It's very, very funny.

I've done a few other bits and pieces for films as well where funding has mysteriously been pulled once I've started shooting my scenes. I won't name them 'cos I don't want to embarrass no one, but I guess people like Lee Phillips are stronger at resisting the anti-Dave leverage from the authorities than others.

I love them old-fashioned Italian families. It don't matter
if you're 14 or 48, you go round Mama's for dinner and get
treated like a kid. Wicked. I know a certain outfit over in
New York who are everything you'd hope for. They watch
The Godfather like it's a home video, if you know what I
mean. Anyway, last year they made me an offer I couldn't
refuse – three days in Sicily, £5,000 in my pocket and all
they wanted me to do was talk. No clumping, no scaring,
no throwing my weight around, just a private 'Audience
With ...' in front of twenty of the Mediterranean's most
respected and well-dressed old gents. For the chance to get
up and rabbit about myself, I'd fucking pay them.

Anyway, I landed at the airport and this blacked-out
stretch limo was there to pick me up from the runway. I had
the full diplomatic immunity bit. 'Don't-a bother about-a
customs, Meester Courtney' and all that. *Touch*. I gave the
tarmac a quick snog like the Pope always does (you know,
when nearly in Rome, and all that), although I drew the line
when this giant chauffeur tried to plant one on each cheek.
Leave it out, geezer, we haven't even been introduced yet.
Anyway, he opened the car door for me and I was taken up
in the hills to this private villa that had more guards than
British Rail. Security everywhere, all of them looking like
they'd just stepped off the Armani catwalk. Even the guard
dogs had bleached hair and Ray-Bans.

Even though they spoke this funny pidgin English, the
important blokes there had their own interpreters for the
finer points of translation: they had no problem with
'cunt' and 'fuck' 'cos when you learn a new language it's
always the swear words you look up first, ain't it? It was
the technical aspects of the legal process I think they had
trouble with, like 'bang to rights', 'done me up like a
kipper' and 'made a proper Charlie of myself'. Anyway,
one of the top men came over and told me what they
wanted. 'Cos he was speaking in his broken English (and

I wouldn't wanna be the soppy fuck who broke it, would you?) it was one of those where you get all these big sentences in just a few words. Impressive? I'm going, 'Woah, this is unreal.'

Anyway, this geezer – 'Don' I think someone said his name was – goes, 'Mr Courtney, please don't give me any gangster stories – I know one million murderers, I know one million bank robbers – my gardener has killed more people than you *know*. All I want to hear about is the day you dressed up as a court jester, went to court and punched a policeman in the face, come out on the steps and said "Guilty". That is the most blatant display of disrespect for law and order I have ever seen anywhere in the world and we would like you to tell us about it.'

When I did that little stunt, I weren't thinking further afield than Peckham. If the national papers in London picked the story up I'd be amazed. I certainly didn't expect the top firm in America to be picking it up on Fox News.

But he was going, 'There's an unwritten rulebook when you're going to court, and you've broken every one.' That rulebook says things like, 'You don't want all your mates coming with you, you wear a suit whether you ever normally wear one or not, you say yes sir no sir, no matter what sort of lairy cunt you are down the pub, and you hand in a letter from someone you say you've known for twenty years saying you're such a good bloke.' That's courtroom law, innit, whether you're in Rome or Romford. But he goes to me, 'You turned up in a black limo with 45 of your hardest-looking mates, dressed as a clown and punched a copper in the head when you went out there and said to the paper, "Have that." You tell me about that.'

So that's what I did. And 'cos I talk a million miles an hour, I'm not sure these gentlemen are following every word, and they don't always laugh when you think they should. I thought, Work with me, people, for Christ's sake. But they just kept quiet and every time one of them whispered into one of the interpreters' ears I never knew if they was looking up a word or ordering an execution. But the funny thing was at the end they all gave me a clap (but the cream soon cleared that up) and there was loads of laughing and joking with a glass of their best wine afterwards. That was a fucking relief. Better late than never, I suppose.

But you can't hurry an Italian, can you? I mean, Rome wasn't built in a day – *although that was the builder's original estimate.*

They love their religion over there, though, don't they? What was all that smoke business about when they chose the new Pope? One of the cardinals puts a bit too much unleaded on the barbie and suddenly they're being asked for a decision. Personally I was disappointed that after calling the last one John Paul they didn't go with George Ringo this time. *Stop it!*

He's got his work cut out for him though, don't you think? Round my way crime's so bad that they've got fourteen confessional boxes in the local church. One of them's got a sign on it that says, 'Eight items or less.'

An old bloke went into one of them the other day and he went to the priest, 'Father, I'm eighty years old, married, have four kids and a dozen grandchildren. I started taking this new Viagra pill, and last night I had an affair and made love to two eighteen-year-old girls. Both of them. Twice.'

The priest said, 'Well, my son, when was the last time you were in confession?'

'Never, Father, I'm Jewish.'

'So then, why are you telling me?'

'Hell! I'm telling everybody!'

(Do you remember when Viagra first came over here?

The first shipment was hijacked as soon as it arrived at Heathrow. Scotland Yard warned the public to be on the lookout for a gang of hardened criminals. *Stop it!*)

Anyway, Italy's been good to me and they even brought out an Italian version of *Stop the Ride* ... You didn't know I could speak Wop, did you? Trouble was, before they went over to the Euro I'd get all these fucking million-lira notes bunged over in royalties, and I thought I'd cracked it, didn't I? There's enough notes coming through the door to wallpaper the fucking house so I'm buying everyone clothes, holidays, cars, witnesses. Just a little bit embarrassing when I found out it was 300,000 lira to the pound. What's that all about? Half a mill to buy a fucking cup of tea?

Actually, since having the accident I've done more travelling than I ever did before. 'Cos I'm aware of how easily it could all end tomorrow if the police get a bit luckier next time, I'm cramming it all in now, so I've been to Spain twice, Tenerife again, Belfast, America, Holland, Lithuania, Poland. What was I doing in Lithuania? None of your business, but it helped with the Air Miles. I was booked to do a show in Denmark a while back, and that was a laugh. I was there to talk on glamorising crime and whether it should be allowed or not. What do you think I said? Anyway, I met loads of people in the same position as myself, all sort of outside the Establishment of their countries, and if I learned one thing from it, it was this: foreign police are still absolute cunts, just in another language. I'm booked for New Year's Eve to appear alongside Jeffrey Archer and Duran Duran in Barbados, and by the time you read this I will have taken part in the 2005 Gumball Rally, thanks to that blinding entrepreneur Maximillian Cooper who invited me and Andy Gardner to enter. We've got the awsome Ford F150 SVT (supercharged) Lightning pickup, we're gonna have all the chaps waving us off, and we'll be racing wheel to wheel through Europe with the likes of Daryl Hannah and loads of millionaires – all ending at the Monaco Grand Prix. It's a hard life.

Actually, 'cos I do a lot of international travelling, I've picked up a few handy phrases. I can say, 'Not Guilty' in eighteen different languages. Chinese ('Rot gruilty', French ('eet woz eem') and even Scouse ('Wot? Me? *Meerder?*'). That's got to be fucking useful, ain't it?

I did have a go at using one of them self-teaching records once. I turned it on and went to sleep to let it sink in; but the record got stuck. The next day I could stutter fluently in Spanish.

But a few of them words came in handy when I went over to Brazil for Ronnie Biggs's seventieth birthday a few years ago. Did you know Brazil is the most colour-blind country in the world? I don't even think they know what racism means. 'Cos it's such a big fucking place the people who live up the top bit are virtually white and the ones what live down south are totally black, but 'cos they're all from the same country they all get on. A little geography lesson there for you, all for the same price.

Anyway, I've already told you I don't do coke – the ice cubes get stuck up my nose. But a lot of the people I was over there with did, and a few of them still had a bit to use or lose by the time we got to Rio airport to come home. The toilet in the airport is tiny but it was still the best place to remove all offending items and get their rocks off. I just wanted a piss but the urinals were chocker, and they had queues outside all the cubicles – there was a lot of people who wouldn't need aeroplanes to fly home, I can tell you. I finally got inside a cubicle and as I was about to shut the door, this fella has shot in with me. So I'm standing there having a piss and he's getting rid of his coke in the best way possible, when suddenly there's this flash over our heads. A wanker photographer who was over there covering Ronnie's party had gone in the cubicle next to us, climbed on the toilet and taken a picture over the partition. I thought that was fucking cheeky considering we'd given him access all areas on everything else. So I said, 'Give us that bit of film' and he started laughing. I said it again and he said, 'Why?' Because, you toerag, you shouldn't have taken that picture. You know what it will look like. And he says he can't because of all the other pictures already on it. How does the song go? That's right, flash, bang – *wallop* – what a picture. I knocked him out in the middle of Rio de Janeiro airport. I took the film and left. Nothing ever happened to those pictures, funnily enough. He's got footage there that must be worth millions of pounds: me, Bruce Reynolds, Roy Shaw, Nick Reynolds, Ronnie Biggs, all the remaining members of the Great Train Robbery gang.

I've even done a bit of work in Mombasa. A couple of my mates went over to do a little deal with the chaps who run the casinos there and I went along as a bit of visual holiday insurance. I can't say I was particularly looking forward to anything kicking off, 'cos the businessmen in question happen to be proper American 'family' men, if you know what I mean. Even the hyenas stopped laughing when they was about. But good as gold to deal with. Total gentlemen, and a good advert for the American way of doing business which, I have to admit, has got me fucking thinking about my future.

It shouldn't be this way, but America is actually offering me a few more options at the moment than my own country.

All my life I have always known that America would be calling for me. I was in no doubt that I would end up there, maybe not living, but that is where my earning potential was going to be. Everything I've done and the associates I've made are all pointing that way. And I'm the sort of man who can meet people and put them on shelves in my head and come back for them later. Me having the accident and Jennifer leaving has made it all come in a little bit of a hurry. I now feel very vulnerable in this country, I'm a sitting duck here, so there's an urgency to me leaving. And what better place to go?

Out there, any one of the things I do over here would make me very, very rich. Starring in my own film over there, I'd make a fortune. Having a number-one bestseller over there I'd be a millionaire. I'm a journalist, I do stand-up, I do chat shows, make records, run a little porn company. The gangsta rap boys over there are pro Dave Courtney. They're striving for reality. I was married to a Jamaican for fourteen years, they know I'm real. I'll be doing some gangsta rap records with them because they want a bit of reality and I want to make some money. They know if I give them a reality check it ain't gonna bounce.

Right now in America is the time and place for Dave Courtney. They'd pay me to fart in a bottle if I could. I've only got to fit myself up a bit where I've had a couple of years of turning into a fucking tub of lard. (I called the local swimming pool the other day and said, 'Is that the local swimming pool?' This geezer said, 'It depends where you're calling from.' *Prick*. So I thought I'd go on the brandy diet instead. I've already lost three days. Then I called a gym and they said I had to come along in loose-fitting clothing. If I had any loose-fitting clothing I wouldn't need the gym, *cunt*.) I'll get fitter than a butcher's dog and go out there as a full action-packed type, full of knowledge, full of jokes, full of laughs, colour-friendly, an actor, singer-songwriter, author. I intend to fully prostitute myself – I'll go to the opening of a fridge if they ask me, 'cos it's the land of opportunities where they make peanut salesmen presidents – so help *me*, you bastards!

Over here, the authorities don't like me 'cos I glamorise crime. In America that's exactly why they love me. Look how they was all over me at Tony Lambrianou's funeral. I've had three bestsellers in England (fingers crossed you're holding number four). They ain't made me two bob over here. In America, one number one will make you $20 million.

America is much more up for someone like me to glamorise their past career. And I don't even feel it's my past I'm gonna be selling, 'cos I still feel I'm living a fucking story anyway. My books aren't really about the gangster things I've done in the past, they're about me now. Come round my house, it's like a film set. Spend two days with me and you'll meet enough people to keep you in stories for a month. So I'm more interested in Dave Courtney now than back then, but it's awkward 'cos it's your past that's made you famous, so to shed it is counter-productive. But America's cool with that.

For notoriety, for famousness, Americans tell me I'm the same over there as John Gotti was over here. Ask any English bloke for an American gangster and they go, 'Al Capone' first then probably 'John Gotti'. He's been dead for years, and in prison for God knows how many years before that, and there's a fucking lot more naughty gangsters than John Gotti. But he's the only one people in England know 'cos he's the one in all the papers. It's exactly the same with me. The Yanks go, 'We're sure there's naughtier gangsters in England than Dave Courtney, but you're the only one we fucking hear of over here 'cos you're all over everything.' I had a chat with a very powerful media man in Los Angeles and he put it this way. He said, 'So if John Gotti brought out a film in England with all his mates running round killing people, would you go and watch it?' I said, 'Yeah.' He said, 'But England's only this big on a map. America's *that* big. If Dave Courtney brought out a film with all his mates, we'd go and watch it. Even if on the first night, everyone walked out and went, "Nah, it's shit," we'd still make twenty million quid 'cos that's how many people went. You bring one record out in Texas and it sells more than all the number ones in the UK for the year. It's that big. You do the lot, Dave: you write books, you act, sing, do stand-up – any one of them makes you a million quid over here, and you do the lot. The full thing. What the *fuck* are you doing over there?'

All right, mate, go easy. But the upshot is, you're now looking at Mr America – Peckham style. If old octopus hands Arnie Schwarzenegger can become governor of California, you know they're gonna love a piece of Dave. Because I think about how I'm seen from abroad, my plan is to keep going over there then come back here and put in the bits I think I'm missing. Whether I deserve it or not, if they've given me the crown for 'Gangster No 1 for the Western World', then I'll try to live up to that. Not just wear the suits and drive the Roller and have the guns and the chaps, but actual walking, talking full-on 24/7 gangster Dave.

I'm taking this serious. I've actually got a CV! And I'm not talking about a silly little Citroën. I'm going to attack from all directions, I've got people in every single position to supply ammunition. I've got people in radio stations, in the music industry, in the gangsta community, the ex-pats, people who are at it in the press, whatever. I've got the Rancids, the porn-film industry in California, the black rappers in the hood, the punk rockers, the Outlaws, the Angels, the mainstream films, the Tarantinos an' that. If they let me get a foothold in that country, I'm off, like I would have been in England if it weren't for the 'Don't Let Dave Get On' campaign.

I went over there this year for the biggest 'Get a load of Dave' tour yet. I did New York for five days, Vegas for five days, Miami for five days and LA for five days. Talk about whirlwind visit. They had weather reports warning about Hurricane Dave blowing in. (What does your missus and a hurricane have in common? At the start they're both wet and wild, then they take off with your fucking house.)

The whole trip was earthy stuff. Of course, you've got to go and meet the high rollers in the city when you want to make a film, but it's the tick-in-the-box people, it's the people on the street, that will make or break you, so I actually had it with them everywhere I went. 'Cos if them people start running round singing your praises, then the cunts upstairs have to listen, 'cos they take notice of the masses. So I weren't just over there for the important meetings and the 'I'll try to find a window for you, Mr Courtney'. I actually done the grass-roots bit and got them on a little buzz as well.

To be honest, I must be doing something right 'cos I was very surprised and flattered by how up on Dave Courtney the American public were. Hardly anyone asked if I was Kojak. They knew what I looked like and most people I met had a favourite little Dave story they wanted to tell me. I think Sky TV have helped me out immensely with the showing of the *Car Sharks* and *Costa Del Dosh* and all them Bravo programmes.

Everything in America's fucking massive, though, ain't it? I've seen arses in California that are so big they had their own postcode. I saw a sign on the highway that said 'Rest Area 25 Miles' – they must have a lot of tired people. And I read this little statistic: eighty per cent of married men cheat on their wives in America – the rest wait till they're in Europe.

But you get all sorts of characters over there, don't you?

This big-shot California lawyer went duck hunting in rural Texas. And I mean rural. We're talking *Deliverance* here. He shot a quacker, but it fell into a farmer's field so, as the lawyer climbed over the fence, this elderly geezer drove up on his tractor and said, 'Get off my land or I'll put a bullet in you.'

The lawyer goes, 'If you don't let me get that duck, I'll sue you and take everything you own.'

The old boy smiled and said, 'In these parts we settle small disagreements like this with the Texas Three-Kick-Rule.'

The lawyer goes, 'What is the Texas Three-Kick-Rule?'

'Well, first I kick you three times and then you kick me three times, and so on, back and forth, until someone gives up.'

The lawyer takes a look at this bony old cunt and thinks, I can have him, so he agrees. The old farmer climbs down from his tractor, walks over to the lawyer and plants one of his heavy work boots right in the geezer's goolies. The lawyer falls to his knees and gets another kick that takes out half his teeth and he falls to the floor. The third one smacks him in the kidneys and he's nearly passing out. But he wants that duck and he's not gonna let some Beverly Hillbilly beat him. 'OK, you old bastard, now it's my turn.'

The farmer just smiles and goes, 'No, I give up. You can have the duck!'

You've got to be aware of little local customs like that when you go abroad and I'm lucky enough to get looked after in New York by the number-one Family there, which is a proper privilege. I'm a sort of British envoy when I go out with them, they show me off out there and I let them know what's going on in England. I used to be called the Yellow Pages of Crime – now I'm the International fucking Directory Enquiries. Just dial 0800-HELP-ME-DAVE and have your credit card number ready.

It's funny how I got in with them, really – I would never compare myself with them on gangster terms, but I've been able to help them out in the UK in lots of different ways over the years. There's been lots of times when I've been asked to chaperone and look after some young people who've come over from America, and they've been connected to the Family in some way. The people who've been showing them round in the day are too old to go to the nightclubs and all that, so they've gone, 'Dave, can you look after this lot?' I don't actually know who these kids' dads and uncles are, I'm just having a good time anyway with them in and out of the clubs, taking them in the Rolls-Royce, giving them both barrels of a good time. The last bunch didn't even want to go back to the hotel so they stayed in the house. So by the time they go back and talk to their dad, Dave Courtney's the only thing that's happening in the UK in their eyes. 'He lives in a fucking castle, man! He has guns on the wall, the white Rolls-Royce . . .'

So, when I go out there now, I'm picked up at the airport and welcomed with open arms by the elders themselves. It was fucking wicked this time. I was there with Brendan, Dane, Dave Archibald (him of the shark suit) and Dave from the Blind Beggar, and we was proper looked after. They took us round loads of different restaurants, I got through my own body weight in fucking meatballs and ravioli, looked at loads of old photographs of people I never knew and got kissed a lot by smart-suited blokes. Fucking respect to them for that.

I weren't there long enough to do everything they had planned for me, and one night I said I had to go and see Jay-Z at his club called 40–40 in downtown Manhattan. These revered old Italian gangsters said, 'We're-a bit-a too old-a to take-a you down-a there, but we'll-a give-a you a lift,' so they pulled out the biggest limo on the planet, bulletproof with all the black windows an' that, and off we went. Talk about a chauffeur who can handle himself. If Tom Cruise had tried to hijack this cab in *Collateral* it would have been a much shorter film.

I'm a believer in say what you see – the old *Catchphrase* saying, you know? – and when we've pulled up, all thirty feet of the fucking car, at the 40–40, what everyone in the place has seen is Dave Courtney piling up to the club with the Gambinos as his fucking taxi, him walk up to the door and go, 'I'd like to speak to Jay-Z if he's in.' If you've never seen four hundred people tighten their sphincter at the same time, that's the way to do it. They don't actually know if I'm on good or bad terms with Jay-Z, 'cos at one stage he thought that highly of me that he put a photo of me and my crew on the cover of his album, with his body superimposed over mine. (Remember that? It was when I guest-starred at the Oxford Union, when I had to speak to the next generation of police chiefs, Freemasons and general posh cunts who'll eventually try to bring me down. That was fucking dreamy. A former criminal teaching the future parliamentarians how to behave.) But after that it went a bit Pete Tong and lawyers got involved and Jay-Z gave us an out-of-court settlement for pirated use of a copyrighted image. That weren't anything to do with me, and I'm over there to sing the guy's praises, but the people at the club don't know that. So the doormen have gone to him, 'Fucking hell, mate, Dave Courtney's just been dropped off by the fucking Firm.' But that was cool, we had a mind-blowing night, me, my gang and a thousand gangsta cunts.

Another mind-bending night we had was 17 March. Check your calendars, that's St Patrick's Day, and no offence to anyone in Dublin, but you will never see a bigger collection of drunken Paddies than in New York on that day. Forget Christmas, Thanksgiving, all that religious crap, this is the biggest day they celebrate. Everywhere you look there's green hats, tits out, Guinness and Baileys on sale everywhere, it's fucking huge. Most of the police seem to be Irish so even they were in a good mood. Not that it helped me ...

We'd been out the night before till five in the morning, and when we got back to the hotel they was setting up the actual carnival, putting all the barricades up in the streets an' that. Brendan, being the staunch Charlton-supporting, South London-talking Irishman, wanted to carry on with it. So we went upstairs, changed clothes, had a cup of coffee and went back out on it for another day's solid partying. So we never really had a chance to get better and eat, sleep, we just went back at it all day, so by the evening I was really, really pissed. And by four o'clock that morning, when we'd ended up in a fantastic strip bar in downtown Queens, I was embarrassingly pissed. I knew it was time for bed when I turned round to my mate and went, 'Fnn nnen nnen nennen nen.' Brendan's sitting there with his hand down some bird's knickers, sticking a score in every ten minutes, and I've decided to walk home.

Outside the fresh air's hit me and I've got the name of the hotel in my head so I stepped out into the road. But like a wanker I've looked the wrong way and this car's come up and screeched to a halt and gone, '*BEEEEEEEEEP*!' Normally I would have gone, 'Sorry, my fault,' but I didn't get a chance this time 'cos he's gone, *vooom*, and moved forward another foot till he's virtually touching me. And this weren't no Mini Metro, this was one of them giant pick-ups they all have. So I've gone, '*What*?' and banged my hands down on the bonnet, and all these doors have flung open and all these geezers with their hats on back to front leaped out going, 'What da fuck is yo problem?' And I'm like, 'Uh oh.' It's no good me giving them a flyer and telling them I'm a celebrity gangster, do you know what I mean? They just saw a fifty-year-old fat bald-headed cunt who's just been a bit cheeky so they decided to give me a little slap. Welcome to America, *prick*. (Of course, the way I'll describe it in the future'll be 'I went to downtown Queens and gave it to the homies.') So when I've really hurt their hands enough with my chin, I thought, I'll lie down here in the gutter for a while and pretend nothing's happening. I thought, I'll just sit here quietly biting the ends of their trainers. They knew they was in a fight, mate.

That little bit of excitement aside, I'll tell you what really amazed me about being in Manhattan. After five years of being snubbed by the UK press, how shocked was I to see I was in the *New York Post* gossip columns *three days running*. I only had to buy a bagel and it's 'Top London gangster Dave Courtney's firm take sugar with their tea'. Proper wank material that was. They covered every move I made, all the bands I saw, how I went to visit Niagara the nightclub, 'cos a friend of mine there is a tattooist, the trip to Jay-Z's, the rather exclusive chauffeur service I had. I kept waiting for the kick in the teeth at the end of the articles like they would in England, but it was straight up, proper reporting. They even said about my meeting with Virgin over there. I owe you, guys. (When I got back home, I found out that in the same week I was in the *New York Post*, *Max* magazine in France, *Empire* in the UK and *Asiania*, this Pakistani magazine. It is actually working for me around the world now. Fucking be afraid!)

Because if I like something or someone I do my utmost to support them and promote them in everything I do, I have a lot of people who want to give me something back. So every town I went to in the States, Harley Davidson gave me a bike just to cruise around on while I was there. This was all set up through Bob down at Dock Gate 20 in Southampton.

I'm a big Harley Davidson fan, they're in all my films, I mention them in my books, I wear their clothes. I drove one every day with no accidents, although I might have caused a few. The funny thing about America is they've got sixty million television channels and fuck all to watch. But I did see a couple of programmes on how they catch villains, and if you think we've got sneaky traffic laws over here with them hiding speed cameras behind bushes and that, listen to this. In some States out there, you have to have a helmet, and in others you don't. So you can start off somewhere where you don't but before you get to the end of the road, 'cos it's so fucking long, you do, and the police just wait there to nick you as you come through. The other thing is, some States use miles per hour and some use kilometres. Don't fucking ask me why. But the signs don't say that, they just say a number. So you could be doing 60mph and get past this bush which is actually the State line, and that's where the coppers are waiting to catch you because that's where it drops to 60kph. Fucking naughty or what?

A friend of mine got done for speeding while we was out there. He saw this cop car behind him, disco lights flashing, and while he's trying to outrun it he's had time to think of an excuse. Like I say, think on your feet and you'll go far. And fast. Anyway, they pull over and the copper walks up and says, 'Listen, fella, I've had a really lousy day, I'm just about to knock off, give me a good excuse to let you off.'

And my mate goes, 'Listen, officer. Three weeks ago my missus ran off with a policeman. When I saw your car in my mirror, I thought it was him trying to give her back!'

Having a Harley was proper useful when it came to meeting up with my old mates the Outlaws. I had one night out with them that was wine, women and song times 8,000. There was fucking hundreds of them. They live by that, 24/7. They don't have fucking Territorial Army part-timers, solicitors by day, dirty, greasy biker scum by night. None of that. They all live the part of being an Outlaw and I've helped them into the criminal world through things like Tony Lambrianou's funeral. It's a very touchy subject, actually, 'cos the hatred between the Angels and Outlaws rivals the black/white thing and the Catholic/Protestant thing over here. There's actually a war going on between them. They're killing each other, actually shooting each other and setting up booby traps. In all wars the most dangerous person is a spy, so they have to be careful that anyone they let into their inner circle ain't a sympathiser for the other side. And that's why it's difficult for me 'cos, like I am everywhere, I'm mates with everyone, the Outlaws and the Angels included. Like I say, people might not like each other, but they all get on with Dave.

One day I went to visit Orange County where they do the chopper bikes and that is an absolute fucking dream of a place. It inspired my friend Matt from Folkestone to have one of them Harley superbikes built. Because I'm a very good friend of Simon Ward from Spearmint Rhino, they're actually going to have a Spearmint Rhino bike made in Orange County. I'll be doing a documentary on that when it comes off.

I don't want to go on about how hard my life is, but I'm afraid I had to do a small documentary on all the Spearmint Rhinos when I was out there this time round. I had to spend time in the branches in LA, Vegas, NYC and Miami. It was absolute hell. The class of actual woman in front of you puts Spearmint Rhino ahead of any other operation in the world – trust me, I've done my research. They all look like they've sauntered down from the cover of *Vogue*. And that's not just the dancers. The clip girls, the women selling the fags, you'd fucking remortgage your house for any of them. I met a rapper called Won G on the plane, a little Filipino, who looks like a Jamaican Hawaiian. We got talking and so he comes to Spearmint Rhino with us and it was mental. The things some people will do for a camera never ceases to ... benefit me. *Stop it!* I walked out of each one of those clubs thinking I was Brad Pitt. I genuinely believed it until I got home and looked in my own mirror. Forget the twenty dollars down their knickers, all the girls in there wanted to dance with us just to say they had. All I can say is, thank fuck for Viagra.

LA was another important one for me. New York's a bit like London when you get down to it, but LA ain't like nowhere on Earth. One night we went to this party on the roof of one of the skyscrapers out there. It was an open-air party with hanging baskets, chairs, fucking ice sculptures, the full nine yards. And because I was there, they actually showed old gangster movies by projecting the film on to the hotel opposite. You're eighty floors up watching *Reservoir Dogs* with Mr Pink an' that, having a dance and a drink like you're in Madame Jo-Jo's. It's fucking mental.

New York was more about checking in with my personal contacts, but LA was all about film business. I had meetings with several people from 20th Century Fox, my old mate Chris Penn, agents, promoters, record producers, publicists. It was really just laying the land and meeting the right people, so when I went to Vegas to meet the main player Billy Clark (you'll meet him in a minute), I already had some people for him who knew what we was doing. Thanks to that little stay in the City of Angels, by the time this book comes out, we'll be well on the Dave Courtney US promotion trail over there, with T-shirts and posters directing everyone to the best places to buy my stuff.

Apart from that, LA was a bit of a fuck-up 'cos they got the hotel rooms wrong. We all ended up having to kip in one room on the first night 'cos everywhere was all full up. On the plus side it was a nice bonding period for everyone, the fighting for the settee, the standing up showering with your mate in the bath. Although I did hear that one of my mates was woken by the bloke next to him with a huge erection in his hand. He says, 'I'm not wasting this, I'm going downstairs to find a brass.'

The mate goes, 'Do you want me to come with you?'

The other one says, 'Why would I want you to come with me?'

''Cos that's my cock you're holding, you *prick*.'

It was only staying in LA that I realised what thieving cunts hotels are with that minibar. If you're gonna rob someone, at least have the decency to stick a balaclava on your head and let them know you're doing it. Don't wait till a geezer's about to check out of his room and hit him with a bill that costs more for a few peanuts than a week in the honeymoon suite. What is that about? Seven quid for a bottle of water. A fucking Toblerone – three quid. What's it made of, Princess Diana's minge?

Vegas was no different, but what another great place for me. The world capital of gambling at your doorstep. (Speaking of gambling, what has little balls and screws old ladies? A bingo machine.) After doing all the groundwork I finally got to meet Billy Clark, who is Mr Fix It when it comes to getting things done out there. He's got offices in NY, Vegas, LA and, soon, Peckham. He's got producers, directors, actors, cowboys, plumbers, you name it, on his books. He was showing off 'cos that Vin Diesel is one of his – so I said I was now gonna be called Red Diesel. A bit smoky and a bit slower but I get there in the end. (Speaking of pikey petrol, did you hear about the gypsy who won the lottery? They paid him in traveller's cheques.)

There was hundreds of fucking good nights out. One night Billy took us to the Stratosphere hotel. The clue is in the name. I don't give a fuck who you are, if you go up a hundred-odd-storey building and on the roof of that there's a funfair, and on the very, very top of that there's a reverse bungee jump which fires you up into the air, it's not natural to run to the front of the queue going, 'Me first, me first', is it? If you imagine, you're strapped down looking at the concrete floor so you can only see the roof of the hotel. But as it fires you up, that's when you see you're eight miles above the desert. With two feet on the ground you might be the scariest fuck alive, but pinged backwards into space on a giant yo-yo you can't help going, 'Ah aha hah!' 'cos it's fucking scary. And no, I didn't have another fucking go.

But things went very well in Vegas, Billy put me in touch with loads of pro-Dave people and he's now arranging for me to do my shows out there. This is the town with hotels that look like pyramids, 24-hour strip bars and fucking Elvis doing the weddings. I live in a castle with eight-foot toy soldiers standing guard – do you think I'm gonna fit in? *Shut the fuck up!*

While I was out there I met Timmy and Heidi who used to own the Aquarium but went out there to buy a hotel. Obviously I ran into my old mate from Rancid Lars Fredrikson as well, and Garry Bushell's mate Andre, another punk geezer from the Men In Black and Ricky Harden, and we went to loads of gigs. But where music was concerned, Miami was the fucking sound machine for me.

Miami's like walking on to a fucking film set. Ocean Drive is just beautiful people, everyone size 6–8, perfect tits, every other car's a Ferrari, all the geezers look like fucking Arnold Schwarzenegger – so I blended right in!

And as the typical Brit abroad, by the time I got to Miami, word had already got round that I was in the country and I had a VIP invite to the Miami Music Festival. It's the biggest party in the world, it's two million people getting off their heads to the music. A load of my old music mates were there, Goldie, Paul Oakenfold, Slip Mat, Fabio and Grooverider and Bailey, and they're gonna help me out in remixing my tunes. So workwise, it was proper successful.

It nearly went a bit Susi Wong, though, thanks to someone who shall remain nameless (for now). I was sitting in the Pelican bar with Goldie, Dave, a few other people and this geezer I'd rather not mention. Goldie's really in with the hotel owner, so the drinks were flowing and I gave them some signed books and posters. After a while, Goldie went to his room and a bit after that I left as well. It ends up with just a few of them there and eventually it's just this one geezer. So what does he do? He fucks off without paying the bar bill. It was only 180 quid for a few drinks, so I don't know what his problem was, but 'cos Goldie had made a big thing of introducing me to the owners, all they know is 'Dave Courtney ran off without settling up'. As soon as I found out I went back there and paid the bill and gave them a hundred quid on top for the embarrassment. Worst of all I'd embarrassed Goldie, which I'd like to publicly apologise to him for. Sorry, mate.

Another downer on the trip was that one of my gang was missing. Storm was meant to be coming but I'm afraid her father died so she had to go to Africa for the five-day funeral instead. She was sorely missed on a personal level but also 'cos she's so good at helping me sell Dave Courtney. Even though I had a fucking whale of a time over there, selling myself is what I was meant to be doing. It's actually very hard to be walking around handing out pictures of yourself – I fucking hate giving away a picture of me, don't I! It's much nicer to have pretty birds running around giving out the leaflets and the flyers for you, which Jen did for me so well in Cannes, and Storm normally does when I do shows in the UK. But by not bringing her, I realised how important it is that she goes everywhere with me next time. She's the first name on the list from now on, but you have to get it wrong to know how to fix it.

Bless her, though, even 10,000 miles away she was still sorting out my mess. She's phoned me all the way from Africa and this cab driver's answered. Turns out Dave has only left his phone in the taxi, ain't he? *Prick*. So she's tried to frighten him into returning the mobile, and he's driven back to the hotel and wouldn't leave till he got forty dollars for it, like a fare. Luckily, just at that time Brendan turned up so I called him over and he had to cough up the readies. He weren't best pleased 'cos he'd bought me the phone in the first place and said, 'It's a fucking tri-band handset, you can use it anywhere in the world. Don't fucking lose it.' So a day after he'd got it for me, he's paying to have it returned. At least it didn't end up at the bottom of the Norfolk Broads like the last one.

To be honest, I'm surprised Storm managed to understand what the cabby was saying, 'cos in Miami they're all Colombians, Cubans and Hispanics. It's actually fucking hard to find an American. Everyone's an Al Pacino and there are actually specialist *Scarface* clothes, shops and bars. Even the supermarkets sell Al Pacino coffee and Al Pacino cornflakes. It's a beautiful, beautiful place. I went to see the room where Scarface did his famous chainsaw scene and came home with a suitcase full of *Scarface* clobber. Proper tasty it is, too.

So it's mission accomplished with America. That's the first of many trips I intend to make in the next eighteen months before I go there and live. They might not let Mark Thatcher in, but they'll let Dave. If you give someone the opportunity to say no to something, normally they will. For example, 'Can I have a visa to go over there?' 'No.' But if you're the guest of someone already working in America, then they handle all that. So if Letterman wants you on his show, they get the visa for you to come over. Perfectly legit. It's sort of made a gift, so you don't have to ask for one. If Leslie Grantham wanted to go over there and be in a film they'd say, 'Come.' They wouldn't say, 'No, you've been in prison for shooting someone.' They can if they want to be nasty and spiteful and they always have that on the shelf. But I imagine the authorities over here are more worried about me leaving than the Americans are about me arriving, 'cos they don't want me to spread the word about how naughty the British upper echelons really are. That's their biggest fear. As for stopping me, I think they find it a bit hard to justify now considering I've been there so many times, and the *New York Post* made a poignant point by saying that 'Mr Courtney comes here a lot as he is allowed to'.

I've sold all the rights to *Hell to Pay* in all territories apart from America, North and South, and I intend to do that one myself because I've already laid the plans for it to be brought out. I'm hoping it will go on to the big screens over there. The financial rewards for getting a film out over there are so vast and I've got such a captive market at the moment it could earn me a couple of mill. I don't need that much to go out there and live, so even if it's only half the success I think it will be, thank you very much.

While I'm actually saying to America, 'Find out what Dave Courtney is,' I'm also realising that, where the accident took them six months off me, it also gave me something – a lot of projects in one go. And 'cos I'm a watcher of these things, I now know it's not how many times you can get in the paper, it's how short a time you can do it in. So in the next six months, any one of my forthcoming projects could do it for me and they'll all be big news over there. I have my own feature film coming out, I have my own documentary, I have this book and I have another one called *Heroes and Villains*, and all of them will be happening at once and I'll be getting press for them all. From a lot of people not knowing Dave Courtney, now they'll all be logging on to the internet and I'll be getting more hits than Mike Tyson's sparring partner. And his missus. There will definitely be something there for them to look at.

Before I go, let me tell you about *Heroes and Villains*. It's one of the best books I've wrote and there's going to be an awful lot of press in America about it 'cos it's about these great American icons and legendary British gangsters. I was asked to write a book in my own words about other people, all my heroes and villains funnily enough, but I can't fucking have that, can I? That's hard for me. I want to talk about me, so I've added a lot of Dave Courtney. It's fucking wicked, I promise you.

But I'm just waiting to see which one goes up first. Whether it's my records, my film, my books, my chat shows, my stand-up, my singing, my dancing, my fucking balloon-bending, midget-juggling, whatever ... Whether it's my connections with the punk scene or the bikers or the gangsters, whatever one starts paying me first to go over there and live while I'm setting the rest up, that's the one I'm gonna concentrate on.

And the thing is, if I've learned one thing about life in the last few years, it's this: find out what you're naturally good at, then find a way to do that as a job, 'cos you'll never have a bad day at it. I know lorry drivers who are the best artists you've ever seen in your life, and they're

EPILOGUE: THE FALLEN ANGEL

Swans, swabs and Stormylicious

When I was active, I'm proud to say, I was one of the best fucking debt collectors in the world. Well, most of the time I was, anyway. There was one occasion when I crept round the back of this row of houses, chucked this garden furniture through the patio doors and went, 'Grrrr!' to the geezer sitting there in his underwear. I chased the bloke through his house, grabbed him by the neck, told him what's what and he's started stuttering, '37b, 37b – you want *next door*.'

Shit.

I'm like, 'Well, here's a tenner for your hinges – do me a favour, tell your neighbour how scary it was, right?'

The moral of that story, apart from the fact that houses should have numbers on their back gates as well as the front doors, is that one man's hero is another's villain. As a debt collector, if I get your million pound back for you, I'm a god. But if you're the geezer I've had up against the wall to get it from, you probably want to shoot me.

And this is what this young bloke came up and started telling me at one of Mick Colby's legendary parties a few years ago. I thought, Mate, are you sure you've come in the right door? You *do* realise whose house you're in, don't you? It's like a fucking blue movie set in here; St Porn's not St Paul's.

But when I've given the geezer a chance to get a word out, it turns out he's an artist and he would like to paint my portrait. His name's Pierre Anstis, and he's actually a religious-artefact restorer by trade, and his job takes him to museums, galleries, churches an' that – fuck knows how he got into that party. But his real talent is doing these amazing artworks (look on his website www.pierre-anstis.com). Anyway, he said to me, 'I paint iconically and I want to paint you.' I didn't want to sound like a div so I said, 'Great.' I thought it was a car. Iconic 500, R-reg, blue.

He said, 'I see you how I think loads of people see you: you're a god to some, and a devil to others.' He's spot on with that one. So he's painted me as a man in a full gangster suit, with a halo, angel's wings and wearing a knuckleduster. He called it *The Fallen Angel* and it's an absolutely wicked picture. The man is a proper genius.

The way Pierre works is to take loads of photographs of his subject to get it as realistic and 3D as possible when he paints in his studio. So he started to come round the house all the time to take all these pictures, and obviously I've hated all that – *shut up!* And during that process he's actually become a very good friend of mine. A proper inner-circle, duster-carrying friend of mine. When I was in the hospital after the crash, him and his lovely missus were fully clued up on the threat to my life and, if there weren't anyone else around, that couple would just hide under my bed and sleep there till the next shift came. And I'll never forget them for that. But Pierre's not a gangster; he just makes an awful lot of money doing these amazing pictures for people I introduce him to.

Anyway, if you paint a bowl of apples you have to have it in front of you or at least a bunch of pictures of it, don't you? So one day, Pierre came round and said, 'I can paint you, Dave, 'cos I've got eight hundred photos of you. But I haven't got any wings.'

Ah.

There was only one thing for it. I had to go out and get a swan and kill it – actually I didn't kill it. I just cut its wings off, put two plasters on it and pushed it back on to the Thames. Just kidding, your Majesty. Actually, trying to kill it was a fucking joke. It was harder than most of the geezers who work for me. I twisted its neck, then I did it again, then again, and again and the cunting thing still wouldn't break. It went round about five times then I let go and it just unravelled at a million mile an hour. And then it fucking attacked me.

For any of Pierre's pictures you're looking at paying about ten grand, minimum. But he's really gone to town on mine, it's worth more like twenty-five. He's made it out of this stuff called Jesso and where the gold knuckleduster is he's actually added real diamonds, and stuck one in my ear for good measure. All the buttons on my suit are Versace, which just knocks me out, and the bracelet's real gold.

When he'd finished it, we took it round to all the different denomination churches and most of them, like the CofE and the Catholics, didn't fancy it hanging in their place. The ones who really wanted it was the Muslims. They thought it was buff. Whereas the bearded geezers down at the synagogue just wanted to know if the diamonds were real. Hmm . . .

Believe it or not, the real jewellery in the painting is not the most incredible thing about it. Pierre said to me, 'Because they won't glamorise you now, we can't reproduce that painting. But after you're dead, it will be worth loads more and copies of that will sell for millions.'

As soon as we've heard these 'after you're dead' words, Storm's seeing pound notes in front of her eyes, isn't she. I've already told her where the money is in case anything happens to me – under the settee. There's eight pence up one end and a quid up the other. But now she knows that that painting is going to be her pension when I've gone. And too fucking right, as well. This is the beautiful lady who actually allowed me to run off with a young girl and she made dinner for all her kids and washed the toys – mine and theirs. This is the lady I've actually had drive down the garage at three o'clock in the morning to buy batteries for the dildo, pass them to me and my bird, then go back to bed. You can't *get* better than that. All dressing-gowned up, she goes out so I can fuck another bird and gets me batteries – and crisps. Luv ya, Storm.

So bearing in mind that they're gonna reproduce this image when I'm gone, what Pierre did to make sure *The Fallen Angel* stayed unique was this: he cut me and put my blood in the paint. Are you with me? He actually added me to the mix for all the flesh. The amount of paint you use for the skin is tinier than you think, and it's all got Dave Courtney DNA in it. I wank over knowing that. How could you not?

The only problem with that is Storm. She reckons, when we weren't looking, she wiped her fanny-battered knickers in the paint as well. That's gonna proper screw up the DNA testers in a few years' time, ain't it? When they finally take a sample swab after I'm dead they'll go, 'Fuck me, it's what we always suspected: Dave Courtney *was* a cunt!'

APPENDIX
THE WIT AND WISDOM OF THE LONDON METROPOLITAN POLICE

And that's it!

A FEW THANK YOUS
F**k *The Ride* and *Hell To Pay* wouldn't have happened without a lot of people.

THE HELL TO PAY CREW

The film is dedicated to the Great Train Robber Ronnie Biggs; Executive Producer Eamonn O'Keefe; Director Roberto Gomez; Producer Austin Vernon; Co Producers Malcolm Martin and Dave Courtney; Film Editor Brian Hovmand; Music Clearance Nicola Fletcher; Distribution Consultant Kevin Crace; Camera/Steadicam Austin Vernon; 2nd Unit Camera Will Chown, Oliver Manzi, 'Andreas'; Special Effects Shoot–for–the–Stars Ltd; Pyrotechnics Alistair Macfarlane, Ross Perkin RM (Ret'd); Armourer Phil Anderson, SFX Gunshots, Ross Anderson; SFX Make–up Micky Goldtooth, Robbie Drake; Re–recording Mixer Julian MacDonald; ADR & Sound Editor Sam Matthews; Lounge Audiopost Consultant Kerrie MacDonald; Smoke On–Line/Colourist Ben Beaumont; Opening Titles Design Anne Foged; Aston Designer Roberto Gomez; CGI Designer Conan McStay; Post–Production Supervisor (NTL) Dominic Selby; Product Manager (NTL) Drew Hosie; Media Centre Manager (NTL) Rhiann McAllister; Engineer Support (NTL); Barnaby Kirk, Babs Gadenne, Andy Biggs; Film Editor's Assistant Rami Bartholdy; Post–Production Manager Satu Ellard; Post–production Advisors Steve Bosnich, David Brady; Audio Consultants Dave Smithers, Darko Mocilnikar; Stills Photographer John Santa Cruz; Location Fixer (Pompey) Kevin Courtney; Production Auditor Andy Bedford; Props Frances Williams @ TFCAS; Runners Dave Courtney, Constantine Georgiou; Best Boy Darren Knight; Stuntman Danilo Gomez–Cravitz; Stunt Co–ordinators Anthony Brown, Jeremy Bailey; Stunt Assistants Malcolm Martin, Brendan Carr.

A Very Special Thanks to Lars, Tim, Matt and Brett – the Rancid boys.

THE HELL TO PAY CAST

John Altman, Angela Bassett, 'Nasty' Nick Bateman, Matt Bearman, Andy Beckwith, Leah Bedford, Jim Benson, Michael Biggs, Sir Charlie Breaker, 'Cowboy' Brian, Gillian Brewer, Kelly Burgess, Garry Bushell, Sue Carpenter, Albert Chapman, Choo & JC Mac, 'Kelly', Peter Conway, Chantel Cummins, Julius Francis, Ian 'The Machine' Freeman, Peter Friel, Owen Gardener, Ian Golding, Jo Guest, Jez, Gary Hailes, Martin Hancock, Paul Haines, Steve Holdsworth, Helen Keating, Jamie Kent, Jimmy 'The Gent' Kent, Dave Laine, Tony Lambrianou, Dave Legeno, Francine Lewis, Steve Lowe, Tony Maile, Mark and Kevin, Malcolm Martin, Roxanne Martin, Johnny McGee, Brendan McGirr, Mark Morrison, Billy Murray, Kelly Noyes, Tony Oakey, Eamonn O'Keefe, Jamie O'Keefe, Lucy O'Keefe, Cass Pennant, Mickey Pugh, Joey Pyle, Joey Pyle Jr, John Pyle, 'Bald' Rob, Marcus Redwood, Nick Reynolds, Adam Saint, Steve Sadler, Scorpion, 'Scouse', Roy 'Pretty Boy' Shaw, Lou Szulc, Tarkan, Terry Turbo, Scott Welch, Steve Whale, Wolfie, Seymour Young.

THE HOODS

Wish, Gary Love, Rickie O'Keefe, Mark Ives, Trevor Mailey, Warren Attitude, Panay Ioutou, Keith Winn, Alex Reed, Bez, Panos Sotirou, Boxer Lester, Adrian 1 & 2, Big Lloyd, Gary Collins, Micky Roth, Colin, Syringes Tony, Rob Sylvester, Mark Hall, Adrian Doughty, Jamie MacDonald, Vic Bishop, Big John x 5, Big Frank x 5, Ken Alexanders, Rich Luff, John Corbet, Andy Gardner, Rob Scott, Adi Woods, Matt Tobin, Le Grande Danoir, Nice Guy Eddie, Alfie Fitness, Mark Lodge, Andre the Wrestler, Dean Coldwell, Tony Maloney, Jack Holman, Martin Lovelock, Andy The Mill, Rob Oakes, Simon Oakes, Jaz, Ricky English, The Six Bend Trap Crew, Jackson Kennedy, Peter Watson, Faz, Frankie Baby, Bernie Davies, Chops, Patrick Courtney, Folkestone Matt, Joey Moore, Big Barry x 3, Pete Henshaw, Andrew Brown, Paul Hughes, Zombie, Christian Kiwi, Big Geoff, Andy Kiwi, Wayne Pursell, Dave Drum, Steve Raith, Damian 1 and 2, Sheffield Ben, Boo, Reece Huxford, Antoni O'Shea, Tank, Danny, Dave Thurston, Musher, Baz, Dukie, Danny Dolittle, Mark Peters, Rubber Ron, Stormin' Norman, Suda, Bob Tanner, Big Ern, Danny Cheltenham, Tim Tivey, Julian White, Paddy, Sheffield Daz, Nick Moorcroft, The RSM, Big Lee, Fat Lawrence, Manny Clark, Neil Wolf and the Tally Ho Crew, Ebo, Bexley Don, Bexley Al, Jay, Costas, Handsome John, Mark Piano, Colin Dunne, Lance Clark, Jaws, The Old Twins, Bismarck, Winkle, Pard, Dave Hurst, Big Dave x 3, Posh John, Chino, Del, Paul and Aaron Stone, Elliot Clark, Neil O'Brien, Fred Batt, Clive McGee, Stretch, Tonbridge Richard, Jamie Taylor, John Farnell, John Boy, Scotty, Geoff Vines, Gary Vines, Paul Haynes, Rico, Lennie Lucas, Fetish Alan, Sam Sharma, Big Mark x 5, Jamie Taylor, Dallas, Ray Steele, Mark Ives, Elpae Georgiou, Brooklyn John, Junior, Handsome Rod, Colin x 4, Kenny Panda, Roy Schnell, Lox, Micky Goldsmith, Juror, Steve, Ken Alexanders, H, Simon Rayner, John Corbett, Chris Hammer, Boogie, Rick Hards, Bruzzie, Shovels, Mad Brian Dival, Dingus McGee, Scully, Fat Lawrence, Woody, Jason Willis, Birmingham John, Big Wayne, Francisco, Fly, Boris, John Tom, Kevin O'Dowd, Rob Andrews, USA Johnny, Louie, Jimmy Cook, Mark McCArthy (Six Bend Trap), John Armour, Jamie Scunthorpe, Mark Fish – Mr Scunthorpe, Sooty and Weep, Big Pete from Pasha, The Animal, Joey Stretch, Pilchard, Linford, James Cohen, Leo, Lee Cross, Perry Benson, Reading Les, Grub Smith, Craig, Birmingham Keith, Lambross, Darren Hearn, Mr T, Mickey Jackson, Steve Foster, Rob from Milton Keynes, Big Ron, Rooster Ian, Mohammed, Mario, Gary Baron, Timmy Abet, Bernie Lee, Paul Scarface, Mick Chapman, Tim Newton, Kiwi and Terry Mallett, Carl Beatty, Busbie, Noel Moyston, Outcast Phil, Rob Hanson, Warrior, Colin Robertson, Byrd Byron, Lee Philips, Bruno Draper, Bradley from the Studio, Boyzie @ Ministry, Black Dave, Dax, James Weatherer, Phil Organ, Terry Currie, Irish Dave McConnell, Tony Simpson, Trevor Tanner, Keith Walker, Lee Murray the Main Man, Roberto Lozano, Gavin the Gatemaker – my Randall to his Hopkirk, Matt Ridley, Peter Fen, Lawrence and the Redz, Ayatollah Massive, Scots Rory, Harry Marsden, Rino, Big Chewy, John Edwards, Cecil @ China Whites, Stilks, Sting, Stuart from Fulham, Roy and the Dirt Track

Boys, Tel Boy, Tally from Tenerife, Eddie from Fulham, Tim @ UB40, Wolves Paul, Fisher Boxing Club, Tony Macmahon, Steve Hooper, Vince from Birmingham, Jay, Big Keg, Big Dennis, Big Don, No Neck Nick, Zac, Zeus, Zig, Chey, Big Ray, Chris Collins, Mark Epstein, Gart Abnet, Ray Bridges, Johnny Jacket, Christian, Dave Legane, Warwick, Lou, Adam, Wilf Pine, Ray Shaw, Mickey Briggs, Amon, Ash, Mick Colby, Charles Bronson, Mad Pete, The Olefontes, Cas Pennant, Carlton Leach, Marc and Tark, Tony, Big Rob, Lee Smith, Frank, Gary, Gavin, Kevin, Blakey, Ben, Shaun, Dave Quelch, Kevin and Steve, James A, Wally, Rocky, Ricky, Ronnie, Mark Bates, Warren, Andy Finlater, Steve 'Tardis' George, Al Benson, Don Crosbie, Eric, Robbie, John, Lloyd, Colin Robinson, Robert Hanson, Russell Carter, Colin Little, 'Agent NO.10', Kevin Jenkins, Dean, Tom Heckman, Vince, Santos, Steve Bogart, Funny Glenn, Nutty Neil, Tony, Basil, Manny, Gary Davidson, Billy Aird, Billy and Harry Hayward, Big Reg Parker, Billy Dalon, Nigel Benn, Julias Francis, Joe Bugner Snr, Joe Bugner Jnr, Mike Tyson, John Harty, Bradley, Flanagan, Mad Tim, Big Memmy, Northern Billy, Mickey, Goldtooth, Mr McGee, Steve McFadden, Costas, Billy, 'Fast Car' Ricky, Mark and Gus at Elite Cars, Eddie the Eagles, Spike, Mickey Taylor, Diamond Dom, Harry Starbuck, Ned Rawlings, Des & Phil and all Outcasts, Dave Ford, Les and Joe, Old Mill Pub chaps, Birmingham Stuart, Gilkicker and Tony, Reemer, Doug, Paddy Sullivan, Bal, Andy Jones, AJ, Jonathan Evans, Ron, Chas, 'Eight Ball', Pard, Pat Brogan, Big Mel, Dean, Danny D, Phil, Des, Kevin Suma, 'Leeds Jimmy', Lord Longford, Lord Fitzgerald, Ken Livingstone, Gyles Brandreth, Bob and Steve, Leon, Leon Lee, Gary Ditton, Jimmy at Tills Motors, Jeremy Bailey, Keith Rose, 'Trisha' security boys, Jason Mariner, Dieter Wittmer, Caesar the Geezer, Jeffrey Archer, Angel, Orry, Chinese Jack, Dave Thurston, Mitch, Medium Ian, Mark Fisher, Dave, Nicky James, Jerry, Dean Cox, Stuart from Reliance Joinery, Phil from Creative Innovation, Scott 'The Tile' Wolstencroft, Dave Courtney Snr, Ray Mudie, Eoin McSorley, Garry Bushell, Ian Edmondson, Martin Brunt, Tony Jackson, Malcolm, Ricardo, Steve Richards, John Blake, Norman Parker, Peter Wells-Thorpe, Scott Walls, Lone Wolf, Big Marcus, Jimmy Kent, John Conteh, Nick Moran, Max Hardy, Stefan, Dave Seaman, Mick Hurst, Guy Agardia, Scott, Riccardo, Mark Munden, Ray Winstone, Jamie Foreman, Quentin Tarantino, Guy Ritchie, David Haeems, Tokes, Bennett Welch, Mr Litham QC, Austin Warnes, Mr Collins QC, DC Tyson, DC Critchley, Dom Sharman, Dean Lambert, Brandon Block, Carl Cox, Terry Ramjam, Tupac, Puff D, Jay-Z, Brian Harvey, Wyclef Jean, Eminem, Dr Dre, Death Row and all boys on the frontline.

THE HOODETTES

Sabrina Libertucci, Holly Thomas, Clare Redman, Annie Deacin Foster, Bella Thekla Roth, Clarellen James, Lisa Henfrey, Ria Jaggard, Sue Moore, Tracy Fenada, Victoria Kay, Daisy Kay, Courtney de Courtney, Bonnie, Marsha, Welsh Helen, Little Tasha, Di, Dionne, Drew, Nadia, Lady Carol, Terri Currie, Leah, Bev 1, 2 and 3, Autumn and EJ, Loretta, Lex, Ruth Lawrence, Bev and Gemma, Welsh Paula, Natasha Taylor,

Staffy, Safi, Sad Happy, My Storm, Ellie, Yasmin, Sugar, Lartey, Tess Courtney, Susan Courtney, Tania Bushell, Denice, Jacky Carr, Claire McNamara, Kate McNamara, Isabella O'Shea, Terri Georgiou, Neke Georgiou, Jessica Georgio-Cross, Sister Beckford, Summer, Katie Campbell, Kat, Lorna Elliott, Ministry Pam, Fru Jaggard, Auntie Myrtle, Caroline Benn, Kaz, Lyndsey Joins, Jane Courtney, Lynn Cooley, Carol Jenkins, Alisha Kusabi, Sue Pyle, Angela Archeleta, Debbie Tucker, Tara Tucker, Baby Angel Pyle, Little Jenny, Candy Floss, Karen Giorgio, Ann Johnstone, Sally Farmer, Caleb Giorgio, Ita, Barbie, Jean, Charlotte Ratcliffe, Blossom, Sandy Farnell, Danielle Elliott, Bev, Mo, Chantelle, Kerry, Connie, Lindsay, Lulu, Sarah Bronson, Sheila, Dave Quelch's lady, Saskia, Brenda, Gilly, Roberta, Lorna, Jackie Vino, Donna Cox, Charlie Breaker's lady, Rhea, Liana, the beautiful Ashley, Sue, Val, Kate, Miss Karen, Marnie Threapleton, Auntie B, Cherie, Phillipa, Naomi, Trudy, Nicole, Meg, Nancy, Rene, Mollie, Tracey, Zara, Sarah, Indiana Courtney, Cathy Barry, Barbara Windsor, Cleo Roccos, Posh Sarah, Christine, Heidi, Jennifer, Elsie Davie RIP.

MUSICIANS & OTHER BITS AND BOBS

Norris Da Boss Windross, J Offenbach, The Business and Steve Whale, Elliott Sagor and Laurence Adeokun, Tricky, Rancid and Lars Fredericksen, Izzy Asco'ta, Joski, Celloman, Sean Flowers, Extreme Music; Lounge Audio Post; Metro Broadcast VMI and Video Europe, London; Satusfaction, London; Peach Ideas, London; NTL and Video Europe, London; NTL – Barnaby and Babs; The Crucifixion by Ronnie Kray courtesy of Phil Mordew and 'John'; Mr Courtney's Wardrobe supplied by Short Stories, Commercial Road, London; Mr Courtney's Harley Davidson Motorcycle kindly supplied by Dock Gate 20, Southampton; Mr Courtney's cigars supplied by Cohibas, Monte Cristo and Romeo y Julieta; Large Rizlas supplied by Mr Courtney; Picture Vehicles supplied by Andy Gardner, Jim's Garage, Teddy and Lenny Webb and Colin Gray; the Crew's late night stand-up comedy by Mr Courtney; Vehicle disposal by TC; Posters by Richard at M1 Print.

THANKS TO

John Pound's Scrapyard, Portsmouth; Jam @ Manhattan's, Woolwich; Gilly @ Gambinos, Gravesend; Lou and Tony Aquarium, Old Street, London; The Dusterman; 'Cowboy' Brian; Beiderbeck's, Portsmouth; Park Tavern Boxing Club, Tooting; Sir Micky Colby; Chris and Sue Vernon; Pierce and Michelle Vernon; Elsie and Jack Vernon; Oliver Vernon RIP; Mirza Fur; Armando and Jayne Gomez-Martin; Catrina Gomez-Martin; Joan Dybowski; Lis and Helmuth Hovmand; Peter Hamden @LipSyncPost, London; Ian Diaz and Julian Boote @ 712 Collective; Ali Catterall; Barry Keefe; Phil Ballard; Steven Moxley; Matthew Owen; Adrian Gardiner; James Pearson; Mitch @ Laughing Buddha, London; Michael @ Jerry's Members Club, Soho, London; Simon Wells; Paul Kennedy @ Inside, London; Premier Despatch; Belle Stennett and the staff at the Dome Cinema, Worthing; John @ the Tower

Club, Littlehampton; Eze and Seamus @ the Crown, Littlehampton; The Peacock Gym; Sin City Films; Victor Films; The Aquarium; For Your Eyes Only; Sugar Reef; Time & Envy; Linnekers; The Belvedere, Peckham; The Business; Mute; Ali Jacko; Maximillian Cooper; And to all the major players in Britain's underworld.

VERY SPECIAL THANKS TO

My Mum, Teresa Courtney; George at the Tardis, Clerkenwell, London; Nick Reynolds and the Cons to Icons Exhibition; Sunny Side Up, Charlton; Karisma; Skin Two; Pure; Rob's Barbers, Forest Hill; Leraze Hair Salon, Portsmouth; Piers Hernu and Front; Capital FM; 1 FM; Millennium FM; News of the World; Sunday Sport; The Voice; Andy Harrison and Delilah Amis; South London Press; Pete Conway and Robbie Williams; Darren Gough; Tony Thompson – Gangland Britain; Jocelyn Bain Hogg; Combat; Nodd, Hector, James and Cyrus @ Ministry Magazine; Chris @ Skinhead and Scooter Magazine; Marcus Georgio and Marc One Security; Titan Security; Brian Adams and Hatch Farm Studios; Mojo; Caesar the Geezer; Mike Osmond and the Naughty Boys; Karaoke Chas; Huey; Aphrodite; Carl 'Tuff Enuff' Brown; DJ Beau Courtney and Blood; Mr Normski; Danielle Montana; MC Cream and Dominic Spreadlove; Mickey Finn; DJ Hurley; DJ Nathan Healey; Huey and the Fun Lovin' Criminals; Stereophonics; Gary G; One Nation and Garage Nation; Clive Button and Lee Patrick; Mal Vango, Lion Design; Steve and Paul; Victoria and Rich; Vanessa Feltz; Zo and Zane; MCPSG; Mark and Jude Coventry; Pasquelle; Maria from Cassidy's; Ralph Haeems; my Ria; Gordon and Juliette; Gerry and Kate; Linda and Frank; Pierre and Helen; John Gillingham; Geraldine and Gail; Liam and Yvette; Francis Bacon RIP; Simon Weston; Les Ferdinand; Neil Hamilton; Max Beasley: Lyndsey Marsh; Dianne and Chris Hackett; John and Kay; John Disley; Diane and Jim, Hayling Island; Diane, Reece and Lulu; Snoop Dogg; HRH Jodie Marsh; Melinda Messenger; Jamie Oliver; James Whale; Welsh Bernie; Adrian Sington and Kirstie Addis at Virgin; Jeff Hudson; all the Scousers, the Geordies, the Paddies, the Jocks and the Taffs and all Bike Presidents everywhere; Sir Paul Condon; HRH the Prince of Wales and Harry and Wills; Dick Emery – ooh, you are awful but I like you; Malcolm McLaren; and all at Her Majesty's pleasure.

TO THE KIDS

Lots of love from Dave: Genson, Drew, Levi, Chelsea, Courtney 'My Lully Girl' and Beau. Joel, Noel, Brogan, Delaney, Bianca, Aspen, John, Brook, Big Jordan, Little Jordan, Brinie, Connor, Tiona, Kayleigh and Ben, Rachel, Zoe, Tommy, Nyasha, Maria and Pedzi.
And a BIG shout to all the doormen and organisers at: Ministry of Sound; Hippodrome; Stringfellows; K-Bar, Chelsea; China Whites; Isola, Knightsbridge; Buzz Bar; Ronnie Scott's; Bagley's; SE24; Caesars, Streatham; Time and Envy, Portsmouth; Submission; Atlantic Bar; the Ten Rooms; Titanic; Limelight; Propaganda; Stage 3; Sophisticats; the

Champagne Bar, Twickenham; Elvis Chipshop; Torture Garden; Driscoll's; Gatecrashers; and all the table top dancers in the country.

MEN OF INSPIRATION

Joey Pyle; Roy 'Pretty Boy' Shaw; Freddie Foreman; Tony Lambrianou RIP; Chris Lambrianou; Ronnie Biggs; Bruce Reynolds; Howard Marks; Charlie Bronson; Charlie Richardson; Johnny Nash; Muhammad Ali; Sir Winston Churchill; Ho Chi Minh; Ernesto 'Che' Guevara; Niccolo Machiavelli; King Arthur and the Knights of the Round Table.

AND FINALLY ...

If I have offended anybody in any way at all it was truly not intentional. Always remember that the moral to the story is what is important, not the story itself.

I would like to take this opportunity to apologise to the following: The police for all the aggravation we caused while making the film; all the hotel staff whilst on location; to all the wives for turning their men it into prima donnas; all the people I owe all that fucking money to. It's coming, I promise! All the people who were cut out of the film in edit. I truly apologise for that; All of you people I forgot to stick on the credits, you know I know that it's the little wheels that make the big wheels go round. I love you and I'm sorry I missed your names out, but if you only knew the fucking aggro it's taken me to get this little lot in you'll understand; to my Stormy, all the kids and anybody close to me. Because this film turned into a fucking person for me. In fact it turned into a *woman*; I have neglected everything and everyone over her, bored people stupid talking about her, spent all my money and more on her. I've laid awake at night thinking about her, defended her to the hilt and wanted everyone to love her. I've lost friends and made enemies over her. So to family I am really sorry – and Thank You.

THE LAST WORD

Hello, my name is Dave Courtney and I want to tell you right from the start that I personally believe that you are born naughty and that gangsters are part of history like pirates, knights in shining armour and cowboys. In no way is this film meant to glamorise crime at all. On the contrary, it shows how disloyal and back-stabbing it gets when greed and jealousy enter the frame. It also shows how close your Judas can be to you without you knowing. CRIME DOESN'T PAY. And that's a fact.

You are no longer pitting your wits against a Sherlock Holmes policeman any more. Once they decide it's your turn they just bug your home, your phone and your car for two years and I don't care if you're Mother Theresa (God bless her). If they heard every word you said for two years they'd find something to either dethrone or incarcerate you. So today it is not the era to be a criminal. You've got it all well stacked against you. So please don't look at this film and think that I am trying to glamorise fuck all about the crime game at all. Because I ain't.

There are an awful lot of bigger and better naughty men around than me in England and just because my face fits at the moment in the media world do not be fooled. The real players you don't even know their names.

'AND AS FOR THIS FILM'

Seeing as 99% of them ain't actors and done it for fuck all, just to show you how it really is and hopefully it gives everyone involved in it a break into a world that normally we never get a chance to. Please excuse me for swearing but I think they were all the absolute bollocks. I am also very proud to say that these are all very good friends of mine.

As Winston Churchill once said: 'Never in the field of conflict have so many owed so much to so few.'

Dave Courtney OBE

INDEX